Digital Media Sport

Technology, Power and Culture
in the Network Society

**Edited by Brett Hutchins and
David Rowe**

Routledge
Taylor & Francis Group

NEW YORK AND LONDON

First published 2013
by Routledge
711 Third Avenue, New York, NY 10017

Simultaneously published in the UK
by Routledge
2 Park Square, Milton Park, Abingdon, Oxfordshire OX14 4RN

First issued in paperback 2016

Routledge is an imprint of the Taylor & Francis Group, an informa business

Library of Congress Cataloging-in-Publication Data

Digital media sport : technology, power and culture in the network society /
  edited by Brett Hutchins and David Rowe.
    pages cm. — (Routledge research in cultural and media studies ; 51)
    Includes bibliographical references and index.
  1. Sports—Computer network resources.   2. Digital media.   I. Hutchins,
Brett, 1973–
  GV568.3.D54   2013
  025.06796—dc23
  2013003431

ISBN 13: 978-1-138-24329-3 (pbk)
ISBN 13: 978-0-415-51751-5 (hbk)

Typeset in Sabon
by Apex CoVantage, LLC

To
Mum for the gift of loving to read

(BRETT)

Daniel, Madeleine, Joanna, Oliver, Alexander, Francesca and a future that burns bright

(DAVID)

Contents

Figures and Tables

FIGURES

TABLES

Abbreviations

ACMA	Australian Communications and Media Authority
AFL	Australian Football League
ASA	Advertising Standards Authority
BAM	Major League Baseball Advanced Media
BBC	British Broadcasting Corporation
BSkyB	British Sky Broadcasting Group
BT	British Telecom
CCTV	China Central Television
CEO	Chief Executive Officer
CNNIC	China Internet Network Information Center
DIY	Do-It-Yourself
DRS	Drag Reduction System
EBU	European Broadcasting Union
EPL	English Premier League
ESPN	Entertainment and Sports Programming Network
FA	Football Association
FFA	Football Federation Australia
FIA	Fédération Internationale De L'Automobile
FIFA	Fédération Internationale de Football Association
HD	High Definition
HDTV	High Definition Television
IMMI	Integrated Media Measurement Inc
IMUSA	Independent Manchester United Supporters Association
IOC	International Olympic Committee
IPL	Indian Premier League
IPTV	Internet Protocol Television
ISP	Internet Service Provider
KERS	Kinetic Energy Recovery System
MLB	Major League Baseball
MUST	Manchester United Supporters' Trust
NBA	National Basketball Association
NBC	National Broadcasting Company
NBL	National Basketball League
NCAA	National Collegiate Athletic Association

NFL	National Football League
NHK	Japan Broadcasting Corporation
NHL	National Hockey League
NRL	National Rugby League
OFT	Office of Fair Trading
PDA	Personal Digital Assistant
PGA	Professional Golfers' Association
SIT	Social Identity Theory
SROC	Sports Rights Owners Coalition
SUAM	Shareholders Unite Against Murdoch
TAMI	Total Audience Measurement Index
TOP	The Olympic Partner program
UEFA	Union of European Football Associations
WAP	Wireless Access Protocol
WCG	World Cyber Games
WNBA	Women's National Basketball Association

Acknowledgments

This collection is the outcome of more than three years research made possible by an Australian Research Council (ARC) grant for the project, "Struggling for Possession: The Control and Use of Online Media Sport (DP0877777)". Thank you to Dr Vibha Bhattarai Upadhyay for her excellent editing and analytical skills, which were of great assistance in the preparation of the manuscript. We would also like to thank Dr Janine Mikosza for her outstanding research assistance over the course of the entire project, and her generosity in the final stage of preparing the manuscript for this book.

Hutchins would like to thank his colleagues in the School of English, Communications and Performance Studies at Monash University who continue to show remarkable patience when confronted by his impatience. Particular gratitude is offered to Shane Homan, Kevin Foster, Sue Kossew, Alison Ross, Deepa Balakrishnan, Robin Gerster, Jodie Wood and Kerry Bowmar. Hutchins also thanks Rowan, a special nine-year-old boy who fills his life with happiness and love.

Rowe registers his gratitude to the people of the Institute for Culture and Society, University of Western Sydney who help make whatever he produces possible—and for serious fun along the way. This time he calls, from the ranks of the professional staff, Simone Casey, Lisa Hanlon (now lamentably working elsewhere at UWS, but spiritually co-present) and Emily-Kate Ringle-Harris to this modest podium. Among the numerous folk who deserve recognition, he can only now pick out Geoff Lawrence for getting him into the media sport caper in the first place, and for being there ever since, and Deborah Stevenson for taking the "D" train. Last, a big shout out to the Rowes, Henders and Hurleys—so distant yet unwaveringly close—and to Dan and Maddy, my favorite emotional baggage.

Brett Hutchins
School of English, Communications &
Performance Studies,
Monash University

David Rowe
Institute for Culture and Society
University of Western Sydney

1 Introduction
Sport in the Network Society and Why It Matters

David Rowe and Brett Hutchins

INTRODUCTION: THE COMING OF NETWORKED MEDIA SPORT

In the early years of the twenty-first century, the long-heralded digital transformation of mediated sport announced its arrival with a force that could no longer be ignored. Newspapers, which had literally marked their readers with ink since the first sport reports more than 300 years earlier, suddenly began to lose them to the much cleaner, more flexible combination of keyboard and computer screen. Analogue radio and television, which had provided sport sound and vision for decades, were given firm notice that their wave-based broadcasts were ultimately to be switched off and replaced by the multiplying binary splits of digital signals. The digital regime rapidly proliferated across mobile telephony and gaming, while computer-based desktop, laptop, notebook and tablet devices created an expanding array of uses and connections that steadily eroded the divide between "old" and "new" sport media, providing many new forms of mediated sport text and ways of accessing them. Thus, as we have argued in *Sport Beyond Television: The Internet, Digital Media and the Rise of Networked Media Sport* (Hutchins & Rowe, 2012), the production and consumption of media sport is in flux, constituting an unstable, unpredictable synthesis of the old and the new, the familiar and the strange, the predictable and the unanticipated.

These are circumstances that demand the close attention of those who are concerned with developments in society and culture in general, and in media and sport in particular. Not only might contemporary transformations in the mediation of sport be instructive in the task of understanding socio-cultural change, but media sport is itself an influential socio-cultural phenomenon that, in a reflexive fashion, is helping to remake the world that has made it. We contend, therefore, that a book devoted to digital media sport is inevitably a study of something much larger—the dynamic "media sports cultural complex" (Rowe, 2004) in the context of national, transnational and global social structures and relations.

SPORT BEYOND TELEVISION ENCAPSULATED

In *Sport Beyond Television* we tracked the development of networked media sport with regard to the intensification of media content production, the acceleration of information flows and expansion of networked communications capacity (p. 17). In these related processes we see the extraordinary growth of the Internet as crucial, not just in terms of the rapidly rising numbers of connections and users across the globe, but in its profound impact on how mediated sport is bought and sold, produced and consumed, accessed and experienced. The "media sport content economy" has shifted from the "scarcity" that was typified by analogue television and radio, and print-based media, to the "plenitude" that is produced by convergent digital media forms that convert cultural data into material that can be reshaped and freely circulated in ways that are difficult to govern. Thus, we contrast broadcast television and its limited "footprints" with the wide-ranging online media sport provision of the "legitimate" likes of Google and the "pirated" live streams of elusive media operators that infringe on the exclusive rights of the television networks. Established broadcast sport interests have tried to adapt to changed market conditions, ranging from harnessing online and mobile content themselves, to undertaking legal action and intensive political lobbying for regulatory change to meet the challenge of new media sport providers.

In the context of the emergent "attention economy" (Lanham, 2006) of the twenty-first century, the relatively static audiences that could be captured and measured via broadcast ratings are pursued in a range of ways in the more variegated online world. Threats to advertising and subscription-based business models call for new metrics to demonstrate who is watching, when and for how long. This networked media world offers new opportunities for sport leagues and established media companies to develop their relationships with fans and customers, but this environment provides a range of other parties with similar communicative and commercial options. Here the website can be shown to be a crucial "meeting point" for sports, fans, sponsors, advertisers and media corporations. Websites are now routinely used both by high-end professional sport and for more modest hobby-based sport pursuits, and can be "mined" for demographic and consumption data in ways that allow more precise targeting and matching of consumers, products and services. Digital media sport, therefore, may be as significant in connecting with people for purposes that have little to do with sport *per se* as in the task of catering to the commodifiable tastes of sport fans.

A critical area of concern is the codevelopment of large institutional media (what we traditionally call "the media" and that is often now labeled "legacy media") and the informal, technologically enhanced human communication that we now call "social media". The latter world of blogging, Facebook friends, Twitter feeds and Tumblrs is of increasing importance to the understanding of a media sports cultural complex that is less easily governed by small clusters of powerful organizations and those who control and operate them. The involvement of participant networks of many shapes and sizes, able to communicate freely across time and space by means of digital technologies, has led to a greater emphasis on user-initiated communication as opposed to producer-led consumption. These users are not only fans, as many athletes themselves want to use social networking to communicate widely without needing to rely on the media and sports organizations as "go betweens". This desire causes consternation for bodies such as the International Olympic Committee (IOC) that seek to avoid "ambush marketing" (athletes trying to promote companies who are not official sponsors and licensed suppliers), political controversy arising from the expression of views beyond the usual platitudes, or scandals caused by ill-advised utterances of a racist, sexist or homophobic nature. There is also a fear that freely communicating sportspeople will provide inside information to sporting rivals or, worse, to those engaged in sports betting. As a result, the management of risk becomes paramount at a time when the means of communication are proliferating and the desire to control public messages still registers powerfully among sports organizations.

Fan-made media communication is, in many respects, as troubling for both media and sport organizations as the involvement of athletes in social networking. The capacity to circumvent the "official" channels creates the possibility of new *loci* of popular power that might, for example, effectively resist a takeover of a football club or the appointment of a new coach. This does not mean that sports hierarchies are suddenly being turned upside down, but they certainly have to take greater account of popular sentiment, exchange and mobilization. Some sport leagues and clubs have displayed intransigence in trying to censor or sue sport fans who use online message boards to criticize them. Others have adopted alternatives to stonewalling and patronizing sport fans, instead choosing to listen to them and harness their energy, expertise and commitment. Here there is often a clash between freewheeling, informal and sometimes-offensive fan discourse and the tightly controlled defense of intellectual property and brand image. The very nature of contemporary sport and fandom is at issue in such disputes: many fans are no longer content to be compliant consumers who might grumble about how the game is run but decline to try to change it. Instead, they might assert "rights of ownership" as the true "custodians" of sport who are able to assemble in convergent media environments with tangible material effects on "mediasport" (Wenner, 1998). At the same time, the "work" of such fans might be harnessed more effectively by sport organizations in, for example, functioning as conduits for consultation on major decisions, or simply by generating interest and consumption through intensive networked communication.

Most sport fans are not paid to communicate about sport, but professional journalists are. The craft of sport journalism has been based in the print media, with radio and television commentary being tied closely to description and discussion of live sport action. The expansion of the media sport sphere has required journalists to be more flexible and multi-skilled in moving across media (for example, print journalists appearing on television and broadcasters writing newspaper articles), but the digitization and convergence of media sport has accelerated and expanded this move towards cross-platform sport journalism. The reason for this change in journalistic practice lies not only in the availability of new technologies and the shrinking journalism workforce caused by the decline of mainstream media business models. It is also because the world of networked media sport contains many competitors with professional sports journalists who are establishing sport websites, blogging, tweeting, podcasting and so on, thereby requiring sports journalists to do likewise in the maintenance of existing audiences and the search for new ears and "eyeballs". As organizationally-based professional sports journalists operate across platforms and increasingly interact with "citizen journalists", both are drawn into the confusing conflicts over ownership and control of content that currently bedevil the media sports cultural complex.

So thoroughgoing has been the transformation of the relationship in the media-sport nexus that the traditional conception of sport *and* media has given way to sport *as* media within a broader leisure framework (Hutchins & Rowe, 2012, p. 10). The line between "reality" and "fantasy" in media sport cultures is blurring as the Internet, computer, console and handheld platforms have made possible new forms of interaction and sports gaming, including the integration of the fictive and the material in sport management games. In this realm of "remediation", sport *as* media can be manifest through Wii-style combinations of technology and athletic skill, and the Olympic-style, international multi-discipline event structure of the World Cyber Games (WCG) (see Taylor, 2012). The futuristic frames of reference for this kind of mediated sporting activity challenge the conventional separation of the human and the mechanical, and the technological and the corporeal. These frames are also indicators of more general disturbances and uncertainties provoked by networked media sport.

As we have noted, the battle over the content, ownership, exploitation and use of mediated sport is being conducted on many fronts, and we are unquestionably going to witness intensified conflict as online distribution meets proprietorial claims over content, and then confronts wider public assertions of media sport-related cultural citizenship (Scherer & Rowe, 2013). The latter concept proposes that access to premium sport content should be widely available rather than confined to the comparatively affluent sectors of the population with the means to partake in media sport culture. Disputation over this matter has deep socio-cultural ramifications. It is clear, then, that concerns with digitally enabled networked media sport cannot be confined to debates about the needs of the sport, media and telecommunications industries. These are matters that go to the heart of debates over the "common culture" and to the essence of what is meant by the "the social" in the contemporary, mediatized world.

THE CASE FOR DIGITAL MEDIA SPORT: TECHNOLOGY, POWER AND CULTURE IN THE NETWORK SOCIETY

In arguing that networked media sport is an important, dynamic and complex subject, we also recognize that it is even more daunting in scale because it can never be about *only* sport and media. These are essentially concepts of heuristic convenience that capture a diverse range of institutions, practices, symbols and values, the multi-faceted elusiveness of which we have signaled in conceiving sport *as* media, and to which we could add, more extensively media/sport *as* culture/society. Here we acknowledge our own limitations—*Sport Beyond Television* covered a great deal of ground, and was determinedly global/transnational/international in scope, but there are many other situationally based "takes" on the subject that we cannot comprehensively articulate and empirical knowledge in other contexts that we do not possess. For these reasons, we have devised *Digital Media Sport: Technology, Power and Culture in the Network Society* as the first international edited collection of its kind that combines contextual reach with thematic scope. Designed as a companion to the monograph but able to stand alone as a contribution to contemporary work on digital media, it identifies the intersecting issues of technological change, market power and social practice that shape the contemporary media sport landscape. The complexity of these related issues demands an interdisciplinary approach adopted in a series of thematically organized essays by international scholars working in media studies, Internet studies, sociology, cultural studies and sports studies.

It is worth recounting why research and scholarship in this area are so urgently required. The number of Internet users worldwide is estimated to have grown by more than 566 percent since the turn of the century, now reaching almost 2.5 billion people (Internet World Stats, 2012). Video content exceeds half of global consumer Internet traffic (Cisco VNI, 2012), while approximately seventy-one percent of Internet users in the US report using a video-sharing site such as YouTube or Vimeo, representing a thirty-eight percent increase in just five years (Moore, 2011). Sport supplies a pivotal cluster of this digital content, especially given the appeal of live sport, highlights packages, and news among users. The 2008 Beijing Olympics, a true sports mega-event, reported impressive online coverage and viewing statistics. Live broadband streaming accounted for 2,200 of the estimated 3,600 total hours shown by the American NBC-Universal networks (NBC, 2008). This pattern intensified at the 2012 London Olympics, with multiplatforming of unprecedented proportion, embracing online, mobile devices, game consoles and broadcast television. Dubbed the "Red Button Olympics" (in referring to digital multichanneling), the British Broadcasting Corporation (BBC) provided 2,500 hours of live coverage, including every competitive event, much of it in high definition and some in three dimensions (Rowe, 2012). The BBC also received twelve million requests for video on mobile phones during the 2012 Games, and reported 9.2 million browsers on its mobile Olympics website and app (O'Riordan, 2012). NBC, the US's Olympic broadcaster, struck partnership arrangements with "Facebook, Twitter, YouTube and Shazam to promote its coverage of the Games onto these popular social media platforms" and provided "Google+, Instagram, Tumblr, and GetGlue with Olympic content" (NBC Sports Group Press Box, 2012). The search engine Google offered browser-customized national medal counts and "updates, news and photos from the Olympic Games on Google+" alongside traffic-generated trending topics (Google, 2012). There is little doubt that the following Summer Olympics, in Rio de Janeiro in Brazil in 2016, will supply an even more extensive range of networked media sport offerings.

As we outlined in *Sport Beyond Television*, such figures and estimates are evidence of a rich and popular second screen experience for fans and viewers (p. 4), with mobiles and tablets now offering increasingly sophisticated additional screens. These multiscreen experiences continue to grow in both volume and detail, particularly in relation to live events. Yet, despite widespread changes in digital media technologies and practices, there is also significant historical continuity evident in the popularity and commercial value of media sport. As was evident throughout the analogue-broadcast era, sport remains a key source of "must-see" content for massive audiences and large cohorts of fans. This appeal positions sport at the epicenter of power and value in a contemporary media setting characterized by multiplying platforms, changing audience behavior and market volatility. It is the immutable demand for sport in the midst of large-scale media transformation that explains the colossal sums paid to secure broadcast and digital coverage rights to sports leagues and events. As Ed Goren, a founding executive at Fox Sports Media Group, states:

> We invested billions of dollars in sports rights . . . with the belief that, as we move forward with more [viewing] options for people, and as the television universe gets more and more diverse, the one segment of network television that would continue to be must-see TV and would continue to deliver large audiences would be the major sports events because that's where the water-cooler talk will be. (cited in Johnson, 2009, p. 114)

The unexpected corollary of Goren's belief is that the increased use of Internet and mobile communications by fans is not eroding audiences for sport on broadcast platforms. This phenomenon runs counter to the initial expectations of many major sports organizations that displayed either indifference or hostility to "their" television content being "cannibalized" by online users. For instance, the general manager of media rights for Cricket Australia, Stephanie Beltrame (2011), describes a marked change of attitude among administrators of the high profile "summer game":

> . . . a positive trend that is emerging is the complementary nature of multi-screens to the overall viewing experience. In a sporting sense,

there was some historical concern as to how the Internet could or would cannibalise the television coverage of an event . . . The reality, as we have seen played out, is that the best arrangement for fans is to be able to watch the content or stay in touch with the progress of an event on whatever device is applicable to them at the time, whether they are working during the day, travelling home on the train, or sitting back in the lounge room of an evening. There is no need to necessarily make a choice—they can have both and more if they wish. (p. 63.6)

Media events like World Cup finals, the Olympics and the Super Bowl continue to record healthy broadcast audience numbers *and* online user statistics. This development is producing new arrangements in the use of content by users across different screens, as well as the deliberate positioning of online platforms and social networking services in terms of their market and advertising value in relation to television. For example, recent efforts by Twitter to translate its extraordinary popularity into consistent commercial revenue have seen its Chief Executive Officer (CEO), Dick Costolo, publicly promote the idea that microblogging "complements all these traditional forms of broadcast media, and in all sorts of fascinating ways that we would have never predicted" (quoted in Ingram, 2012). This overall expansion in "transmedia attention" demands the type of analysis provided by contributors to this book.

As the sixteen chapters show, digital media sport exemplifies the entanglement of print, analogue, broadcast, digital and mobile media in a large and messy contemporary communications ecology (Goggin, 2011, p. 4). Media sport is, therefore, an important dimension of social, cultural and economic life in "the network society". Developed over many years, Manuel Castells's empirically grounded theory (see 2000a, 2000b, 2002, 2004a, 2004b, 2009; Castells, Fernandez-Ardevol, Qiu & Sey, 2007) has been a touchstone in the planning of this collection; a fact that is both implicitly and explicitly evident in the pages that follow. It is noteworthy that two of the contributors—Peter Millward (2011) and Matthew David (David & Millward, 2012)—have been especially active in applying Castells's concepts to globalized media sport and, particularly, to soccer (or, to use its strictly correct name, association football). The deep intermeshing of sport and leisure activities in capitalist systems and global communications means that media sport is both a "mirror" and "motor" of the conditions characterizing the network society (Giulianotti & Robertson, 2009). It is for this reason that we coined the term "networked media sport", seeking to capture the role of digital communications networks and the power of networking logic in the mediation of sports content, events and experiences (Hutchins & Rowe, 2012; Hutchins, Rowe & Ruddock, 2009). This book advances this line of inquiry through case studies and evidence drawn from North American, British, continental European, East Asian and Australasian contexts. Given the importance of sport as a media commodity, cultural form and social activity, it is crucial that this internationalizing trajectory continues to advance in scope and depth into the future, especially as the effects of the "informa-tion technology paradigm" are globally felt (Castells, 2000a).

Media sport provides crucial evidence of a momentous historical tran-sition in modes and systems of communication.[1] In Castells's terms (2009, pp. 55–70), this development involves a shift from a social world domi-nated by a combination of: (i) *interpersonal communication*—"the message is sent from one-to-one with feedback loops"—and (ii) *mass communica-tion*. The latter is often one-directional communication where "the message is sent from one to many, as with books, newspapers, films, radio, and tele-vision", but also features limited forms of interactivity through talkback radio, letters to the editor in newspapers and magazines, and call-in tele-vision programs (pp. 54–55). Industries, markets, institutions and systems of regulation were built over the course of the twentieth century that both shaped and responded to changes in mass media technologies and interper-sonal social norms, with sport featuring directly and indirectly throughout. A distinguishing feature of the network society has been the emergence of (iii) *mass self-communication* through the Internet, web-based platforms and wireless communications: "self-generated in content, self-directed in emission, and self-selected in reception by many who communicate with many" (p. 70). As Castells outlines, uploading a video to YouTube, sending a tweet and posting on an online message board are acts of self-communication *and* mass communication for a potentially global audience. Rather than acting as competitors or substitutes, the three forms of commu-nication "co-exist, interact, and complement each other" (p. 55) for the first time in human history:

> What is historically novel, with considerable consequences for social organization and cultural change, is the articulation of all forms of communication into a composite, interactive, digital hypertext that in-cludes, mixes, and recombines *in their diversity* the whole range of cul-tural expressions conveyed by human interaction. (original emphasis, Castells, 2009, p. 55)

The overlaps, contradictions and disputes generated in the course of this articulation are manifold and are felt acutely at the level of organizational, institutional, political and economic relations. Sport highlights these devel-opments in media and consumer technology markets because of its enduring and profitable affinities with broadcast television. Unpredictable commer-cial and social outcomes are generated by the digitization and networking of digital sports content, and the individual "enhanced autonomy" (Benkler, 2006) enabled by mass self-communication. Much is at stake as those sports organizations, leagues, teams and media corporations that enjoyed long-standing competitive advantages during the era of mass media attempt to protect their position and/or profit from digital-convergent media environ-ments. Telecommunications providers, information technology companies and digital media specialists are now "players" in the global media sport industries. There is also now a need to take into account the hordes of users consuming and producing sports-related media content on a daily basis via television, social networking services, websites, mobile media, online streams, news sites, blogs, message boards, user-generated video platforms and games. Organized into three sections, *Digital Media Sport* analyzes these developments and, in so doing, accounts for the emergence and operation of mass-self communication in the key context of sport.

BOOK STRUCTURE AND CONTENT

This book capitalizes on the effectiveness of professional sport as a primary focus of attention around the watercooler, in the boardroom, on screen and in digital networks. Broadcasters, digital media operators, sports leagues and fans are all responding in different ways to the changes created by online media, and the vicissitudes of digital television formats and mobile devices. These are conditions of continuity and discontinuity underpinned by emergent viewer and user practices. Each of the chapters in *Digital Media Sport* addresses how the form, function, value and/or practices of media sport are changing in a manner that is both theoretically focused and empirically based. In analyzing the state of contemporary media sport and its trajectories and futures, it highlights both local specificities and global patterns.

Part I, **Evolving Technologies, Platforms and Markets**, opens with Gerard Goggin's "Sport and the Rise of Mobile Media" (Chapter 2). He explores the rise of sport in mobile media and the issues presented by their use and promotion, through to their operation across a range of social contexts and significant media-entertainment enterprises. Goggin identifies a far-reaching tension between the formal economy of media sport and the informal economies of cultural participation and user cultures. This conflict, it is emphasized, has been most obvious in battles over mobile media rights to sports content. In the following chapter, "Desktop Day Games: Workspace Media, Multitasking and the Digital Baseball Fan" (Chapter 3), Ethan Tussey examines how the websites, apps and digital programming strategies implemented by Major League Baseball (MLB) have created new arrangements for digital sports fandom. This chapter shows that league executives encourage "multitasking" viewing habits in order to distinguish digital media users from television viewers, with a key to this process being the cultivation of the workplace audience as a prime target for digital ventures. By catering to these online viewers and infiltrating work places and spaces, MLB and other sports leagues are contributing to the redefinition of the forms and spaces of sports fandom in the digital era.

Ben Goldsmith, by contrast, returns to the dominant communications technology of both the analogue and, to date, the digital media sport environment—television. "'SporTV': The Legacies and Power of Television"

(Chapter 4) argues that sports-related programming is often overlooked in favor of event coverage in the study of sports television. His analysis focuses on three areas—platform interaction, technological innovation and content ecologies—and describes technological innovations arising from television coverage of sports, with a particular focus on online video, audience measurement, and 3D production and viewing. Goldsmith's emphasis on the persistent centrality of sport to television as an entertainment medium throws light on the empirical deficiencies of declarations of television's imminent demise, given that it is still immensely popular and is adapting to and incorporating online and other technologies. Television's continuing significance in the mature continental European media market is well recognized in Tom Evens's and Katrien Lefever's "The Struggle for Platform Leadership in the European Sports Broadcasting Market" (Chapter 5). They analyze the transition of power in the sports broadcasting rights marketplace, noting that almost everywhere in Europe free-to-air broadcasters are losing their dominance as providers of soccer games. Instead, pay television operators and telecommunications carriers are starting to assert serious claims in the marketplace. This "struggle" for platform leadership is discussed in a broader European perspective and is illustrated by a case study of Belgian soccer, with the authors concluding that these changes are not always in the "public interest", and specifically as it applies to the aforementioned issues of national cultural citizenship (Scherer & Rowe, 2013). Here, the key distinction between free-to-air and subscription sport television is recognized, as well as the rising importance of corporations whose primary involvement has not been historically in broadcast television, but in online and mobile delivery systems.

The first part of the book ends with a consideration of one of the key problems for companies such as the British Sky Broadcasting Group (BSkyB), the Entertainment Sports Programming Network (ESPN) and British Telecom (BT), who expend billions of dollars, euros and pounds on purchasing exclusive media sport rights. In "The Challenge of Unauthorized Online Streaming to the English Premier League and Television Broadcasters" (Chapter 6), Andrew Kirton and Matthew David examine the case of English Premier League (EPL) soccer, which they nominate as "the global football league" (Millward, 2011). They treat the EPL as a paradigmatic instance of the excessively commodified sporting leagues that exist in today's global media sports cultural complex, outlining the web of economic relations that work to produce live broadcasts of EPL matches. In discussing the emergence and nature of unauthorized online live-streaming as a challenge to these existing economic arrangements, they argue that this practice has the potential to intensify financial instability in the EPL and among its broadcast partners. The practices of online "piracy" that stimulate so much disquiet among media rights holders are, for many sport fans, legitimate forms of resistance to commercial sport and media organizations that they see as exploiting their love of sport. It is to these sport fans and users to which the book turns in Part II: **Fans, Audiences and Identities**.

"Online Belongings: Female Fan Experiences in Online Soccer Forums" (Chapter 7) by Deirdre Hynes and Ann-Marie Cook engages with one of the common "blind spots" in celebratory accounts of digital and online media—gender. They address what is often ignored in the study of sport, community and online interaction: how women experience and express their identities as fans in online forums. The authors analyze the experiences of female fans online, examining discourses that emphasize the position of women within a male-dominated soccer culture, as well as its management of gendered identities. In exposing the means by which identity is expressed in these forums, they shed light on the implications of these processes both for online and other media sport environments. Gender, as well as race and sexuality, is also a focus of David J. Leonard's "Eye Candy and Sex Objects: Race, Gender and Sport on YouTube" (Chapter 8). Leonard examines YouTube videos of several US female athletes, including Serena Williams (tennis), Brittney Griner (basketball), Allison Stokke (track and field), Alex Morgan (soccer) and Hope Solo (soccer). His analysis seeks to understand the ways in which race, gender and sexuality operate in this online space, paying particular attention to how user comments address female athletic bodies. These comments illustrate the power of gendered, racial and heterosexist logics. Although US-focused, the discussion is relevant to other national cultures characterized by the commercial control of media sport and widespread engagement with user-generated media platforms such as YouTube.

Jimmy Sanderson also addresses divisions and identities in the online world, examining how US sports fans use digital media platforms to repair their "fractured identities". In "Facebook, Twitter and Sports Fans: Identity Protection and Social Network Sites in US Sports" (Chapter 9), Sanderson shows what happens when sports teams make unpopular decisions, athletes leave teams, or much-loved sports figures are the subject of negative media attention. He provides evidence of fans striving to make sense of these events and to defend themselves, with digital media tools amplifying opportunities for identity expression, and fans increasingly using these channels to bolster and express a range of identities. Sport fan expression and resistance in networked environments is central also to Millward's "Fan Movements in the Network Society: Project, Resistance and Legitimizing Identities among Manchester United Supporters" (Chapter 10). This chapter explores the emergence of "project," "resistance" and "legitimizing" identities among supporters of Manchester United, a genuinely global club and brand. These issues are connected to the private ownership of the club, and relate to the role of fan interaction and digital communications in the network society. Applying (as noted earlier) the concepts of Castells, the author focuses on the responses of Manchester United fans to the commercialization of "their" sport and club, especially with regard to its controversial US owners the Glazer brothers, who are renowned for "leveraging" the debts of sport clubs.

In the closing chapter of Part III, Andy Ruddock investigates soccer fan practices in Australia that have been largely borrowed from the EPL, and that are constructing "new" yet familiar traditions in another hemisphere via a combination of digital media and embodied practice. " 'Born on Swan Street, Next to the Yarra': Online Opinion Leaders and Inventing Commitment" (Chapter 11) is concerned with the media practices of Melbourne Heart (a club in Australia's professional A-League soccer) supporters, with a particular emphasis on "digital opinion leading." This process is understood through the content of an Internet message board where potential Heart fans debate the appeal of this new team (founded in 2008). Ruddock explains how online opinion leading complements contemporary analytical approaches to audiences and media power, focusing on the active participation of fans in the circulation and creation of media content. The social networking among sport fans addressed here with regard to soccer resonates with that of many other domains of media sport, such as so-called "lifestyle sports." These are the subject of the first chapter in the third and final section of the book: **Content Ecologies, Social Software and Games.**

In Chapter 12, "New Media Technologies in Lifestyle Sport", Paul Gilchrist and Belinda Wheaton explore the location and use of media technologies in the lives of lifestyle sport participants, reflecting on the uses of social networking sites and online video platforms in parkour. Sometimes known as "free running", parkour is a form of human movement that focuses on "efficient motion" over, under, around or through "human-made" or naturally occurring obstacles by jumping, vaulting and climbing. The authors contextualize social communication around parkour historically by discussion of the established pursuits of climbing and surfing. In assessing the impact of various digital media technologies, Gilchrist and Wheaton highlight the ways in which seemingly novel "do-it-yourself" media practices are actually a longstanding feature of lifestyle sport cultures. This historically informed skepticism about some aspects of digital social media takes on an explicitly political character in the Chinese context in Haiqing Yu's "Blogging the Beijing Olympics: The Neoliberal Logic of Chinese Web 2.0" (Chapter 13). She critiques the incorporation of digital media and blogging in the presentation of the 2008 Beijing Olympics by Chinese mainstream media, telecommunications operators, commercial content providers, local tabloids and individuals. Yu illuminates the dynamics of blogging and the neoliberal logic of the Internet in the context of the Chinese media sports cultural complex and, in the process, questions the relationship between professional sports journalists, bloggers and "citizen journalists".

The changing practices of journalists discussed by Yu are then appraised in "Sports Journalism and Social Media: A New Conversation?" (Chapter 14) by Raymond Boyle and Richard Haynes. Authors of the pioneering monograph *Football in the New Media Age* (2004), they assess the extent to which social media platforms are transforming sports journalism, focusing in particular on media-source relations. The chapter canvasses how the relationships between sports journalists and their audiences are changed by "a new conversation" taking place inside social networking media, adopting an approach that recognizes the specificities of news cultures within different sports. Sports journalists find themselves having to come to terms with a media sports cultural complex that has developed well beyond the simple structure of mediated sport performance and journalistic reportage and commentary. The "real" and the "imagined" are constructed in and amongst sport fans in ways that may involve journalists, but do not necessarily give them pride of place. This point is exemplified in "Carnival Mirrors: Sport and Digital Games" (Chapter 15) by Steven Conway and Mark Finn, with video games shown to market themselves as faithful reproductions of sport. The authors focus on soccer, but also reflect on other pursuits such as motor racing. These digital products, they suggest, are more than simple "remediations" of sports performance and activity. Conway and Finn introduce the term "reludification" to describe how these games incorporate certain realist forms of representation and models of interaction, but also embrace rules and mechanics that are not conducive to traditional physical competition. Their analysis reveals that digital sport games now have a tangible impact upon the physical world of sport and its media representation. How journalists and media sport corporate powerbrokers, with their commitment to describing or investing in the relatively "solid" world of sport, negotiate this evolving combination of the physical and the virtual is one of the striking dilemmas posed by contemporary networked media sport.

The final chapter returns us to one of the abiding questions of the media sports cultural complex given the foundational role of gender, and, specifically, of masculinity in the making, practice and interpretation of sport. What prospect is there that the gender order of digital sport will be substantially different from that of its predigital incarnation? In "Privileged Men and Masculinities: Gender and Fantasy Sports Leagues" (Chapter 16), Luke Howie and Perri Campbell seek to understand the types of masculine practice enacted in online fantasy sports leagues. In the process they reveal these settings to be masculinized "fantasyscapes", explaining that, whilst some attention has been paid to fantasy gambling, communications and participant motivations, an understanding of fantasy sports leagues as gendered and cultural experiences is comparatively lacking. For illustrative purposes, the authors offer a case study of the selected roles played by gender in a fantasy sports league, with data drawn from the online platform where the league is conducted.

This closing chapter is symptomatic of the state of the field in media sport studies. It has travelled some distance from much that was recognizable in the predigital age, and yet is a sound reminder of the profound, inevitable link between media sport culture and the "great world" that has produced it, and within which it plays a notable part. Networked digitization does not altogether shape the social world, but nonetheless its influence cannot be discounted. There is also much legitimate disputation about the concept of the network society but, irrespective of one's preferred theoretical framework and conceptual model, the evidence presented in this collection announces clearly that digital media sport is a major force in twenty-first century global society and culture.

NOTE

1. John B. Thompson (1995, 2005, 2011) also offers an insightful and complementary account of this historical transition in communications and media and its sociological implications. Similarly, Goggin (2012) supplies a helpful analysis of the relationship between Castells's concepts and mobile communications and media.

REFERENCES

Beltrame S (2011) The new world of selling content: Cricket as a case study. *Telecommunications Journal of Australia* 61(4): 63.1–63.7.

Benkler Y (2006) *The Wealth of Networks: How Social Production Transforms Markets and Freedom*. New Haven and London: Yale University Press.

Boyle R & Haynes R (2004) *Football in the New Media Age*. London: Routledge.

Castells M (2000a) *The Rise of the Network Society*. 2nd ed. Oxford: Blackwell.

Castells M (2000b) *End of Millennium*. 2nd ed. Oxford: Blackwell.

Castells M (2002) *The Internet Galaxy: Reflections on the Internet, Business, and Society*. Oxford: Oxford University Press.

Castells M (2004a) *The Power of Identity*. 2nd ed. Oxford: Blackwell.

Castells M (ed.) (2004b) *The Network Society: A Cross-Cultural Perspective*. Cheltenham, UK: Edward Elgar.

Castells M (2009) *Communication Power*. Oxford: Oxford University Press.

Castells M, Fernandez-Ardevol M, Qiu JL & Sey A (2007) *Mobile Communication and Society: A Global Perspective*. Cambridge, MA: The MIT Press.

Cisco VNI (2012) *Cisco Visual Networking Index: Forecast and Methodology, 2011–2016*. Online. Available from: http://www.cisco.com/en/US/solutions/col lateral/ns341/ns525/ns537/ns705/ns827/white_paper_c11-481360_ns827_Net working_Solutions_White_Paper.html (Accessed 11 November 2012).

David M & Millward P (2012) Football's coming home? Digital reterritorialization, contradictions in the transnational coverage of sport and the sociology of alternative football broadcasts. *British Journal of Sociology* 63(2): 349–69.

Giulianotti R & Robertson R (2009) *Globalization and Football*. London: Sage.

Goggin G (2011) *Global Mobile Media*. London and New York: Routledge.

Goggin G (2012) The iPhone and communication. In: Hjorth L, Burgess J & Richardson I (eds.) *Studying Mobile Media: Cultural Technologies, Mobile Communication, and the iPhone*. New York and London: Routledge, 11–27.

Google (2012) *London 2012 Olympic Games*. Online. Available from: https://www .google.ca/campaigns/olympics/ (Accessed 14 December, 2012).

Hutchins B & Rowe D (2012) *Sport Beyond Television: The Internet, Digital Media and the Rise of Networked Media Sport*. New York: Routledge.

Hutchins B, Rowe D & Ruddock A (2009) "It's fantasy football made real": Networked media sport, the Internet, and the hybrid reality of MyFootballClub. *Sociology of Sport Journal* 26(1): 89–106.

Ingram M (2012) Dick Costolo says Twitter is a reinvention of the town square—but with TV. *Gigaom*, 27 November. Online. Available from: http://gigaom.com/2012/11/27/dick-costolo-says-twitter-is-a-reinvention-of-the-town-square-but-with-tv/?utm_source=General+Users&utm_campaign=cdd4edd ba4-c%3Amed+d%3A11-28&utm (Accessed 28 November 2012).

Internet World Stats (2012) *World Internet Users and Population Statistics*. Online. Available from: http://www.internetworldstats.com/stats.htm (Accessed 19 November 2012).

Johnson VE (2009) Everything new is old again: Sport television, innovation, and television for a multi-platform era. In: Lotz AD (ed.) *Beyond Prime Time: Television Programming in the Post-Network Era*. New York: Routledge, 114–37.

Lanham RA (2006) *The Economics of Attention: Style and Substance in the Age of Information*. Chicago, IL: University of Chicago Press.

Millward P (2011) *The Global Football League: Transnational Networks, Social Movements and Sport in the New Media Age*. Basingstoke: Palgrave.

Moore K (2011) *71% of Online Adults Now Use Video-Sharing Sites*. Washington, DC: Pew Internet & American Life Project. Online. Available from: http://pewinternet.org/~/media//Files/Reports/2011/Video%20sharing%202011.pdf (Accessed 3 November 2012).

NBC (2008) NBC's complete Olympics. *nbcolympics.com*, 9 July. Online. Available from: http://www.nbcolympics.com/newscenter/news/newsid=148556.html (Accessed 7 November 2008).

NBC Sports Group Press Box (2012) NBC Olympics' media partnerships contribute to record viewership and digital traffic. *NBC Sports Group Press Box*, 14 August. Online. Available from: http://nbcsportsgrouppressbox.com/2012/08/15/nbc-olympics-social-media-partnerships-contribute-to-record-viewership-digital-traffic/ (Accessed 14 December 2012).

O'Riordan C (2012) The story of the digital Olympics. *BBC Internet Blog*, 13 August. Online. Available from: http://www.bbc.co.uk/blogs/bbcinternet/2012/08/digital_olympics_reach_stream_stats.html (Accessed 15 August 2012).

Rowe D (2004) *Sport, Culture, and the Media*. 2nd ed. Maidenhead, Berkshire: Open University Press.

Rowe D (2012) Opening ceremonies and closing narratives: The embrace of media and the Olympics. *JOMEC Journal: Journalism, Media and Cultural Studies* 2: 1–13. Online. Available from: http://www.cardiff.ac.uk/jomec/jomecjournal/2_november2012/rowe_openingceremonies.pdf (Accessed 28 November 2012).

Scherer J & Rowe D (eds.) (2013) *Sport, Public Broadcasting, and Cultural Citizenship: Signal Lost?* New York: Routledge.

Taylor TL (2012) *Raising the Stakes: E-Sports and the Professionalization of Computer Gaming*. Cambridge, MA: The MIT Press.

Thompson JB (1995) *The Media and Modernity*. Cambridge, UK: Polity Press.

Thompson JB (2005) The New Visibility. *Theory, Culture & Society* 22(6): 31–51.

Thompson JB (2011) Shifting Boundaries of Public and Private Life. *Theory, Culture & Society* 28(4): 49–70.

Wenner LA (ed.) (1998) *MediaSport*. London: Routledge.

Part I

Evolving Technologies, Platforms and Markets

2 Sport and the Rise of Mobile Media

Gerard Goggin

> . . . sports content is among the most popular and engaging genres and well positioned to thrive in an increasingly fragmented media marketplace and rapidly evolving multi-screen world.
>
> (Nielsen, 2012a)

> . . . sport holds the key to attaining dominance in convergent media environments where television, online, and mobile media overlap, interact, and compete.
>
> (Hutchins & Rowe, 2012, p. 20)

INTRODUCTION: THE NEW POLITICS OF DIGITAL MEDIA SPORT

It is axiomatic to speak of the symbiosis of media and sport in the contemporary conjuncture that defines the power relations of culture (Boyle & Haynes, 2009; Miller, Lawrence, McKay & Rowe, 2001; Rowe, 2011). With subscriptions to cellular mobile technology reaching an estimated six billion subscribers worldwide in 2012, mobile media in all their varieties plays a vitally important role in how networked, digital media constellate power and identity in contemporary networked societies (Goggin, 2011). As part of this dispensation, mobile phones and media are well established as an important conduit for the representation, distribution and consumption of sport. Mobile media raise a paradox that media scholars identified some time ago. Sport and new technologies have often gone hand-in-hand in key phases of innovation in newspapers, radio and television. Like many other new communication technologies, mobile phones were hailed as revolutionary in the early phase of their introduction, or, at the very least, were believed to hold great potential in changing the coverage of media sport. Some fifteen years after such technological boosterism flourished in the late 1990s, the actual contribution of mobiles to the "marriage" of media and sports (Rowe, 2004) remains tricky to specify.

In approaching the question of mobile media and sport, Raymond Boyle's pioneering 2004 paper on third-generation (3G) mobiles makes two valuable points that remain valid. First, echoing many new media researchers, Boyle reminds us of the inherent difficulty of "identifying future trends of new media consumption", as the "way these digital technologies become embedded in our everyday social lives has not always been in a manner that has been easily envisaged" (Boyle, 2004, p. 81). Second, Boyle predicts that "much will change over the coming years as mobile technologies become more deeply rooted in our everyday lives" (Boyle, 2004, p. 81). What he sees as critical to this process is "substantial continuity in how sport fans use media":

> The previous waves of media innovation from the print and broadcast media suggest a sense of a continuing evolution in the relationship between technologies, sport and supporters rather than the full scale revolution that was so widely predicted. (Boyle, 2004, p. 82)

Boyle's comments largely ring true almost a decade on from the first concerted push of sport into mobile media in the 3G era. Mobiles are profoundly constitutive of everyday life for many people in the second decade of the twenty-first century. Indeed, leading mobiles scholar Rich Ling has suggested that the mobile phone has qualified as what Émile Durkheim termed a "social fact" (Ling, 2012). That is, the mobile is now a mediation technology central to society's functioning.

To flesh out this contention, let us consider available data on the use of media by sport followers. In 2011, soccer was the top sport followed in six of eight countries featured in the *Global Sports Media Consumption Report*—Great Britain, Germany, Spain, France, Italy and Brazil. In the US, the National Football League (NFL) was ranked first, and in China it was table tennis (Perform, KantarSport & TV Sports Markets 2011, p. 19). In all these markets, television was the medium of choice, followed by the written press (magazines and newspapers) and then the Internet (although it should be noted that the Internet was second favorite in the US, Brazil and China). Actual attendance at sports events often came fourth. When the data on sport consumption via the Internet are broken down, the main method of interacting with sport content online is via a PC/laptop. Of the methods used by sports fans to consume sport online, only about ten to twenty percent of fans in the UK, Germany, Spain, France and the US watched via an Internet-enabled mobile device (mobile phone, smartphone, or table computer), compared to forty-six percent in China, forty-two percent in Brazil and twenty-six percent in Italy (Perform et al. 2011, p. 21). This study also finds "mobile consumption of sport is skewed towards the affluent, men, and those aged 18–34" in these countries (Perform et al. 2011, p. 33). Brazil is an interesting exception to this rule, with online consumption of sport having a broader reach across all demographics (except the over-55-year-olds),

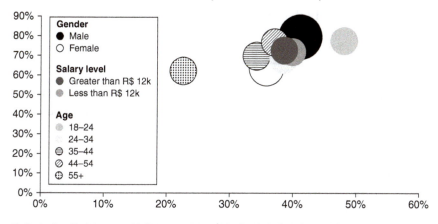

Vertical axis = % of demographic that consumes sport online including via a mobile
Horizontal axis = % of demographic that consumes sport via an internet enabled mobile device
Size of bubble represents interest in sport among demographic

Figure 2.1   Profile of fans accessing sport content online in Brazil. Source: Perform *et al.*, 2011, p. 33. Extracts from the *Global Sports Media Consumption Report 2011* reprinted with kind permission of Perform, TV Sports Markets & KantarSport.

including roughly equal consumption of sport by women and men using mobiles and the Internet (see Figure 2.1).

Market research surveys of this type have their limitations, especially when undertaken in the midst of significant media transformations. However, this snapshot is useful when considering the scale and scope of mobile media's role in the media and sport couplet. It also directs our attention to thinking about the influential, if not decisive, ways in which mobile media are involved in transformations in sport and its consumption.

This chapter charts the rise of sport in mobile media, from their strategically important early role in underwriting speculative investments in new technology, through to their present function across a range of everyday settings, as well as large industrial media-entertainment engagements. I argue that there are complex new politics of digital media sport that can be clearly observed through mobile media. A constitutive tension is being played out between the organized and formal economy of media sport on the one hand, and the informal economies of new modes of cultural participation on the other. Such politics are enabled by the new dynamics of sport in society, as much as by the affordances and user cultures of mobile media platforms. The tension has been most visibly and controversially on display in the industrial, economic and legal battles over media rights to sports content (Hutchins, 2013).

Before proceeding, a note on definition is important. By mobile phones, I mean mobile handsets, devices, software and applications that rely upon cellular mobile telecommunications networks. Cell phones, as they are called in some countries, were famously categorized into technological stages of first, second (2G), third (3G) and now fourth generation (4G) mobile networks. The mention of 4G networks confronts us immediately with the challenge that mobile phones are deeply involved in processes of media convergence. Specifically, mobile phones are involved in a series of specific and complicated convergences. First, telecommunications networks are being reengineered as data networks that will continue to carry voice communications. But the architecture of these networks resembles the Internet and data communications more than the telephone networks of the twentieth century. Secondly, central to fourth-generation networks is the intermixing and fusion of Internet-based wireless networks, such as WiMAX (the successor to WiFi), with cellular mobile-based networks. With WiFi-capable mobile handsets, users are already well accustomed to switching between wireless and mobile networks. Now such hybridity is enacted at the level of the networks. Thirdly, there are significant convergences emerging regarding the messy phenomenon referred to as mobile Internet. As we have seen from the statistics on sport fans in China and Brazil, mobiles are increasingly being used to access the Internet, something that smartphones like the iPhone, Android system, Blackberry and their clones make easy to do. Locative media, then, involve a crossover between locational, navigational, mapping technology and mobiles. Finally, mobiles are a significant part of the new television ecologies that exist in relation to television infrastructures and cultures (Goggin, 2011, 2012).

STARTING THE AFFAIR

The diffusion of mobile phones in the 1980s and 1990s positioned sport as a key cultural activity for new forms of communication. While we do not have direct studies to establish the contours of adoption at this time, the role of mobiles in the lives of sport participants, managers and followers began to be noted in the research of that time (Palen, Salzman & Young, 2001). Mobile phones were used in micro-coordination of team members and fans (Boyle, 2004), and played an often controversial role in elite sporting events. With the portability of mobile phones, participants could, for example, place a bet on a horse directly from their phone while at the racecourse (Observer, 1992). Players pushed the boundaries of acceptable conduct by using mobile phones on the field—such as when West Indies cricketer Brian Lara was censured in 1995 for making a phone call while fielding in the slips (a fielding position in cricket) (Williams, 1995). The potential interruption to particular sports in which the crowd is expected to be quiet at key points, such as in tennis when spectators received mobile phone calls (especially ringtones) while the ball was in play, was a much ventilated theme. For instance, venues such as Wimbledon placed a ban on their use in the royal box on center court (Hyde, 2001).

While the rise of the Internet in the 1990s triggered growing interest in the potential of mobiles to change the consumption of sport, this was a slow process. In 1992 in the UK, a tussle unfolded among three rival broadcasters, BBC, ITV and BSkyB, for the broadcast rights to the new EPL soccer competition. News coverage of these negotiations saw the mobile phone feature as a communicative conduit for the twists and turns of corporate treachery (Guardian, 1992). Sports and mobiles were also conjoined relatively early in the developing area of sport celebrity. Many mobile phone companies promoted their products through the new figure of the global sports celebrity. Many sport stars were provided with mobile phones and airtime and became the vehicles for advertising campaigns. The most famous instance was the contract of Manchester United captain, David Beckham, with mobile giant Vodafone (Goggin, 2006)—a good example of the new mobile phone culture's involvement in the "media sports cultural complex" (Rowe, 2004).

Where mobiles did feature directly as media occurred in relation to the portable predecessor technology of radio:

> . . . the general decline in supporters carrying radios into football [soccer] grounds indicates that for many the function of keeping in touch with other games has been taken over by the mobile phone (with of course recent models now incorporating a radio into their range of functions). (Boyle, 2004)

By 1996, the mobile phone was being used to provide a new sense of "liveness" in the older media form of talk radio:

> Talk Radio, the national commercial phone-in station, isn't interested in match commentaries but sees huge scheduling benefits in ever more sports programming, including its quirky updates from mobile-phone users at football [soccer] grounds. (Guardian, 1996)

This new kind of commentary proved popular, leading to specific sponsorship deals for celebrity phone-in guests. In the early 2000s, mobiles began to be widely used as a means to distribute information about sport. The BBC trialed the distribution of online news, including sport, to Internet portal and mobile phones, and was criticized by some for using its public service broadcasting status to try and dominate the new commercial platforms (Wells, 2000).

A milestone moment occurred at Wimbledon in 2000 when scores were accessed through the Internet and mobiles in "record numbers" (Cassy, 2000). In addition to its popular website, IBM provided fans with match scores via mobile text messaging and computer-based email. The managing director of Sports.com, Tom Jessiman, opined:

> Sports results is killer content for mobile internet devices . . . Events change so often during the day and sports fans want to be kept updated on changing scores wherever they are . . . They can wait until they get home to watch the highlights on television but they need to know the score as soon as it changes. (Cassy, 2000)

Sky UK offered users real-time news and information via the mobile Internet Wireless Access Protocol (WAP), including a makeshift location media service:

> In football [soccer] for example, users can find live scores and fixture information about every British league team, premiership fixture lists, team news and scores and have access to the official Premier League Opta statistics. The service also provides users with the latest news updates in rugby, cricket, golf, motorsport, boxing, tennis and athletics . . . A novel feature of the Sky mobile internet service will direct users to the nearest pub equipped with Sky Sports—simply by the user entering their postcode and matching their location to the nearest Sky-screening venue. (British Sky Broadcasting, 2000)

The use of WAP mobile Internet technology, text messaging and the emergence of mobile data services—featuring ringtones, video and picture downloads and wallpapers of sports stars—saw mobile phone culture and sport mutually implicated. However, the next frontier of mobile media and sport was firmly believed to be that of the 3G mobile.

MOBILE TELEVISION

3G mobiles made video communication a reality, providing video calling and mobile television. Video calling managed to attract much interest, but only a modicum of actual take up. The combination of mobile television and sport provided a much more complicated set of outcomes. As we have seen, the initial "pitch" for mobiles and sport revolved around providing key information and news to eager fans, while leaving the broadcast experience to those not at the ground, or to the enjoyment of the post-match replay. The mediated experience of "liveness", however, was not far from the minds of media technology developers. For instance, in 2000 it was claimed that Borussia Dortmund striker, Joerg Heinrich, made history when his goal against FC Freiburg in the German *Bundesliga* soccer league competition became the first key sporting moment to be shown live on a mobile phone. As it turned out, those participating in the trial conducted by technology company Worldzap received an alert on their mobile phone that a goal had been scored, but then needed to turn to their handheld computer to view it (Observer, 2000). This stitching together of technologies now strikes us as rather awkward, yet it underscores how the movement of television into the realm of mobile media proceeded by fits and starts rather than in a smooth progression.

The advent of mobile television systems, integrated with the rest of digital television, seemed an exciting prospect for sports content providers. The promise of mobile television was to offer sports broadcasts whenever and wherever the viewer wished to see them. This vision relied upon digital technology supporting direct broadcast of television signals to mobile phones, involving the development of a number of standards worldwide, including Digital Video Broadcasting-Handheld (DVB-H) in Europe. In Japan and Korea, the emphasis evolved towards multimedia broadcasting for mobile reception, with standards including DMB in Korea, ISDB-Tmm and SEG in Japan. Around the world, trials of direct broadcast to mobiles commenced in 2003, but the full commercial broadcast of sport via mobiles occurred in earnest only from 2006–2007 onwards (Curwen & Whalley, 2008). Sport proved highly attractive in many studies of these trials and in early commercial offerings of mobile television (de Renesse, 2011).

In the meantime, video and televisual excerpts of sport were broadcast and widely consumed via other methods—especially what was termed "unicasting" or the distribution of mobile video content over the cellular network. Here a consumer is able to choose which programs or channels they wish to watch. Mobile carriers sought to acquire rights for key sports and to build a specific audience and consumption habit. This development added fuel to the already phenomenally valuable market for sports coverage rights: "The wide use of mobile phones resulted in the development of new broadcasting intermediaries and platforms in the sport broadcasting landscape" (Tsiotsou, 2012). For example, the Hong Kong-based international carrier associated with 3G, Hutchison, developed highly publicized sporting coverage and services on mobile television that were tailored to specific national markets. In the UK, the company offered sporting highlight packages of EPL games, while in Australia Hutchison's "3" covered the cricket, accompanied by prominent advertising and sponsorship packages (Goggin, 2011).

Early in the diffusion and development of mobile television, the power of existing brands and players in sports media was clearly apparent. In the UK, the dominant satellite provider, Rupert Murdoch's BSkyB, launched its Sky Mobile TV in 2007. The service was available on Vodafone, Orange and T-Mobile, and offered three simulcast channels, Sky 1, 2 and 3. At the time, Sky felt that it was seeing "real demand for live football [soccer] on a mobile phone" (Mobile, 2007). Sky Mobile TV eventually became an "app", and was then phased out in favor of a new service called Sky Sports TV in 2011. Subscription television providers such as BSkyB were well placed to offer their curated and aggregated services to mobile carriers. Not only did subscription television properties migrate their services to the new mobile television platform, but particular networks and channels also took the opportunity to find new distribution openings. A good example of this shift is ESPN, the world's largest dedicated sports network, with its ESPN Mobile.

The marketing of mobile television was driven strongly by the major national and international sport events. This is an obvious strategy given that such events attract the largest television audiences worldwide. In 2006, mobile television was trialed in the Melbourne Commonwealth Games and the Fédération Internationale de Football Association (FIFA) World Cup held in Germany. The latter trial of mobile television was considered a "key event" in the technology's development and attracted widespread interest (Kretzschmar, 2009). By this time, the potential market was clearly believed to be significant by those companies vying for the rights to broadcast sport. In the lead-up to the 2004 Athens Olympics, the US network broadcaster NBC and the European Broadcasting Union (EBU), respectively, struck deals with the International Olympic Committee (IOC). The deals included all coverage rights, and specified rights to mobiles, as well as to television, radio, audio, video-on-demand and the Internet (Tsiotsou, 2012). Since this time, negotiations over mobile rights have grown in intensity, as have the sums paid and the energy put into enforcing the rights obtained. The actual consumption of sport on mobile television has, however, been difficult to pin down until recently.

The 2008 Beijing Olympics was acclaimed as the moment when sport broadcasting via mobile television "arrived". The EBU dubbed these the "digital games":

> The 2008 Games were the first time that digital media coverage of the event—including live broadband internet coverage and mobile phone clips—was widely available throughout the world from websites of official rights holders. In China, over the seventeen days of the Olympic Games, 153 million people watched live broadcast of the Olympic Games online, with 237 million watching video on demand footage and an average 20 million page views per day on the mobile phone platform provided by CCTV.com. (EBU, 2008)

However, when the nature of this media experience is scrutinized, its implications are not so clear-cut. P. David Marshall, Becky Walker and Nicholas Russo (2010) argue that the consumption of Olympic events was low in many countries. Furthermore, the actual construction of the television coverage for mobiles was less than inspiring:

> . . . the official mobile television broadcasts in many countries were heavily mediated and framed not just in a nationalistic way, but also in a way that delayed and trickled information to audiences, or repeated the format and broadcasts already broadcast on conventional television. In several countries, mobile content was only provided through paid subscription services, and the only content available was the retransmission of previously transmitted television broadcasts. (Marshall et al., 2010, p. 273)

A key reason for this unimaginative use of mobiles for sport lies in the tension between "new" and "old" media. Instead of mobiles providing a distinctly different and compelling new mode of sport consumption via live television or streamed video (as with the Internet), their contribution to digital sport lies in the various kinds of information, data, interactions and engagements that they make possible—from scores and weather updates, through subscription-based mobile phone newspapers and text messaging athletes, to viral video, games and social activities (Marshall et al., 2010).

What is evident in the Beijing Olympics, then, and certainly thereafter, is the existence of a rich mobile technology ecology in which sport now finds itself mediated. It is replete with commercial services that started in the early days of WAP mobile Internet and supported by 2G (or rather 2.5G) networks (Goggin, 2006). This ecology also takes its energy and shape from the new kinds of "unofficial" mobile phone and media cultures, of which text messaging was an early harbinger. For instance, the attempts of Chinese state and corporate interests (Yu, 2009) to control and license the media space of the Beijing Olympics were only successful up to a point, namely in controlling the distribution of official Olympic content via mobile devices (Marshall et al., 2010). If, though, the links between amateur mobile phone footage and the user-generated content platforms of the Internet were not so easily activated at the Beijing Olympics, this is no longer the case in China and elsewhere. The 2012 London Olympics were dubbed the "social media" Olympics. The Opening Ceremony featured Sir Tim Berners-Lee, the man credited with the invention of the World Wide Web, sending live tweets from the stadium. A key part of the cinematic and musical extravaganza of the Opening Ceremony revolved around young people's use of mobile and social media, with romance blossoming between two lovers due to a lost-and-returned mobile phone. Despite heavy intellectual property restrictions on user-generated content (discussed in a later section), athletes and spectators alike took to Twitter, photo apps like Instagram, Facebook and other software on mobile platforms.

FANS, MOBILE INTERNET AND SMARTPHONES

The proposition that highly lucrative sports content would be the flagship of the mobile television "revolution" has not been realized. Yet, sport and mobiles, I would argue, remain symbiotically related. What occurred is quite different from what was imagined in the early 2000s. There are various reasons why this is so, but I'll focus on two decisive factors. First, television itself has mutated dramatically, with the media organizations and producers, and audiences who have "invested" in television, locked in a process of intense and, at times, radical innovation that varies greatly around the world. Second, the evolution of mobile telephony and telecommunication into fullblown mobile media has taken forms that were not foreseen and are still unfolding. Looming large here are the complex convergences referred to as "mobile Internet" and, especially, the mobile aspect of social media.

Television has retained, and in many ways strengthened, its place as the most lucrative and popular form of media for consumption of sport (Rowe,

2011). The long awaited technological transformation in this nigh-century-old media form has been digital television, with countries in the process of switching over from analogue systems. As this transition occurs, the mainstream television industry—whether free-to-air or subscription—is undergoing a radical makeover through Internet-based forms of video and television. The emergence of television ecologies is probably a more accurate way of characterizing this media form than "television" per se. Viewers have a growing range of television consumption options depending on their country, providers and infrastructure, levels of access and literacy, income, time and expenditure preferences. Television is transmitted in traditional modes, via download or catch-up on the Internet, broadcast via Internet TV, video-on-demand or purchased via iTunes. It can be stored and viewed on a wide range of devices from the "box" or digital video recorder, through "connected TV" or home media server, to portable laptop computer, game or mobile media devices. Mobiles have become a key player in these new television ecologies, but not, as we have seen, through the extension of broadcast television to mobile platforms (Goggin, 2012). Rather, the consumption of video via mobiles has emerged as a popular activity, including the viewing of YouTube videos on mobiles (Nielsen, 2009).

A key issue for sports media organizations is how to configure access to content across the contemporary Babel of devices and contexts, understand the consumer demand for these, and construct appropriate business models. A major assumption is that mobiles will be a significant media platform for sport in these new television ecologies, but that mobiles will operate in a cross-media or transmedia platform environment. It has long been recognized that the "active audience" of television has enjoyed watching programs and interacting with this content, as well as communicating about it with co-present and absent others. This activity of audiences often now occurs via mobiles (telephone calls and SMS being early examples of this practice) and Internet (with Twitter catalyzing this phenomenon). Such conversations among viewers and between audiences and content also lead to engagement with other kinds of media, such as games. Cultures of use of this kind are now built into the communicative architecture and formats of televised sport, as Bjørn Taalesen, sport editor of Norwegian public broadcaster TV2, explains:

> It starts with text messages to elect the best player. Then you develop it so that you can make substantial revenues from creating a manager game on Tour de France, where the viewers are engaged to "join" the program. (quoted in Solberg & Helland, 2011, p. 26)

Making sense of such participant-oriented accounts of innovation, Harry Arne Solberg and Knut Helland contend:

> Broadcasting has been characterized by rapid technological innovations during the first years of the 21st century . . . The borders between

media activities that previously were separated have been more or less removed. Using the Internet and mobile telephone as a supplement to traditional TV viewing is now very common . . . [S]ports broadcasting has had an important role in this development, for example by familiarizing viewers with the new products and services . . . [and] . . . product innovations *per se* have made integration more advantageous. (Solberg & Helland, 2011, p. 31)

It is this kind of environment that Nielsen trumpeted in its 2010 report, *The Changing Face of Sports Media*:

Sports are also perfectly suited for the current three-screen media age. On average 81 million people in the US visited sports websites each month to keep tabs on their fantasy teams or follow any one of the captivating stories this year. Leagues have used websites, social networks, and smart phones to create a virtual sports bar for fan dialogue to help the buzz surrounding major televised sporting events. (Nielsen, 2010)

Recently, such cross-platform, integrative digital media television has been dubbed "social" or "connected" television—and it is a phenomenon in which mobiles play a key role. As Brett Hutchins and David Rowe note, the "key to the future of media sport is the relationship between screens" (Hutchins & Rowe, 2012, p. 76).

Convergence between mobiles and the Internet is also proceeding apace. With mobiles a family of key devices by which consumers access the Internet, the various media forms important to sport can be accessed in this way. In addition, the advent of mass media mobile Internet—high bandwidth, software-driven, mobile computing devices that span a continuum from classic cell phone through smartphone and tablet to Internet-equipped portable media of other provenance (whether an e-book reader, game device or other technology)—has been accompanied by the creation of new affordances and cultures of use. The most obvious recent example of this innovation is the "apps phenomenon"—software applications for smartphones and tablets (Goggin & Crawford, 2011). As approved apps in the Apple Store passed the 500,000 mark in April 2011, one estimate was that sports apps accounted for some three percent of all apps downloads (Scott, 2011). This figure compared to fifteen percent for games, fourteen percent books and eleven percent entertainment, which raises questions about the extent to which sport media actually feature within other categories. A 2011 Nielsen study found that thirty-one percent of US tablet and smartphone users had downloaded sports apps (free and paid) in the previous thirty days (Nielsen, 2012b). Another Nielsen study ranked the top five mobile sports apps as: ESPN (sixty-two percent), NFL Live (eighteen percent), Yahoo! Sports (seventeen percent), MLB.com (Master League Baseball) (sixteen percent) and Fox Sports Mobile (thirteen percent) (Nielsen, 2012a).

Apps have provided a means to bring together different aspects of the mediated experience of sport, offering new kinds of personalization and choice. Multichannel television vastly increased the amount of sport available, focused on particular sports (one sport per channel), and offered the opportunity to reaggregate sporting content on a grand scale (hence the megasports networks such as ESPN). The Internet increased the potential coverage even further by offering websites, blogs and other technologies as supplements to official information and media. The Internet also provided a many-to-many infrastructure for the amateur sharing and broadcast of sport. Television and video content is also now widely accessed by apps.

As well as their involvement in the consumption of sport via mobile media, apps play a heightened role in the prosaic logistics and coordination of individuals and groups participating in and watching sport. The role of mobiles in the microcoordination of sport fans—not to mention communal activity at many cultural and social events—has been long acknowledged. These social functions of mobiles interweave not only with mobile social media, but also mobile commercial applications. For example, tickets for major events such as the 2012 Rugby Championship could be purchased via the "M-Ticket" portal, and then individual tickets distributed to friends via SMS. Apps now frame much of social media for mobiles, whether these are social media applications initially developed for, and popularized on, the desktop or laptop computer-based Internet, or "mobile"-native social media applications. Again, the world of mobile Internet and apps varies greatly across cultural and social settings, including pioneer social networking systems such as Cyworld (Korea), Mixi (Japan), QQ and Weibo (China), and Facebook, Twitter and LinkedIn (US).

Apps provide new ways to repackage existing kinds of media coverage and to replace or extend them through innovation. This trend is observable in the many newspapers and magazine apps that are driven as much by the plunging revenue models for traditional print media as by the excitement surrounding digital forms. For instance, sport websites have taken over, or displaced, the traditional role of the match program purchased at a sporting event to gain information about the game, profiles of players and statistics. Sport websites are also the prime destination for information, with many sports and events providing websites that are customized for browsing on mobile websites. The 2012 London Olympics had an official website (http://www.london2012.com/) offering a comprehensive array of information, allowing users to navigate the event and its media. It also offered a mobile site (http://m.london2012.com/) that was stripped down for quick loading, but with a link to the full site. Then there were two official apps, "Join In" and "Results". The Join In app was billed as "a mobile guide to help you plan, enjoy and share your Games experience". This "pocket guide" presented:

> . . . an essential planning tool for everyone, whether you have tickets for a sporting event or not. From the start of the Olympic Torch Relay to

the Olympics and Paralympics, the Opening and Closing Ceremonies, plus all the cultural, city and community celebrations happening across the UK, Join In is your essential companion. (http://www.london2012 .com/mobileapps)

By contrast, the Results app provided:

> . . . results, live updates, calendar schedule, details of sports, medal tables and athlete profiles. Users can also follow specific countries, receiving official news and updates tailored to them all in one app.

Apps can be also used to coordinate the consumption of media associated with a sporting event across different devices. TV 2 Norway, for example, claimed the first live synchronized companion app for iOS and Android devices during live coverage of the Tour de France in 2010. Billing this as a complementary and "fully immersive two-screen experience", the app pushed content to a viewer's tablet or mobile device in synchronization with the action happening on the TV screen (Dennis, 2011). Other apps incorporate features of location and positioning technologies that characterize smartphones as locative media (de Souza e Silva & Frith, 2012; Farman, 2012). For instance, the Official Qantas Wallabies app, developed by the Australian Rugby Union for the 2012 Test season, "takes you off your seat and into the coaches box" (Australian Rugby Union, 2012). As well as player profiles and live match statistics, the Wallabies app also provides "live GPS tracking" of stars (in home matches at least).

The ultimate significance of apps culture for media sport is still being played out. Due to the nature of the mobile as an intimate, personal technology, apps have allowed new kinds of connection between fans and sport because of their potential to bring together a wide range of information deriving from the individual mobile users and the sport that they like. In terms of the media industry and economy, apps have provided a rapidly growing platform for innovation, tapping into the potential of mobile computing, data and software. The apps stores have breached the "walled garden" of telecommunications carriers and mobile vendors by allowing even relatively small software producers to offer their wares to a global audience. This development offers new avenues for sports clubs, sporting leagues and communities of fans to strengthen their hand as new media intermediaries, as has occurred with earlier phases of Internet development. Yet, the smartphone, tablet and apps ecologies come with their own politics requiring much wider discussion (Goggin, 2011). Moreover, apps culture evolves as rights holders take increasingly aggressive measures to police what users do with the technology.

For instance, alongside the innovative official apps for the 2012 Olympics (such as the *Ceremonies Explorer* tumblr blog) came strict rules that concern the use of user-generated content and social media by athletes, accredited media and ticket-holders. In venues, for instance, ticket-holders were prohibited to make:

> . . . unauthorised transmissions and/or recording through mobile telephones or other instruments (video cameras, tape recorders, etc). (19.3.2, LOCOG, 2012)

In the event that a ticket-holder did not take heed of this instruction, sharing of such content online was specifically banned also:

> Images, video and sound recordings of the Games taken by a Ticket Holder cannot be used for any purpose other than for private and domestic purposes and a Ticket Holder may not license, broadcast or publish video and/or sound recordings, including on social networking websites and the internet more generally, and may not exploit images, video and/or sound recordings for commercial purposes under any circumstances, whether on the internet or otherwise, or make them available to third parties for commercial purposes. (19.6.3, LOCOG, 2012)

Athletes and other "accredited persons" were only permitted to use social media during the Olympics within narrow bounds:

> The IOC encourages participants and other accredited persons to post comments on social media platforms or websites and tweet during the Olympic Games . . . However, any such postings, blogs or tweets must be in a first-person, diary-type format and should not be in the role of a journalist—i.e. they must not report on competition . . . (IOC 2011)

Like other instances of over-zealous policing of rights concerning the Olympic rings logo, this ban on social media caused an international controversy, although the IOC and London Olympics Organizing Committee tried to downplay its actual effects (Kermond, 2012).

CONCLUSION: MOBILE MEDIA CULTURE AND DEMOCRATIZATION?

The place of mobiles in digital media sport is multifarious. In mid-2012, I attended a baseball game in Phoenix, Arizona between the local Diamond ("D") Backs and the Los Angeles Dodgers. At the ground itself, the game took shape through a mix of media. Familiar baseball rituals, including the national anthem and music played to fuel the crowd's enthusiasm, punctuated the action on the field. New elements also made an appearance: Twitter feeds; an interlude in which crowd members danced with a cartoon character appearing on the scoreboard and public screen; and figures and text scrolling across the border of the roof on the stands. The divide between watching the game live at the venue, and its mediated representation else-where, had been seriously breached—a point made by Steve Redhead in his discussion of "the way in which [during] mediatized sporting events in ac-celerated modernity the stadium is effectively transformed into a television set" (Redhead, 2007, p. 237). Internet and mobile media are also increas-ingly integral to how the game itself transpires and is followed at the venue, and the deeper social underpinnings that such media entail.

This experience underlined the contemporary manner in which mo-bile media are a pervasive, highly significant element of "sport as media" (Hutchins & Rowe, 2012). The rise of mobiles has coincided with a great intensification of sport and media in society. From the use of mobile com-munication for a range of purposes, mobiles themselves developed sub-stantial roles as sports media. Telecommunications and mobile companies compete for sports content for their new mobile channels, as is evidenced by the production of ringtones, wallpapers and video downloads from mobile portals, as well as the broadcast of sport via mobile television. While mo-bile sports rights are more fiercely fought over than ever, the role of mobile media has dramatically shifted. Again, we can look at this altered state of mobile media from various perspectives.

The political and cultural economies of mobile media have changed pro-foundly in the space of a few short years. As Castells demonstrates in *Com-munication Power*, there is an intermingling of old and new media interests in the transnational corporations that dominate digital media (Castells, 2009). Telecommunications and mobile companies are powerful players in the new digital media landscape, challenging the television broadcasters for control of sports media. Yet, for their part, they are now seriously chal-lenged by the likes of information technology corporations such as Apple and Google. Furthermore, the television networks generally include tele-communications, mobile, broadband and Internet companies as substan-tial, if not dominant, corporate shareholders. The technologies and cultural practices associated with mobile media have altered dramatically—with the mobile's imbrication in new television ecologies, and the rise of mobile social media and apps, obvious indications of this change. These socio-technical innovations, in particular, are marked by great tensions, as was evident in the case of the Beijing and London Olympics. The scale of "unofficial", un-regulated user activity in contemporary sport is also remarkable. An AT&T manager noted in a corporate blog that in 2012:

> AT&T customers at the Superbowl uploaded nearly 40 percent more data than they downloaded—posting lots of video, pictures and taunt-ing messages to friends who weren't lucky enough to experience the game live. (Donovan, 2012)

The widespread use of mobile media is an integral aspect of everyday media culture, and this kind of customer take up of mobile media is a boon for mobile companies preoccupied with their profitability in the great battle for sport between the screens. For other powerful interests in media sport, such as the rights owners and holders, a clear line is drawn between official reliance upon, and harvesting of, user-generated content and mobile practices, and what unofficial, unsanctioned users are permitted to do. Where this development leads in terms of the commodification of sport, and public access to and participation in it, are highly contested issues. The pressing question is, finally, whether the "social turn" in television, Internet and mobile media amounts to something much more democratizing than it has been thus far.

ACKNOWLEDGEMENT

My thanks to Rosemary Curtis for her excellent research assistance. This chapter was supported by Australian Research Council Discovery Grant DP120101971 *Moving Media: Mobile Internet and New Policy Modes*.

REFERENCES

Australian Rugby Union (2012) *Wallabies*. App. Online. Available from: itunes. apple.com/lv/app/wallabies/id379883692?mt=8 (Accessed 1 June 2012).

Boyle R (2004) Mobile communication and the sports industry: the case of 3G. *Trends in Communication* 12(2–3): 73–82.

Boyle R & Haynes R (2009) *Power Play: Sport, the Media and Popular Culture*. 2nd ed. Edinburgh: Edinburgh University Press.

British Sky Broadcasting (2000) Sky offers enhanced mobile package: offering mobile users the most comprehensive, real-time sports & news information. 22 September. Available at: *M2 Presswire*.

Cassy J (2000) Net service is a winner for Wimbledon. *The Guardian*, 20 July. Online. Available from: www.guardian.co.uk/technology/2000/jul/20/internetnews. onlinesupplement (Accessed 27 January 2012).

Castells M (2009) *Communication Power*. Oxford and New York: Oxford University Press.

Curwen P & Whalley J (2008) Mobile television: technological and regulatory issues. *info* 10(1): 40–64.

Dennis T (2011) Norway get immersive 2-screen experience thru never.no. *gomonews.com*. Online. Available from: www.gomonews.com/norway-get-immersive-2-screen-experience-thru-never-no/ (Accessed 25 March 2012).

de Renesse R (2011) *Mobile TV: Challenges and Opportunities Beyond 2011*. London: Open Society Foundation. Online. Available from: www.soros.org/reports/mapping-digital-media-mobile-tv-challenges-and-opportunities-beyond-2011 (Accessed 14 August 2012).

de Souza e Silva A & Frith J (2012) *Mobile Interfaces in Public Spaces: Locational Privacy, Control, and Urban Sociability*. New York: Routledge.

Donovan J (2012) A different take on the big game—stats from the stands. *Innovation Space*. Online. Available from: http://www.attinnovationspace.com/innovation/story/a7780988 (Accessed 26 March 2012).

EBU (European Broadcasting Union) (2008) Beijing 2008: the digital games. *EBU News*. Online. Available from: http://www.ebu.ch/en/union/news/2008/tcm_6-62839.php (Accessed 25 January 2012).

Farman J (2012) *Mobile Interface Theory: Embodied Space and Locative Media.* New York: Routledge.

Goggin G (2006) *Cell Phone Culture: Mobile Technology in Everyday Life.* London and New York: Routledge.

Goggin G (2011) *Global Mobile Media.* London and New York: Routledge.

Goggin G (2012) The eccentric career of mobile television. *International Journal of Digital Television* 3(2): 119–140.

Goggin G & Crawford K (2011) *Young, Mobile, Networked: Mobile Media and Youth Culture in Australia.* Report of ARC Discovery project. Sydney: Department of Media and Communications, the University of Sydney.

Guardian (1992) Premier League Football Contract—late winner leaves ITV sick as parrots. *The Guardian,* 22 May, 3.

Guardian (1996) Tune in—and kick up your ears. *The Guardian,* 12 August, 14.

Hutchins B (2013) Sport on the move: the unfolding impact of mobile communications on the media sport content economy. *Journal of Sport and Social Issues.* Online. Available from: http://jss.sagepub.com/content/early/2012/09/11/019372 3512458933.abstract?rss=1 (Accessed 1 December 2012).

Hutchins B & Rowe D (2012) *Sport Beyond Television: The Internet, Digital Media and the Rise of Networked Media Sport.* New York and London: Routledge.

Hyde M (2001) Diary—the warmest of salutes to Mark Byford. *The Guardian,* 3 July, 16.

IOC (International Olympic Committee) (2011) IOC social media, blogging and internet guidelines for participants and other accredited persons at the London 2012 Olympic Games. 15 September. Online. Available from: www.olympic.org/ Documents/Games_London_2012/IOC_Social_Media_Blogging_and_Internet_ Guidelines-London.pdf (Accessed 14 August 2012).

Kermond C (2012) Olympics ban image, video sharing. *The Age,* 15 June. Online. Available from: www.theage.com.au/business/marketing/olympics-ban-image-video-sharing-20120614–20d11.html (Accessed 14 August 2012).

Kretzschmar S (2009) Journalistic content and the World Cup 2006: multimedia services on mobile devices. In: Hartmann M, Rössler P & Höflich JR (eds.) *After the Mobile Phone?: Social Change and the Development of Mobile Communication.* Berlin: Frank & Timme, 85–100.

Ling R (2012) *Taken for Grantedness: The Embedding of Mobile Communication into Society.* Cambridge, MA: MIT.

LOCOG (London Olympics Games Organising Committee) (2012) Terms and Conditions of Ticket Purchase. Online. Available from: www.tickets.london2012. com/homepage (Accessed 14 August 2012).

Marshall PD, Walker B & Russo N (2010) Mediating the Olympics. *Convergence* 16(3): 263–78.

Miller T, Lawrence GA, McKay J & Rowe D (2001) *Globalization and Sport: Playing the World.* London: Sage.

Mobile (2007) Live football booming for Sky. *Mobile,* 21 December, 1.

Nielsen (2009) *Tuned into the Phone: Mobile Video Use in the US and Abroad.* New York: Nielsen.

Nielsen (2010) *The Changing Face of Sports Media.* New York: Nielsen.

Nielsen (2012a) *State of the Media: 2011 Year in Sports.* New York: Nielsen.

Nielsen (2012b) *State of the Media: Consumer Usage Report 2011:* New York: Nielsen.

Observer (1992) Horse-sense on bookies' day of rest. *Observer,* 26 July, 12.

Observer (2000) It's good to watch. *Observer,* 22 October, 15.

Palen L, Salzman M & Youngs E (2001) Discovery and integration of mobile communications in everyday life. *Personal and Ubiquitous Computing* 5(2): 109–22.

Perform, KantarSport & TV Sports Markets (2011) *Global Sports Media Consumption Report 2011: Analysis of Sports Media Consumption and Preferences across Eight of the World's Major Markets*. London: TV Sports Markets.

Redhead S (2007) Those absent from the stadium are always right: accelerated culture, sport media, and theory at the speed of light. *Journal of Sport and Social Issues* 31(3): 226–41.

Rowe D (2004) *Sport, Culture, and the Media*. 2nd ed. Maidenhead, Berkshire: Open University Press.

Rowe D (2011) *Global Media Sport: Flows, Forms and Futures*. London: Bloomsbury Academic.

Scott J (2011) App store milestone: 500,000 applications approved. *148Apps*. Online. Available from: http://www.148apps.com/news/app-store-milestone-500000-applications-approved/ (Accessed 8 April 2012).

Solberg HA & Helland K (2011) Sports broadcasting: an accelerator of business integration in the media industry. *Nordicom Review* 32(2): 17–33.

Tsiotsou R (2012) Entrepreneurship in sports broadcasting. In: Chadwick S & Ciletti D (eds.) *Sports Entrepreneurship: Theory and Practice*. Morgantown, WV: Fitness Information Technology, 97–120.

Wells M (2000) BBC faces inquiry into online giveaway. *The Guardian,* 17 July, 2.

Williams R (1995) Cricket—Lara's run for cover. *The Guardian,* 29 November, 2.

Yu H (2009) *Media and Cultural Transformation in China*. London and New York: Routledge.

3 Desktop Day Games
Workspace Media, Multitasking and the Digital Baseball Fan

Ethan Tussey

INTRODUCTION: DIGITAL TECHNOLOGIES AND THE MULTITASKING SPORTS FAN

ESPN's wildly popular online personality, Bill Simmons, is fond of claiming that digital technology has greatly improved the lives of US sports fans. Simmons (*The B.S. Report with Bill Simmons*, 2011) cites multiplatform subscription services such as the National Basketball Association's NBA League Pass, MLB.TV and NFL Sunday Ticket, social networking sites like Twitter and Facebook, and mobile devices such as tablets and smartphones, as the tools that have changed sports fandom. Unique digital services allow sports leagues to engage with fans via emerging technologies without jeopardizing existing primetime broadcast business models. Leagues justify their decision to differentiate digital services from television content by claiming that the digital viewer is different from their television counterpart. This appeal to technological determinism informs the design and functionality of online services, positioning digital access as a supplement to established broadcast viewing practices.

Media scholar Max Dawson (2011, p. 210) has argued that content providers use technological limitations and assumptions about the digital audience to develop a distinctly digital aesthetic or "aesthetic of efficiency"—"characterized by streamlined exposition, discontinuous montage and ellipsis, and decontextualized narrative or visual spectacle." According to Dawson, media producers have embraced the "aesthetic of efficiency" because it offers a distinct solution to the problem of emerging media, allowing companies to define certain content as "digital" without having to change programming and business strategies. Media producers use online user data to justify this strategy. For instance, ComScore (2007) states that digital audiences spend an average of 2.5 minutes on each online video, which provides a convenient rationale for developing a distinct "new media" business. Through the creation of digital platforms, sports leagues reinforce assumptions about digital spectatorship that help them reach new fans while maintaining current viewers.

Digital sports services encourage users to multitask not simply because digital audiences are "multitaskers," but because leagues are able to offer clips, highlights and textual information without violating existing television contracts. This strategy is ideal for sports leagues because, according to television studies scholar Victoria E. Johnson (2009, p. 123), sports are

> . . . predisposed to being parsed out in small "bytes" of information or highlights and news alerts best suited for miniaturized technologies and a la carte delivery.

Digital sports services encourage sports fans to check-in for content while attending to other activities such as work. Thus, new media theorist Anna Everett argues that digital viewers adopt a "pixilated gaze" (2003, p. 8) that is more "hyper-attentive" and "active" than the traditional television viewer because they tend to interact simultaneously with multiple windows and technologies. It is not the technology alone that creates this multitasking expectation. As cultural studies scholar, Melissa Gregg, has shown,

> . . . with the increased use of digital technology, workloads that may have been acceptable to begin with are shown to accumulate further expectations and responsibilities that aren't being recognized. (2011, p. 2)

Because employers are requiring more time from their employees, people are incorporating their pastimes into their work day as a coping mechanism, and as a way to stay informed about their favorite media franchises.

William Boddy (2004, p. 1) notes that the emergence of any new communication technology includes the "public rehearsal of contested and self-serving fantasies of the new product's domestic consumption". This rehearsal process is well under way. The creation of digital products and services for online sports fans implies foundational cultural beliefs about digital technology, viewing contexts and audience behavior. In this chapter, I argue that digital products and services developed by MLB have set standards and expectations about digital sports fandom that are changing the ways in which people watch sports. MLB websites, apps and digital distribution strategies are arguably as influenced by the business strategies of the league office as they are by so-called revolutionary digital technologies. I reveal that league executives encourage multitasking viewing habits in order to distinguish digital viewers from television viewers. Key to this process is the courting and cultivation of the workplace audience as a prime target for digital ventures because multitasking employees produce large amounts of web traffic. MLB's successful targeting of the workplace audience has helped to establish the league brand beyond its relationship with its television network partners. Workplace fans are now the same fans courted by the recently launched cable network, the MLB Network. The baseball fandom promoted on digital platforms has enabled MLB to identify a lucrative niche audience that is more interested in the action of the entire league than the activities of only their hometown team. By catering to these viewers, MLB and other sports leagues are redefining sports fandom for the digital era.

These developments suggest that success in the post-network/multiplatform/global distribution era is dependent on cultivating a lucrative niche audience and creating a 24-hour multiplatform presence. MLB identified the workplace audience as fans who would best suit their digital brand strategy and privileged their consumption habits over those of other baseball fans. Johnson (2009, p. 115) notes that the majority of sports leagues are following this strategy, as "quick-hit, highlight-oriented, 'instant access' " appeals to a particular type of multitasking consumer, and not to the average fan that is looking for the communal experience that watching a ball game traditionally represented. When Simmons applauds the MLB.TV app, he represents the type of fan invested in the entire league because they are engaged in fantasy sports and/or they are cultivating the cultural capital required to be a "true" baseball fan. Dawson (2007) points out that advertisements for these tech savvy consumers are pitched at:

> affluent, technologically advanced male consumers between the ages of 18 and 34 who, on account of their age, gender, and class status, experience limits on neither their movements nor their consumption habits. To consume mobile television is, in the context of these advertisements, to escape the social and spatial constraints of the home—as well as the feminine connotations of domestic viewing—for more interactive (and appropriately masculine) forms of perambulatory public leisure and consumption. (p. 233)

Targeting young males with the time, money and desire to make sport a major focus of their lives might be a good business strategy, but it also limits the democratic potential of digital distribution.

MAJOR LEAGUE BASEBALL IN YOUR CUBICLE

The decision to target the lucrative demographic discussed above was made in 2000 when the MLB pursued a digital strategy vastly different from the one that it had used for television licensing and audiences. To implement this strategy the league created MLB Advanced Media (nicknamed BAM) to standardize the digital presence of each MLB team. This decision ended contracts that team owners had pursued with third party web developers. A unanimous vote by league owners consolidated all digital rights to ensure that each team would share in the digital dollars. This meant that the website for the New York Yankees would not be run by the team but by the league office. The decision to cede control to the league and share profits represented a radical departure for this famously regional sports league.

While the league office negotiates national and international broadcast rights, the majority of baseball's television revenue is generated team-by-team and region-by-region, with profits dependent on the size of the media market. These broadcasting rights have contributed to a league of "haves and have-nots". Teams in major media markets, like New York and Los Angeles, earn record revenues for their television rights, while those in smaller markets survive on the comparatively limited money that they earn from regional television market contracts. Commissioner Bud Selig approached the digital frontier as an opportunity to achieve greater parity in a famously unbalanced league (Leitch, 2008).

Selig compared the creation of BAM to the historic broadcast licensing strategy of former National Football League (NFL) commissioner, Pete Rozell (Levy, 2007). Rozell's strategy is part of the reason why the NFL is the most popular sport in the US. He convinced league owners that sharing television revenue was in the league's best interests, explaining that the success of the then fledgling sport was dependent on getting people who did not have a local team to watch NFL games. By negotiating with national broadcasters for rights to the entire league, Rozell was able to ensure that NFL action appeared in every living room in the country. The networks promoted the entire league instead of individual teams, and viewers became fans of the NFL instead of just a particular team. The MLB's commissioner Selig believed that he might be able replicate the NFL's success on digital platforms. Seven years later, the strategy appears to be working as BAM made nearly US$400 million, served fifty million visitors and ranked in the top one hundred of all websites on the Internet (Levy, 2007). A key to BAM's success is its targeting of the workplace audience. In 2001, during the press announcement of baseball's streaming media service, MLB.TV, the league made its appeal to workplace viewers clear to reporters by providing two explanations. First, executives pointed out that most offices, as opposed to homes, had the broadband Internet speed to facilitate streaming video. Second, MLB.TV would be secondary to television, offering only out-of-market games (see below). This service would then require a different type of baseball fan who was interested in more than their local team (Hu, 2001).

Local games are "blacked-out" on MLB.TV in accordance with the terms of television contracts that baseball teams sign with regional broadcasters. These exclusive broadcast deals divide the nation into regions that define the broadcast jurisdictions of particular teams. For example, a baseball fan in Las Vegas cannot watch the games of the Oakland Athletics, San Francisco Giants or Arizona Diamondbacks on MLB.TV because Las Vegas is not part of those teams' regional broadcast jurisdictions. Most baseball viewers are fans of the particular team in their home region or city, and thus cannot watch their favorite team on MLB.TV. These blackout restrictions force fans to find a television if they want to see their team's games being broadcast, meaning that MLB.TV is a service popular only with those fans of "out-of-market" teams (for example, an Arizona Diamondback fan living in

Atlanta can watch their team as long as they are not playing in their home market against the Atlanta Braves), or for fans that simply want to watch baseball during the workday.

BAM is technologically capable of showing in-market games on MLB. TV. However, the MLB wants its digital properties to supplement television—not compete with it. BAM Chief Executive Officer, Bob Bowman, said of MLB.TV, "It's not as good as TV, but if you can't be near a TV, this is not a bad second place" (Hu, 2001). MLB.com spokesman Jim Gallagher also explained, "We are slaves to our rights holders. We are proceeding very carefully and in a very cordial fashion" (Hu, 2001). This "cordial" attitude has shaped the digital strategies of many sports leagues, as digital executives reassure nervous broadcast partners that digital products are helping, rather than hurting, television ratings.

MLB.TV and the majority of digital products produced by BAM are examples of what I term "workspace media"—they target a particular type of consumer and viewing experience that complements the television industry. Workspace media describes content produced for, and consumed by, the workplace audience (Tussey, 2009). Entertainment companies increasingly treat the workplace like a television "day part", programming content for desktops and mobile devices to be viewed in cubicles during lunchtime. Engaging the workplace audience is crucial for media conglomerates with digital aspirations, as work hours are peak times for web surfing (Stetler, 2008). Most television franchises, like Fox Sports Digital's "Lunch with Benefits" (a daily Web series designed for the cubicle dweller), update their digital offerings over the course of the work week through a combination of marketing and storytelling. This content is designed to give audiences a "touch point" that reminds them to watch their favorite shows during regularly scheduled broadcast times.[1] At its most creative, workspace media programming relates to Henry Jenkins's (2006) concept of transmedia storytelling in which narrative elements and world creation are presented on multimedia platforms. More routinely, workspace media content resembles what Jonathan Gray (2010) refers to as promotional "paratexts"—short video clips, audience opinion polls and contests designed to contextualize audience understanding of television content.

Targeting the workplace audience is especially important to MLB because, unlike other professional sports, the league schedules games every day of the week, with many games beginning during the workday. Employees are a natural audience for these games, particularly as more than half of all online videos are watched in the workplace (Nielsen, 2010). Yet, people do not watch baseball in their office cubicles as they would in their living rooms. Viewing habits change dramatically depending on the viewing context (McCarthy, 2001). Anna McCarthy (2004) has observed that digital screens are important cultural objects that are factored into the politics of office environments. Thus, studying the use of workspace media in office politics requires site-specific observations to understand digital spectatorship, and includes visits to office cubicles, observation of the role of media texts in interpersonal relationships and interviews with employees about their media habits. In my own research on workspace media, I visited several offices, observing habits for a week at a time and supplementing my notes with employee interviews. These methods reveal distinctive patterns and customs in the workplace viewing experience.

When combining my site-specific research with larger studies of workplace viewing, it becomes clear that people use workspace media to complement the rhythms of the workday. The typical workspace media viewing day can be divided into three parts, beginning with a settling-in period where employees check email and catch up on news. During this early part of the day, employees access workspace media that provide "digital white noise", which is often something that can be listened to like streaming radio or podcasts. In the middle of the day, typically during the lunch hour, employees engage workspace media as digital "break room television", catching up on television episodes that may have aired earlier in the week or the night before. The third workspace media habit is "media snacking", a term coined by *Wired* columnist Nancy Miller (2007). Snacking occurs throughout the day as employees search for relief from the monotony of work. During these times, employees look to workspace media for short videos, news stories or games.

Digitally distributed sports content is well suited to these workspace media viewing habits. Streaming audio of sports broadcasts provides digital white noise for the early "settling in" period of the workday. As employees plan out their day, the dedicated sports fans might organize their lunchtime to correspond with the start of sports events such as the National Collegiate Athletic Association (NCAA) Men's Basketball Tournament, the Olympics, soccer World Cup, MLB games or a golf tournament. Online sports coverage is also a perfect workspace media snack, as it provides an ongoing event to check throughout the day. For example, sports fans can set a goal of completing a task by a particular time and reward themselves by checking the score of a game. Analysis of workspace media viewing during the 2006 FIFA World Cup indicated that fans surfing FIFA webpages at work visited eighty pages per day on each day of the tournament (ComScore, 2006). The online audience was looking for score updates and information, rather than simply watching while at work. Workspace media products and services facilitate this media snacking by including programmable functionality that alerts viewers to particularly relevant moments in the game via text message, instant message or accumulated highlights that can be conveniently accessed by the user.

THE BOSS BUTTON

The "boss button" is worth considering as a significant example of "check-in" functionality. Boss buttons allow an audience to camouflage workspace media content by transforming it from a game or streaming video window into an image that looks like a spreadsheet or a word processing document. This feature has existed since the earliest forms of digital workspace media. Computer games like solitaire used boss buttons to conceal game play at the click of a button when "nosy" supervisors came to check on the productivity of employees. This button is the kind of added content that is easily included in software design and is unlikely to be blocked by intellectual property law, coding restrictions and retailer complaints. The streaming media player for the annual NCAA Men's Basketball tournament was equipped with a boss button when it premiered in 2006. The button converted the screen from a digitized broadcast to a window that looked like an empty spreadsheet. The functions of the boss button have also become more elaborate over time, gaining interactive features that work like a real email inbox complete with messages that the user can read. These messages often feature information about the corporate sponsors of the event, making this functionality both a creative accessory and an attribute of the digital marketing experience. Most workspace media products come complete with a version of the boss button, or with an interface that allows the screen to conceal or partition the viewing area.

These features enable workspace media sports snacking that some groups find concerning. In 2006, the consulting firm, Challenger, Grey and Christmas, published a report that claimed that workspace media snacking (13.5 minutes of web surfing a day) during the NCAA Men's basketball tournament cost an estimated US$3.8 billion in worker productivity (Vasquez, 2006). This staggering number was quoted widely and then rejected as invalid by journalists after identification of several methodological flaws. As Jack Shafer of *Slate.com* (2006) explained:

> Workers routinely shop during office hours, take extended coffee breaks, talk to friends on the phone, enjoy long lunches, or gossip around the water cooler. It's likely that NCAA tourney fans merely reallocate to the games the time they ordinarily waste elsewhere.

In contrast, researchers at the University of Melbourne in Australia have suggested that those employees who "snack" on workspace media are actually more productive, with Brent Coker stating:

> Short and unobtrusive breaks, such as a quick surf of the Internet, enables the mind to rest itself, leading to a higher total net concentration for a day's work, and as a result, increased productivity. (University of Melbourne, 2009)

These findings suggest that workspace media sports snacking—engaged in by twenty percent of the entire US "active at work audience" during the 2008 Olympic Games—may be as restorative and important to office cohesion as a trip to the water cooler (Nielsen, 2008).

Evidence of the sometimes-transgressive pleasure that workspace media sports viewing can provide is observable in the social network activity that accompanies daytime baseball games. During the 2011 post-season, eleven of forty games began their broadcast during work hours. I tracked the interactions of fans by monitoring Twitter at these times. The following tweets reflect the sense of satisfaction that viewers get from using sports to rebel against the constraints of the professional workplace:

> They don't like it when I watch a lot of baseball at work. That won't stop me. #postseason [@Lists Twitter ID]
>
> watching from work but getting the updates! This'll be another tight game. Hang in there CJ! @str8edgeracer #throwstrikes #postseason.—[@Lists Twitter ID]
>
> always refreshing to be able to check your favorite team's game from work at 3effing30 and see they're losing #postseason [@Lists Twitter ID]
>
> watching the rangers on your phone because you're stuck at work!! #texasgirlproblems #postseason [@Lists Twitter ID]
>
> Missing the Rangers game today due to work @Rangers keep a fan posted! #TeamRangers #postseason #winning [@Lists Twitter ID]
>
> #postseason @MLB on the desktop thanks to postseason.tv nothing makes the day fly by like homeplate collisions and homeruns [@Lists Twitter ID]

These tweets help to demonstrate how people incorporate sports viewing into their work routines. For some it is an act of defiance, while for others it is a way to connect to others that share their passion.

Many workspace media fans are grateful to MLB for providing services that improve their workday. This attitude is translating into commercial returns, as BAM is by far the most successful digital sports division in professional sports. The 2012 MLB At Bat mobile application is the most downloaded sports app in the Apple iTunes store, despite a base cost of US$14.99 and premium cost of over US$100 (Ogg, 2012). The app enhances media snacking through an interface that can be customized and informs the user of game progress via alerts and highlights. Both the MLB At Bat app and the MLB.com website offer live "look-ins" that give fans the ability to watch games in ten-minute intervals during tense games. Through these live look-ins, a baseball fan can view every pivotal moment of each game live without ever watching one entire game. The "snackable" concept is so popular that MLB has partnered with Yahoo! Sports to offer another app, MLB Full Count, which automatically takes the audience from one game to another so that they never have to miss a crucial play. Across the globe, sports leagues are creating similar highlight, check-in and live look-in digital services, as is evident in offerings from the BBC, NBC, YouTube's Olympic platform and the PGA's @Live app. These workspace media products are redefining what it means to be a sports fan, offering a multitasking pixilated gaze as the "natural" digital viewing context.

DIGITAL SPORTS SPECTATORSHIP: FROM TELEVISION TO THE WEB AND BACK AGAIN

The hyper-attentive spectator targeted by sports apps is assumed to be much more active than television or film viewers. Digital sport fans are considered to be deeply engaged consumers who use sports in their daily lives, interpersonal relationships and hobbies. As Matthew Purdy of the *New York Times* (2001) explains:

> The Great American Pastime has intersected with the great American way of passing time, and surfing the World Wide Web has given every fan a ticket to sit in the digital dugout. Baseball is broadcast and dissected so completely on the Internet, where it is then recreated in fantasy leagues, that you never know what you will miss leaving the keyboard for the ballpark.

Purdy's belief that the Internet enhances baseball is reflective of a fan who uses sports to interact with other people through fantasy sports leagues and sports gambling. These activities rely on the statistics of baseball to create a more involved entertainment experience.

Attracting fantasy baseball fans is exceedingly important to sports leagues because fantasy players are a valuable market demographic (see Chapter 16). Research shows that fantasy sports and online sports gambling are the fastest growing hobbies for online sports fans (Boyle & Haynes, 2002). By 2010, fantasy sports provided US$800 million of revenue for global sports leagues, with nineteen percent of full-time US employees participating in them (Good, 2011). Media sport fans are also much more likely to spend money on advertised products than live event attendees (Pritchard & Funk, 2006). In fact, BAM earned US$600 million in revenue from these fans through merchandise, out-of-market broadcasts and radio feeds (Salter, 2012). MLB is so dedicated to monetizing fantasy sports that the league has attempted to stop other websites using baseball statistics to create competing fantasy games (Pollack, 2006). MLB's efforts to block this competition failed after a legal challenge, but the money spent trying the case demonstrates the league's dedication to binding fantasy players to official MLB products and services (ESPN News, 2006). The MLB website currently offers five types of fantasy games requiring various levels of engagement. BAM creates variations on its games to complement the busy work schedules of its fans. As Bowman states:

> These games are popular with fans who had played fantasy baseball before but had left it, who said, "I don't have 20 minutes a day." These games only take a minute or two. They take up a lot less time and are a lot more fun. (Lemke, 2008)

It is Bowman's belief that digital baseball fans want to be able to "talk smack with a coworker"[2] about their baseball knowledge, and he ensures that BAM creates content that facilitates this social activity (Lemke, 2008).

While Bowman is celebrated for creating a business around the valuable workplace audience, BAM had few other options other than to pursue this market. Forbidden from replicating the experience that most baseball fans want—live in-market games—BAM products then encouraged different viewing behaviors. League owners, though, are so concerned that digital distribution of their games will "cannibalize" television revenue that they have even expressed concerns about BAM's use of highlights (Liberman, 2002). Digital content producers must maintain a good relationship with television broadcasters because they rely on regional broadcasts for the audio and visual content that appears in their products. By respecting the business models and distribution windows of local broadcasters, BAM is able to create content without the enormous overhead of live production costs. In the process, they have framed the digital sports spectator as a different kind of viewer than the television sports fan.

It is perhaps ironic that the strategies employed by BAM to attract a digital audience are the same as those used to start its own cable television network, the MLB Network. This network could easily be a competitor with MLB's television partners, but it is instead designed to *complement* the league's existing television contracts. The language used by network president, Tony Petitti, to describe MLB Network is similar to that used by Bowman to describe MLB.TV:

> We want to be the next choice for baseball fans, we want them to know that we're here, and we can get you caught up. We're another tool to enjoy the game. (Sandomir, 2008)

Petitti's description of the network as "the next choice" and as "catch-up" viewing speaks to the same niche audience targeted by MLB.com. In the ideal scenario for MLB executives, the modern baseball fan logs into MLB. com at the beginning of the workday to update their fantasy selections, checks in at lunch time to MLB.TV to watch part of a day game on their desktop computer, and goes home to watch their local team's broadcast while clicking-back and forth to the MLB Network to follow events in the rest of the league. Bowman expresses enthusiasm for the synergistic possibilities that exist between the network and the website:

> There's going to be a pretty thick pipe between our two shops, and on the ad side, we now have the ability to go after sponsors and offer TV while they have the ability to offer clients an established name in digital media. (Fisher, 2008)

The level of cooperation between MLB's digital businesses and broadcast arms, from editorial decisions to aesthetic characteristics, represents an attempt to replicate the behavior of the digital sports fan on multiple screens.

MLB Tonight, the signature show of the MLB Network, translates the hyper-attentiveness of workspace media to the living room. It makes use of the league's "live look-in" rights to help viewers stay updated on games occurring across the league. As *Sports Business Journal* reporters John Ourand & Terry Lefton (2010) explain, this live look-in feature is the key distinction that makes *MLB Tonight* a different experience from other popular baseball studio shows like ESPN's *Baseball Tonight*. While traditional highlight shows like *Baseball Tonight* recap games after they have finished, *MLB Tonight* gives fans a way to follow all the games as they happen, including from when the first game starts in the afternoon until the last game ends late in the evening. The audience is not expected to watch the entire broadcast. Rather, viewers act as they do at work, checking-in throughout the evening on games in progress.

The success of BAM and the MLB Network paves the way for other sports leagues to create cable programs for the modern multitasking spectator. BAM's influence is far reaching, providing the digital infrastructure for other sports leagues and networks including the NCAA, the Olympics, ESPN and Turner Sports (Salter, 2012). Bowman anticipates BAM's digital products being "cross-marketed" and integrated with ESPN's content offerings to provide greater cohesiveness in the digital presentation of MLB's brand (Fisher, 2008). Given BAM's dominance in the digital sports landscape, it is reasonable to assume that the strategies that it has pioneered to generate a distinct digital sports audience will be replicated around the world. Indeed, the National Hockey League (NHL) Network's "NHL Tonight", NBA TV's "NBA Gametime", the NFL Network's "NFL Redzone" and ESPN's "Goal Line" already offer fans snack size sports viewing based on live look-in rights. MLB's pursuit of a digital viewer to complement its television offerings has produced a template for sports leagues looking to expand their brand and to attract a valuable niche demographic.

CONCLUSION: ACCELERATED SPORT FAN CULTURE AND "PRESENCE BLEED"

A combination of public discourse, industry innovation, commercial practices and employer expectations is connecting particular user behavior to digital technologies. The business strategy behind digital sports services contributes greatly to the association of digital technology with multitasking. The privileging of certain forms of sports fan behavior over others is contributing to our understanding of emerging technologies and shaping the ways in which we integrate them into our lives. Digital platforms have emerged for sport at the same time that leagues are looking to the international market for new fans. Charles Acland (2003) has written that the media industry's focus on expansion, particularly on international markets and ancillary revenue, has resulted in a reconceptualization of the entertainment product as a "mutating global product". Paul Grainge's *Brand Hollywood* (2008) pursues Acland's point, suggesting that branding has increased importance in the globalized and digitized entertainment era, especially as it relates to attracting the more active consumer. According to Grainge, pursuing the active consumer requires an increased emphasis on marketing, synergy and intellectual property rights enforcement, while entertainment businesses continually repurpose their content by making it available for purchase or rental on as many platforms as possible. In this context, sport is recast as a daily hobby requiring constant engagement.

MLB's dedication to developing its brand is apparent in the decision to unify its web presence, develop a television network and adopt highly restrictive intellectual property enforcement policies. The last of these strategies is especially concerning, as Steven Levy of Newsweek (2007) explains:

> MLB.com says that a big part of its mission is spreading the gospel of baseball; its attitude toward sharing video is definitely old school. Every day four BAM staffers prowl the back channels of YouTube and the like, seeking video highlights of recent and classic games that they can tag for the site's copyright censors to remove.

MLB is distinct from the National Basketball Association (NBA), NFL or NHL in the level of aggression that it exhibits in copyright restrictions. The strategy is designed to make MLB.com and its licensed affiliates the only places to find online content, on the basis that the more time that audiences spend on officially licensed and ad-supported websites, the more they interact with the official brand of MLB. This centrally controlled strategy clashes with the baseball "anytime anywhere" idea that the league sells to its digital customers.

The notion that digital technology is accelerating the spread of culture and creating a highly interactive citizenry is a concept that has intrigued new media theorists. Hutchins (2011) has described this accelerated culture, arguing that disruptive digital platforms such as Twitter challenge the level of control exercised by sports leagues and increase the autonomy of fans and athletes. While it is undeniable that global information networks facilitate the rapid distribution of information as it happens, it is also important to identify how sports leagues are attempting to maintain control over the presentation of their leagues. The prepackaged highlights, the blackout restrictions, the aggregated clips and the emphasis on fantasy sports limit the ways in which sports fans can access content and multitask. Many digital sports services like MLB.TV do not allow fans to watch their local teams when the games are on television, so there is no incentive to take an extended work break to watch the final hour of the game on a desktop monitor. Instead, MLB.TV encourages fans to watch across the league and wait for alerts that bring reports of what has happened in games while they continue working at their desks. As highlight programs such as *MLB Tonight* also bring multitasking practices to the living room, we are likely to see an increase in "presence bleed" (Gregg,

2011, p. 2). This term describes the encroachment of work responsibilities into private leisure spheres because of expectations of digital accessibility. In effect, digital multitasking represents a set of media practices that work both in favor of and against employees, contributing to an expectation that they always be contactable, working *and* consuming, even when at home. Digital sports services are, therefore, a link between multitasking spectatorship and modern connected labor in the global network economy.

NOTES

1. I have written about Workspace Media production at length in my dissertation, "Workspace Media: The Rise of the Procrastination Economy and the Future of Entertainment," which at time of writing is yet to be completed. A good example of the tone and purpose of this production is summed up in the press release announcing the launch of "Lunch with Benefits" (Fox Sports Digital, 2009).
2. "Talking smack" refers to boasting about sports knowledge, a preferred team's prowess or an opposing team's futility.

REFERENCES

Acland CR (2003) *Screen Traffic: Movies, Multiplexes, and Global Culture.* Durham: Duke University Press.

Boddy W (2004) *New Media and Popular Imagination.* Oxford: Oxford University Press.

Boyle R & Haynes R (2002) New media sport. *Culture, Sport, Society* 5(3): 95–114.

ComScore (2006) *Official FIFA Cup Web Site Attracts Millions of Viewers and Billions of Page Views from Around the World in June.* Press Release, July 13. Online. Available from: http://www.comscore.com/Press_Events/Press_Releases/2006/07/Top_50_US_Websites (Accessed 30 July 2012).

ComScore (2007) *3 Out of 4 U.S. Internet Users Streamed Video Online in May.* Press Release, July 17. Online. Available from: http://www.comscore.com/Press_Events/Press_Releases/2007/07/US_Online_Video (Accessed 14 May 2012).

Dawson M (2007) Little players, big shows: format, narration, and style on television's new smaller screens. *Convergence: The International Journal of Research into New Media Technologies* 13(2): 231–50.

Dawson M (2011) Television's aesthetic of efficiency: convergence television and the digital short. In: Bennett J & Strange N (eds.) *Television as Digital Media.* Durham: Duke University Press, 204–30.

ESPN News (2006) Fantasy leagues permitted to use MLB names, stats. *ESPN. com*, 8 August. Online. Available from: http://sports.espn.go.com/mlb/news/story?id=2543720 (Accessed 10 July 2012).

Everett A (2003) Digitextuality and click theory: theses on convergence media in the digital age. In: Caldwell JT & Everett A (eds.) *New Media: Theories and Practices of Digitextuality.* New York: Routledge, 3–29.

Fisher E (2008) MLB Net, BAM growing closer as launch nears. *Sports Business Journal,* 15 December. Online. Available from: http://www.sportsbusinessdaily.com/Journal/Issues/2008/12/20081215/This-Weeks-News/MLB-Net-

BAM-Growing-Closer-As-Launch-Nears.aspx?hl=MLBAM&sc=0 (Accessed 16 April 2012).

Fox Sports Digital (2009) Fox Sports creates digital programming unit. Press release, 9 September. Online. Available from: http://static.foxsports.com/content/fscom/binary/migrated/20027/10044456_37 (Accessed 16 April 2012).

Good (2011) *The Fantasy Sports Economy*. Online. Available from: http://www.good.is/post/infographic-the-fantasy-sports-economy/ (Accessed 16 April 2012).

Gregg M (2011) *Work's Intimacy*. Malden, MA: Polity Press.

Gray J (2010) *Show Sold Separately: Promos, Spoilers, and Other Media Paratexts*. New York: New York University Press.

Grainge P (2008) *Brand Hollywood: Selling Entertainment in a Global Media Age*. New York: Routledge.

Hu J (2001) Baseball officials plan live video streaming. *Cnet*, 30 October. Online. Available from: http://news.cnet.com/2100-1023-275123.html (Accessed 6 March 2012).

Hutchins B (2011) The acceleration of media sport culture: Twitter, telepresence and online messaging. *Information, Communication & Society* 14(2): 237–57.

Jenkins H (2006) *Convergence Culture: Where Old Media and New Media Collide*. New York: NYU Press.

Johnson VE (2009) Everything new is old again: sport television, innovation, and tradition for a multi-platform era. In: Lotz AD (ed.) *Beyond Primetime: Television Programming in the Post-Network Era*. New York: Routledge, 114–38.

Leitch W (2008) MLB's digital dominance: as the world scrambles to master online video, crusty old baseball already has it figured out. *Fast Company*, 1 April. Online. Available from: http://www.fastcompany.com/magazine/124/mlbs-digital-dominance.html?page=0%2C0 (Accessed 16 April 2012).

Lemke T (2008) Bite-sized fantasy baseball; MLB.com seeks to lessen amount of time required to play. *The Washington Times*, 19 March. Online. Available from: http://www.washingtontimes.com/news/2008/mar/19/sportzbiz-bite-sized-fantasy-baseball/ (Accessed 16 April 2012).

Levy S (2007) Covering all the online bases. *Newsweek*, 25 June. Online. Available from: http://www.thedailybeast.com/newsweek/2007/06/24/covering-all-the-online-bases.html (Accessed 16 April 2012).

Liberman N (2002) Teams worry that baseball's web highlights will hurt TV ratings. *Sports Business Journal*, 8 April. Online. Available from: http://www.sportsbusinessdaily.com/Journal/Issues/2002/04/20020408/Special-Report/Teams-Worry-That-Baseballs-Web-Highlights-Will-Hurt-TV-Ratings.aspx?hl=MLBAM&sc=0 (Accessed 30 March 2012).

McCarthy A (2001) *Ambient Television: Visual Culture and Public Space*. Durham: Duke University Press.

McCarthy A (2004) Geekospheres: visual culture and material culture at work. *Journal of Visual Culture* 3(2): 213–21.

Miller N (2007) Minifesto for a New Age. *Wired* 15(3). Online. Available from: http://www.wired.com/wired/archive/15.03/snackminifesto.html (Accessed 4 March 2012).

Nielsen (2008) *Web Traffic to U.S. Sports Sites Grew in August*. 3 October. Online. Available from: http://blog.nielsen.com/nielsenwire/online_mobile/web-traffic-to-us-sports-sites-spiked-in-august (Accessed 11 April 2012).

Nielsen (2010) *How People Watch-The Global State of Video Consumption*. 4 August. Online. Available from: http://blog.nielsen.com/nielsenwire/global/report-how-we-watch-the-global-state-of-video-consumption/ (Accessed 11 April 2012).

Ogg E (2012) With 3M downloads, MLB app hits out of the park. *Gigaom*, 12 April. Online. Available from: http://gigaom.com/2012/04/12/with-3m-downloads-mlb-app-hits-it-out-of-the-park/ (Accessed 12 April 2012).

Ourand J & Lefton T (2010) The veteran vs. the upstart. *Sports Business Journal.* 12 July. Online. Available from: http://www.sportsbusinessdaily.com/Journal/Issues/2010/07/20100712/This-Weeks-News/The-Veteran-Vs-The-Upstart.aspx?hl=%22MLB%20Tonight%22&sc=0 (Accessed 3 March 2012).

Pollack P (2006) Fantasy baseball case may have First Amendment implications. *ArsTechnica*, 22 May. Online. Available from: http://arstechnica.com/old/content/2006/05/6888.ars (Accessed 10 April 2012).

Pritchard MP & Funk DC (2006) Symbiosis and substitution in spectator sport. *Journal of Sport Management* 20(3): 299–321.

Purdy M (2001) Who's on first? Wonder no more. *New York Times*, 7 June. Online. Available from: http://www.nytimes.com/2001/06/07/technology/who-s-on-first-wonder-no-more.html?pagewanted=all&src=pm (Accessed 10 April 2012).

Salter C (2012) Who's streaming March Madness? You'd be surprised. *FastCompany*. 16 March. Online. Available from: http://www.fastcompany.com/1825193/who-s-streaming-march-madness-you-d-be-surprised (Accessed 16 April 2012).

Sandomir R (2008) A network to satisfy the appetite of baseball-hungry fans. *New York Times*, 2 October. Online. Available from: http://www.nytimes.com/2008/10/03/sports/baseball/03sandomir.html?_r=1 (Accessed 29 March 2012).

Shafer J (2006) Productivity madness. *Slate.com*. 20 March. Online. Available from: http://www.slate.com/articles/news_and_politics/press_box/2006/03/productivity_madness.html (Accessed 8 December 2010).

Stetler B (2008) Noontime web video revitalizes lunch at desk. *New York Times*, 5 January. Online. Available from: http://www.nytimes.com/2008/01/05/business/media/05video.html?_r=4&ex=1357362000&en=6229cf8d4abdac05&ei=5088&partner=rssnyt&emc=rss&oref=slogin&oref=slogin (Accessed 19 October 2009).

The B.S. Report with Bill Simmons (2011) Podcast radio program. ESPN, October 20. Online. Available from: http://espn.go.com/espnradio/play?id=7126430 (Accessed 22 October 2011).

Tussey E (2009) Foam finger cubicle: selling ESPN360 as workspace media. *Flow TV* 10(10). Online. Available from: http://flowtv.org/2009/10/foam-finger-cubicle-selling-espn360-as-workspace-mediaethan-tussey-ucsb/ (Accessed 17 October 2009).

University of Melbourne (2009) *Freedom to Surf: Workers More Productive if Allowed to Use the Internet for Leisure.* Press Release. 2 April. Online. Available from: http://newsroom.melbourne.edu/news/n-19 (Accessed 15 July 2009).

Vasquez D (2006) The dreadful price of March Madness. *medialife*. 16 March. Online. Available from: http://www.medialifemagazine.com/artman2/publish/Sports_TV_52/The_dreadful_price_of_March_Madness_3477.asp (Accessed 8 December 2010).

4 "SporTV"
The Legacies and Power of Television

Ben Goldsmith

INTRODUCTION: PRODUCTION INNOVATIONS AND CONTENT HYBRIDS

Any assessment of the present or future of digital media sport needs to be grounded in an understanding of the legacies and enduring power of sports television. By "television" I am referring specifically to "broadcast-like" television, by which I mean real-time, streamed, curated services transmitted either over-the-air via radio waves, by cable or satellite, as distinct from on-demand, downloadable "television-like" services delivered primarily via broadband or mobile Internet. Convergence and digitization have undoubtedly broadened participation in media production, and allowed content that could once only be seen on broadcast television to be accessed on multiple platforms, devices and services. Yet broadcast television is still a key driver of innovation in production technologies and techniques and remains the principal site for developing new or hybrid programs and content. These production innovations and content hybrids are particularly evident in the coverage of sport and sports-related programming. With its capacity to aggregate large audiences, especially around sporting events, broadcast television is also still a vitally important site for advertising and audience measurement.

This chapter examines television in three key areas: (i) platform interaction; (ii) technological innovation; and (iii) content ecologies. I begin by briefly contrasting the production of sports content and the sale of sports rights on television and on Internet-based video services like YouTube. Next, I describe some of the technological innovations arising from television coverage of sporting events, with a particular focus on audience measurement practices and 3D television production. The third part of the chapter discusses the ways in which sport is central to television as an entertainment medium. Sports-related programming is often overlooked in favor of event coverage in scholarly analysis of television, but I argue that these programs and program types are enormously important when thinking about the form and direction of contemporary television.

SPORT, TELEVISION AND THE INTERNET

More than fifteen years ago, Robert W. McChesney claimed that sport was "arguably the single most lucrative content area for the global media industry" (McChesney, 1997, p. 95). If anything, this statement is even more valid today, and especially so regarding television. Writing about the American context, Johnson argues that sport programming "represents a symbolic and actual 'bridge' between network-era practices and post-network realities", with sport positioned as "*both* epitome of network-era television *and* quintessential element of post-network developments" (Johnson, 2009, p. 116). Sports coverage and related content continue to undergird and sustain traditional forms of television, while simultaneously drawing viewers online and promoting sales of High Definition (HD), 3D and "smart" or "connected" Internet enabled television sets. This situation ensures that television remains at the heart of the "media sports cultural complex" (Rowe, 2004).

In terms of production, the total volume of sports content made especially for and distributed first over the Internet already far exceeds that produced by television, although this content is by no means as prominent in terms of media profile or viewing figures. Much of this online content is user-generated, although there also is an increasing amount of professionally produced material. Several of the "YouTube Original Channels"[1] launched in late 2011 and early 2012 are sports oriented, with a strong bias towards action sports and sports news. These channels, launched as part of this online video service's efforts to provide and promote more professional content, support Markus Stauff's argument that YouTube "works above all as a secondary resource, making accessible what is defined as relevant by other media" (Stauff, 2009, p. 241). For instance, action sports such as skateboarding and motoX have been important components of ESPN's content offerings ever since the network created the X Games in 1995. Part of Stauff's point is that the majority of sports content on YouTube (which is a reasonable proxy for online video as a whole by virtue of its volume of content and the fact it is by some considerable margin the most popular online video service) consists of sporting highlights, "taken from television, often only slightly modified" (Stauff, 2009, p. 242). Much online content has, then, its origins in, or is indebted to the forms, styles and practices of sports television.

In terms of sports rights, the amounts paid for online rights, for the moment at least, are still dwarfed by those paid for free-to-air or subscription television. For example, in Australia the free-to-air and subscription television rights to Australian Football League (AFL) matches for the period 2012–2016 were sold for just over AU$1 billion in April 2011 (Witham, 2011). The online rights were sold for AU$153 million, or about fourteen percent of the television rights. The largest online video service, the aforementioned YouTube, took some tentative steps into live sports, streaming Indian Premier League (IPL) Twenty20 cricket matches, Copa America soccer matches and America's Cup sailing races worldwide in 2011. However, it was "unclear if YouTube paid any production costs or rights fees" for this coverage (Mickle & Ourand, 2011). In terms of ratings or views, the most popular sports videos on YouTube number in the tens of millions of hits. But the comparison with television ratings is inexact. While television audience measurement is a combination of those watching a broadcast "live" (that is, at the time that a program is broadcast) and up to seven days later (Balnaves, O'Regan with Goldsmith, 2011, pp. 115–18), views of videos on YouTube and on other online video services are cumulative and not restricted to a particular time period. The convergence of television and the Internet in the form of connected televisions, or broadband-enabled set-top-boxes capable of gathering and reporting enormous amounts of data, suggest that it will become possible to generate comparable figures for television and Internet viewing. The reality at this time, however, is "few common standards exist, and proprietorial systems dominate" (Balnaves et al., 2011, p. 107).

TELEVISION AND TECHNOLOGICAL INNOVATION

Throughout the history of television, coverage of sports events has consistently occasioned technological innovation, with sport regularly assisting in the promotion of new kinds of television sets and systems. To give just one historical example, in the 1950s, as television rolled out across Australia (in the wake of the Melbourne Olympic Games), set manufacturer STC used a variety of sports images in its advertising. The advertisements, featuring a boxer throwing a punch and a pair of hands catching a cricket ball, appear to anticipate the arrival more than five decades later of 3D sets, as each image juts out of the screen on which it appears towards the viewer, much as 3D does today. There are many examples of both analogue and digital media technologies developed or modified specifically for the production of sports television. These include innovations in camera technologies, such as the in-car Racecam developed by engineers at Channel 7 in Australia in the 1970s for coverage of the annual Bathurst 1000 motor race (Thomas, 2006) or the HD Plunge Cam developed by the BBC for coverage of diving events in the 2000s (Pennington, 2007, p. 18).

While John Ellis mounts a convincing argument that sport, along with news, has been at the cutting edge of technological innovation in television "because of its insistent need to analyze and explain" (Ellis, 2007, p. 122), there are other reasons for the "happy confluence" described here. Historically, the bulk of the audience for sports television has been male. In a general sense, technological innovation in television via sport can be read as masculinizing a medium traditionally associated with the feminine. In their work on the promotion of HD television (HDTV), Michael Z. Newman and Elana Levine argue that in the discourses surrounding HDTV, "television becomes technologically sophisticated, masculinized, and both economically and aesthetically valued" (Newman & Levine, 2012, pp. 104–05). The emphasis on sports in marketing HDTV sets "is in response to a widespread belief that consumers who purchase HD sets typically see sports viewing as the key appeal of the new technology" (Newman & Levine, 2012, pp. 104–05). Sports television is a key site of technological innovation because of its popularity with audiences, its capacity to generate enormous revenues and because it provides a platform for television broadcasters and providers to distinguish themselves from their rivals. Douglas Kellner describes global sports media events such as the Olympic Games or the soccer World Cup as technologically sophisticated spectacles or "technospectacles" whose purpose is "to seize audiences and increase the media's power and profit" (Kellner, 2003, p. 1). This is the case for commercial free-to-air broadcasters and for pay television providers for whom sports coverage and its attendant technological innovations are a key means to attract and retain premium subscribers.

Global media events such as the Olympic Games or the soccer World Cup provide an opportunity for content providers, equipment manufacturers and even audience measurement firms to showcase their latest innovations and test possibilities. Among content providers, the BBC has a long history of technological innovation through the work of its Research and Development unit, often in partnership with other broadcasters and related organizations. The BBC used the opportunity presented by its role as host broadcaster of the 2012 London Olympics to trial Super Hi-Vision or Ultra HD in partnership with the Japanese public broadcaster NHK (Carter, 2012). The BBC also televised the Opening and Closing ceremonies, and the men's 100 meters athletics final live in 3D, with nightly highlights also provided in 3D. Roger Mosey, the BBC executive in charge of its Olympics coverage, described the 3D "experiment" as "part of the story of innovation around the London Games" that will provide the industry with "actual data on [the] use of 3D" (Mosey, 2012). The American commercial network NBC, in partnership with the Japanese manufacturer Panasonic and the Olympic Broadcasting Service, screened more than 200 hours of Olympics coverage in 3D in the US. This development sustains and develops the arrangements via which Panasonic and Sony subsidized 3D production at major sporting events like the 2010 soccer World Cup in South Africa, the 2011 Rugby World Cup in New Zealand, and the 2010 and 2011 US Open tennis tournaments.

NBC used its coverage of the 2008 Beijing Olympic Games to conduct audience research across its television channels, website and service for mobile audiences in order to produce the Total Audience Measurement Index (TAMI), a combination of data from different media, panelists and research firms. Quantcast tracked unique browsers, video streams, page views and time spent online at NBCOlympics.com. Knowledge Networks recruited 500 different Olympics watchers per day who kept a media diary that recorded how they watched the Olympics, including where, when and on what media. Integrated Media Measurement Inc (IMMI) equipped a panel of forty people with cell phones capable of recording sound bites in program signals that allowed time spent watching or interacting with Olympics coverage on all platforms throughout the day to be measured. Interviews and focus group sessions were conducted with an "Olympics Qualitative Panel" comprising eighty people in two major markets. IAG conducted surveys of consumer recall of ads, brands, marketing intent and consumer behavior across television, Internet and mobile platforms. Nielsen measured television ratings, and Rentrak monitored video-on-demand usage and viewing through personal video recorders. Around 3,600 hours of video were distributed by NBC over broadcast and cable television, via the website and over mobile telephone networks. NBC repeated and augmented its research at the Vancouver Winter Olympics in February 2010. Up to 15,000 respondents were recruited during the Games, including 2,000 equipped with Arbitron People Meters, and forty with IMMI's mobile technology, both of which can report out-of and in-home viewing. Keller Fay also monitored social networking sites and viral communication for the broadcaster (Balnaves et al. 2011, pp. 109–11; Sigismondi, 2011, pp. 108–13).

As many of these Olympics examples show, sport has been a consistent feature of industry research and development in both HD and 3D production, just as it has been used in consumer markets to promote sales of HD and 3D equipped sets. While in the past some broadcasters and television pioneers experimented with analogue HD and 3D, the recent prominence of both formats coincides with the transition from analogue to digital television services. This development is also due, in no small part, to the enormous sums invested in research and development by equipment manufacturers (principally Sony and Panasonic), broadcasters (most prominently NHK, ESPN and BBC), the European Union through its various Framework Programs (Hilton, Guillemaut, Kilner, Grau & Thomas, 2011, p. 462; Grau, Borel, Kauff, Smolic & Tanger, 2011, p. 2), as well as the boom in 3D cinema since 2009. Yet, it is precisely the *difference* between live events coverage and feature film production that has placed sport at the heart of worldwide research activities in standards development, technologies and production facilities for 3D. Live event production presents different challenges and requires different techniques than film production, precluding the kinds of modification or augmentation that are common during feature film post-production, with graphics and captions needing to be added "on the fly". In addition, camera locations for live event production tend to be in fixed positions, while television directors have considerably less control over the unfolding action than their film counterparts (Jolly, Armstrong & Salmon, 2009, p. 2).

Producing and transmitting 3D sports events is also a significant engineering challenge, with increased costs and complexity for production services companies and broadcasters, as well as new spectrum or bandwidth management issues. Furthermore, 3D or stereoscopic production is more costly than 2D, and 3D workflows are more labor-intensive than for equivalent 2D or monoscopic production. Outside broadcast or mobile units require additional equipment and crew in order to set up, operate and produce in 3D, with each unit costing between two and three times as much as 2D HD trucks (Grotticelli, 2010, p. 33). Each 3D production unit must employ a stereographer—an entirely new production role—to check and correct the 3D image, along with additional processing engineers. Another novel technical problem in 3D sports coverage includes the difficulty of accurately aligning zooming stereo camera pairs:

> since the "telecentricity" property of lenses—the extent to which the image moves perpendicular to the lens optical axis during a change of focal length—is not tightly controlled by lens designers at present, and two randomly selected lenses are unlikely to be well-matched. (Jolly et al., 2009, p. 3)

To date, coverage of major sports events has been the main focus of 3D television production by some margin. The world's first digital terrestrial 3D broadcast in Australia in 2010 covered one of the annual State of Origin rugby league matches, with coverage of the soccer World Cup in South Africa following several weeks later. These broadcasts were only possible because the media industry regulator, the Australian Communications and Media Authority (ACMA), made spectrum available and issued licenses for 3D broadcasts for a trial period (ACMA, 2010). The need for additional broadcast spectrum, coupled with the cost of production in 3D, discouraged Australian free-to-air broadcasters from applying for further trials until the 2012 London Olympic Games, and it has principally been pay television providers that most vigorously pursued 3D. The Disney-owned, US-based ESPN pay television network has been a pioneer in 3D sports production, with boxing, American college football and the network's own X Games action sports series regularly shot and broadcast in 3D. In the UK, both ESPN and BSkyB broadcast live EPL matches in 3D. Subscriber numbers are still small compared with those watching in 2D, which influenced French pay television provider Canal Plus' decision to close its 3D channel in January 2012 because of "the lack of enthusiasm among subscribers for stereoscopic programs" (Keslassy, 2012).

While sales of 3D capable sets are increasing—with the realistic expectation that 3D will soon be a standard feature of all sets with screens over 32 inches in diameter—a lack of available content, coupled with resistance to the unusual strictures of 3D viewing, has inhibited the spread of the new format. At the time of writing (mid-2012), all commercially available 3D television sets require viewers to wear special glasses. The two most common types are polarized (or passive) and shuttered (or active). Polarized glasses are commonly used in cinema: two views of a scene appear on the screen, and are then filtered by the lenses of the glasses, each of which has a different polarization to allow only one image to reach each eye. Shuttered or active glasses are controlled by an infra-red signal from the television. Left and right images rapidly alternate onscreen, with the shutters in each lens switching in time with the onscreen images from transparent (allowing the correct image to reach the eye) to opaque (to mask the image intended for the other eye). Given that 3D requires the person watching to conform to a new regime of television watching, it may be more correct to term 3D viewers "observers", from the Latin *observare* meaning to conform one's actions, or to comply with rules, codes, regulations and practices (Crary, 1991, p. 6). In addition to wearing special glasses, observers must sit directly in front of the screen and not move around or the effect will be lost. In this way, 3D complicates Ellis's well-known assertion that television's "regime of vision . . . is a regime of the glance rather than the gaze" (Ellis, 1982, p. 137).

The sustained and directed attention of 3D viewing demand new audience behavior and bodily arrangements that discipline and constrain the practice of viewing while also opening up visual possibilities. These requirements also limit 3D's attraction in public venues such as pubs and bars that, traditionally, have been popular sites for sports viewing. Sport has again been at the forefront of research to address these difficulties, with efforts to develop autostereoscopic 3D television (using lenticular lens systems that do not require special glasses), and to generate stereoscopic content from 2D recordings typically revolving around sports coverage (Grau & Vinayaga-moorthy, 2009; Grotticelli, 2011a; Hilton et al., 2011). Notwithstanding the difficulties of predicting how consumers will behave, it seems unlikely that 3D will become a mainstream television technology until autostereoscopic displays become the norm, thus allowing multiple simultaneous viewers and mobility around the room, as has always been permitted by 2D displays (Surman, Hopf, Sexton, Lee & Bates, 2008, p. 498).

SPORTS TELEVISION CONTENT

The previous section of this chapter traced the role of sport in innovation in television technology. Next I turn to television content in order to look at the ways in which sport has become central to television as an entertainment medium. This function is evident both in the coverage of sport, and in its expanding influence across the content spectrum. In the 1920s, Lord Reith, Director General of the BBC, defined the public broadcaster's mission as "to inform, educate and entertain". This ethos has influenced television systems across the world, although for commercial and subscription television today (and perhaps also for much public service television) it has been reduced mainly to only the last of this triumvirate. As television scholar Frances Bonner has written, "The primary reason for television's existence is now to entertain" (Bonner, 2011, p. 43). Sport, in terms of both event coverage and related programming, is a core component of television entertainment.

As I have written elsewhere, "sportv" is a collective term for the range of sport-themed or -inflected programming, and is not restricted only to event coverage and related news/discussion programs (Goldsmith, 2009). I break down sportv into seven interconnecting types:

1. Coverage of sports events is termed *actuality sportv*, referencing the commonly used industry term for the recording of events as they happen, as distinct from programs using archival material and studio-based programs (although presenters and commentators often introduce and discuss the event in a small studio at the venue). Actuality sportv is location-based, in stadia or venues often built or set up with television coverage in mind, so that the needs of the television audience in terms of camera and microphone positions are as much a priority as those of the live audience. It is increasingly common for coverage to be relayed on screens at the venue for the benefit of the live audience (Grotticelli, 2011b). This event-based, large-screen "ambient television" (McCarthy, 2001) mirrors the common practice of large and often multiple screens being part of the studio set of panel and news sportv programs. Both are examples of contemporary sports television's "hypermediacy" (Bolter & Grusin, 1999), in which the visibility of the medium—and of mediation itself—is a core component of programming.

2. *Wraparound sportv* encompasses pre-event interviews and introductions, commentary and special comments, and highlights and interviews immediately post-game. Wraparound, along with actuality, is the most common type of sportv. Together with replays of old matches, wraparound sportv makes up almost all of the content of the dedicated club and competition channels that are becoming increasingly common at the highest level of many sports. Examples of such channels include the American basketball channel NBA.TV, and MU.TV, the channel of the EPL's Manchester United.

3. Some of this coverage will be recycled in *newsportv*. Newsportv is strongly grounded in the conventions of television news coverage and contains two main types. The first, typified by the Eurosportsnews 24-hour sports news channel, consists of a rolling sequence of short news items, often highlights, introduced and connected by a voiceover (allowing for multi-language versions) rather than an on-screen presenter. The second type of newsportv, exemplified by *Sky Sports News* in the UK, *Fox Sports News* in Australia, and ESPN's *Sport Center* in the US, is typically filmed in a studio, involves one or more on-screen presenters reading sports news from a teleprompter, introducing short reports and providing live voiceover for highlights. Presenters usually sit at a desk, addressing the viewer directly in front of

a backdrop of a working newsroom or a bank of screens. In common with news channels, newsportv channels typically include a number of visual information streams such as a scrolling text bar at the bottom of the screen that relays results and news, often repeating (though on a different timer) the visual highlights onscreen. Male presenters, like male newsreaders, will typically wear a jacket or sports coat and a tie. In its division of categories of sports programs, ESPN makes shifting distinctions between "Talk and Debate" and "News and Analysis" shows. The two forms bleed easily into each other.

4. *Panel sportv* is a flexible and resilient television form dating back to the medium's earliest days. The panel of sports pundits, often current or former professional sports players, journalists and commentators, and usually led or hosted by a sports journalist or network star, can itself form the basis of a show. In combination with newsportv, sport-variety and television sports segments, panel sportv can be part of a longer program. In Australia, this latter hybrid form was the basis of the long-running sports program *Wide World of Sports*, which aired during Sunday lunchtimes from 1959 to 1987, and *The Footy Show*, which offers two versions reflecting the historically rooted geographical division between rugby league and Australian rules football. Panel sportv is typically studio-based and features an "expert panel" seated at a presentation table (*NRL on Fox*), on a raised podium arranged in a semi-circle in chairs (*ESPN Soccernet Press Pass*) or in armchairs or couches around a coffee table (*On the Couch, The Offsiders, Match of the Day*). Presenter backdrops include colorful "flats" in abstract designs (often related to the particular topic sport) and the ubiquitous large screen or bank of screens that panelists and presenters do not watch, preferring to look at monitors hidden out of camera view. This form has been adapted by ESPN through the use of the "celebrity squares" bank of monitors linking panelists in studios across the US with the host in *Around the Horn*. Sky Sports (UK's) *Soccer Saturday* is a hybrid of newsportv and panel sportv in which former players in the studio view and report live on matches in progress that they, un-like the everyday viewer because of licensing and technological restrictions, are able to watch on monitors embedded in the desk in front of them. Sports quiz programs such as the British *A Question of Sport*, the Australian *The Squiz* and New Zealand's *Game of 2 Halves* might be considered variants of panel sportv.

5. *Variety sportv* is magazine television, which draws from the other program types. It may comprise panels; expert commentary; clips and highlights usually chosen for comic value; (typically) less serious interviews with sports professionals, administrators and sometimes fans; games or contests involving sports professionals, celebrities and ordinary people; and, occasionally, live music performances. Variety sportv can feature sports stars in unusual locations or situations, as

in the enormously popular New Zealand series starring two former rugby players, *Matthew and Marc's Rocky Road to . . .* Other leading examples of this type include Australia's *The Footy Show* (based on panel sportv) and the UK's *Soccer AM* (a much looser, studio-based production), both of which are filmed live in front of raucous studio audiences wearing club colors.

6. *Reality sportv* includes scripted and non-scripted sports-themed reality television programs, such as the growing number of talent identification formats like *Super Soccer Star, The Contender* and *Cricket Superstar.* These programs pit young players or aspiring professionals against each other in a series of challenges, with the ultimate prize of a professional contract or a place in a leading professional club's youth academy. Other examples include the Scandinavian format *FC Nerds*, in which a group of people chosen for their lack of sporting aptitude are trained to become a team and, ultimately, play against a professional side.

7. The final type, *telesportv*, is of most interest to this chapter. Telesportv comprises programs that are either made for television, or are hybrids of sport and other program types. The former set of programs consists of shows like *Wipeout, It's a Knockout* or the German format *Schlag den Raab* (remade in the UK and Australia, albeit briefly, as *Beat the Star*). The second group of hybrid programs includes familiar international formats like *Masterchef* or *Iron Chef* (sport-cooking) and *The Biggest Loser* (sport-makeover). Telesportv has been dismissed by some television scholars like Garry Whannel as "quasi-sports", "trash sports" or synthetic events (Whannel, 1990, pp. 111–14; Whannel, 1992, pp. 59, 170). In contrast, I argue that they are characteristic of contemporary television in the post-broadcast era, in which sports styles, values and languages combine with television's imperative towards entertainment. In his work on games and play, Roger Caillois discusses the "pure space" of the game's domain, "a restricted, closed, protected universe" (Caillois, 2001 [1958], p. 7). There is a case to be made for telesportv like *Wipeout* (discussed below) as a pure television space existing for and because of television. This type may have an existence beyond television, but it is primarily designed and made for this medium. Telesportv is not like sports events or the "elite competition" that "sports television" is usually understood to mean and yet shares a foundation as a competition based on physical aptitude. More so than other forms of sports television, the coverage of telesportv is determined absolutely by the needs and demands of television.

An instructive example of telesportv is *Wipeout*. All of the various formats of the program are filmed on the same course in Argentina, which was specifically designed to produce the best camera angles and a sense of visual drama. Studio-based telesportv like *Schlag den Raab* are especially good examples of set or course design in the interests of television. *Schlag den Raab*, like *Wipeout*, is a format. This is a German program in which contestants are challenged to beat host Stefan Raab (or a local celebrity in other versions) in a variety of contests, many of them explicitly sports-like, others involving different kinds of physical challenge. This format has been sold and remade around the world. The show has spawned a number of similar "celebrity sports events", including another German show, *Stars in Danger*, in which celebrities compete in a number of contrived sports such as Wok Bobsleigh.

The sports hybrid group of programs proliferates in the post-broadcast era, as program makers seek "the 'feel' of competitive uncertainty that is central to sports" (Rowe, 2011, p. 100). These hybrid programs are good examples of the way in which television, as Garry Whannel has observed, can turn "almost anything into the stuff of competition" (Whannel, 1990, p. 111). At the same time, these programs demonstrate the recycling or hybridization of sports television's forms and styles, with slow motion replays, interviews with contestants and voice-over commentary complementing the adoption of the forms and styles of sport. The cooking competition format, *Masterchef*, is a prime example of the sports hybrid or sports-inflected program. The Australian version of the format is set in a cavernous warehouse, "dressed" like an arena, with non-participating contestants (and some cameras) looking down on the action from a mezzanine. On the floor the contestants engage in various competitions marked by physical exertion, under a set of rules, with a group of referees or judges determining the outcome. The competition is punctuated by commentary from the judges, and interspersed with interviews with participants. There are frequent replays of key moments, typically immediately after a commercial break. *Iron Chef* utilizes similar techniques and is set in a "Kitchen Stadium" where master chefs compete in culinary contests explicitly framed in gladiatorial terms. Importantly, telesportv tends towards skill or aptitude-based contests, which may involve elements of physical competition but, rarely, bodily contact between participants. This character is in keeping with John Fiske and John Hartley's observation, "television sport differs from sport itself in rejecting as 'unsportsmanlike' the more physical manifestations of competitive conflict" (Fiske & Hartley, 1978, p. 116). Fiske and Hartley are discussing sport on television, but this point applies equally to telesportv, in the majority of which there is no prospect of one competitor physically harming another. Even in physical game shows like *Wipeout* and *Hole in the Wall*, or the Japanese originals like *Takeshi's Castle*, *Most Extreme Elimination Challenge* and *Ninja Warrior*, the physical challenge is centered on the individual.[2] There are exceptions, but even in programs such as *Gladiators* and MTV's *Bully Beatdown*, in which a bully is pitted against a professional fighter in a ring, participants wear protective headgear and padded clothing to minimize the chance of serious injury.

The proliferation of these programs and program types is a consequence of the importance of sport to television in general. They play on the features of sports including regulated, physical competition, and also adopt some or all of the stylistic features and forms of visualization typical of sports coverage, such as voice-over commentary, slow motion instant replays, special comments, highlights and multi-camera coverage. These programs can tell us a great deal about contemporary television, and about the role of sport in media transformation. While they may be segmented and recirculated online, their principal platform is television and, as yet, they have few if any online equivalents.

CONCLUSION: THE "SPORTIZATION" OF TELEVISION

Jay David Bolter and Richard Grusin's (1999) influential concept of "remediation"—in which a new media form takes on and refashions its predecessors, while older media forms adapt to new circumstances—reminds us that, in order to understand media change, we need to hold together the old and the new, to recognize the presence of the new in the old, to assess the consequences of the old for the new, and to consider where the old and new diverge as well as converge (O'Regan & Goldsmith, 2002). Television in its various modes and forms simultaneously instantiates both media convergence *and* divergence or media specificity. Via "connected" or "smart" sets with Internet connectivity, either built-in or facilitated by a broadband-enabled set-top box, television can be seen as the principal medium of convergence. But this coming together of broadcasting, telecommunications and online platforms in the television set masks persistent differences in the ways in which content and services may be produced and delivered. Television content may be viewed via broadcast spectrum, fiber optic cable, the Internet or wireless mobile networks, and an increasing variety of devices. At the same time, television continues to be a site of innovation in production technologies, with its visual style and expanding range of sports-inflected or related content often setting television apart from user-generated and modified content available online.

This chapter has explored instances of convergence, divergence and innovation through analysis of the transformations and legacies of sports television technologies and content. The creation of 3D coverage of sports events and of sports hybrid programming would not be possible without the institutions, infrastructure and financial clout of television. To some extent, these elements can be seen as evidence of the "sportization" of television (as distinct from the mediatization of sport) to adapt Norbert Elias's description of the process by which pastimes became sports (Elias, 1986, p. 22). Elias argued that the evolution of sport cannot be explained by the ideas and actions of individuals, but was developed over time by many people, and subject to chance, coincidence and shifting social conditions. The same can be said of sportv, both in terms of what it enables technologically, and in its content forms that typically are hybrids or adaptations of existing program forms or styles.

NOTES

1. See http://www.youtube.com/yt/advertise/original-channels.html (accessed 24 February 2012).
2. Japanese broadcaster Tokyo Broadcasting System (maker of *Takeshi's Castle, Most Extreme Elimination Challenge* and *Ninja Warrior*) sued the American network ABC and production company Endemol (producer of *Wipeout*) in 2008 alleging copyright infringement. The case was settled out of court in 2011.

REFERENCES

Australian Communications and Media Authority (ACMA) (2010) *Temporary Trials of 3DTV and Other Emerging Technologies*. Discussion Paper, ACMA, Sydney, September.

Balnaves M, O'Regan T, with Goldsmith B (2011) *Rating the Audience: The Business of Media*. London: Bloomsbury Academic.

Bolter JD & Grusin R (1999) *Remediation: Understanding New Media*. Cambridge, MA: MIT Press.

Bonner F (2011) *Personality Presenters: Television's Intermediaries with Viewers*. Farnham: Ashgate.

Caillois R (2001) [1958] *Man, Play and Games* (trans. Barash M). Urbana and Chicago: University of Illinois Press.

Carter J (2012) BBC talks Super Hi-Vision plans for London 2012. *techradar.com* 13 March. Online. Available from: www.techradar.com/news/television/bbc-talks-super-hi-vision-plans-for-london-2012–1068914 (Accessed 13 March 2012).

Crary J (1991) *Techniques of the Observer: On Vision and Modernity in the Nineteenth Century*. Cambridge, MA: MIT Press.

Elias N (1986) Introduction. In: Elias N and Dunning E, *Quest for Excitement: Sport and Leisure in the Civilising Process*. Oxford: Blackwell, 19–62.

Ellis J (1982) *Visible Fictions: Cinema, Television, Video*. London and Boston: Routledge & Kegan Paul.

Ellis J (2007) *TV FAQ: Uncommon Answers to Common Questions about TV*. London and New York: IB Tauris.

Fiske J & Hartley J (1978) *Reading Television*. London: Methuen.

Goldsmith B (2009) Sportv: beyond the sport event. *FlowTV* 10.10. Online. Available from: flowtv.org/2009/10/sportv-beyond-the-sport-event-ben-goldsmith-university-of-queensland/ (Accessed 19 July 2012).

Grau O, Borel T, Kauff P, Smolic A & Tanger R (2011) 3D-TV R&D activities in Europe. *BBC Research & Development White Paper*. WHP 215, BBC, London, December.

Grau O & Vinayagamoorthy V (2009) Stereoscopic 3D sports content without stereo rigs. *BBC Research White Paper*. WHP 180, BBC, London, November.

Grotticelli M (2010) 3-D clouds mobile production picture. *Broadcast Engineering World*, 32–35.

Grotticelli M (2011a) TV2 Norway tests cost-effective 3-D distribution over IP. *Broadcast Engineering Online*. 17 October. Online. Available from: http://broadcastengineering.com/news/tv2-norway-tests-cost-effective-3-d-distribution-over-ip (Accessed 19 July 2012).

Grotticelli M (2011b) In-stadium entertainment. *Broadcast Engineering* 53(10): 20, 22–24.

Hilton A, Guillemaut J-Y, Kilner J, Grau O & Thomas G (2011) 3D-TV production from conventional cameras for sports broadcast. *IEEE Transactions on Broadcasting* 57(2): 462–76.

Johnson VE (2009) Everything new is old again: sport television, innovation, and tradition for a multi-platform era. In: Lotz AD (ed.) *Beyond Prime Time: Television Programming in the Post-Network Era*. New York and Abingdon: Routledge, 114–37.

Jolly SJE, Armstrong M & Salmon RA (2009) Three-dimensional television—a broadcaster's perspective. In: Woods AJ Holiman NS & Merritt JO (eds.) *Stereoscopic Displays and Applications XX, Proceedings of SPIE-IS&T Electronic Imaging*, San Jose, USA, 19–21 January 2009, 1–11. Bellingham, WA: SPIE.

Kellner D (2003) *Media Spectacle*. New York and London: Routledge.

Keslassy E (2012) Canal plus shutters 3D service. *Variety*. 3 January, np.

McCarthy A (2001) *Ambient Television: Visual Culture and Public Space*. Durham: Duke University Press.

McChesney RW (1997) *Rich Media, Poor Democracy: Communication Politics in Dubious Times*. New York: The New Press.

Mickle T & Ourand J (2011) With new channels, YouTube edges into rights market. *SportsBusiness Journal*, 14 November. Online. Available from: www.sportsbusinessdaily.com/Journal/Issues/2011/11/14/Media/YouTube.aspx (Accessed 24 February 2012).

Mosey R (2012) Olympic ceremonies and 100m final will be in 3D on the BBC. *BBC Sport Roger Mosey's Blog*, 15 February. Online. Available from: www.bbc.co.uk/blogs/rogermosey/2012/02/olympic_ceremonies_and_100m_fi.html (Accessed 13 March 2012).

Newman MZ & Levine E (2012) *Legitimating Television: Media Convergence and Cultural Status*. New York and London: Routledge.

O'Regan T & Goldsmith B (2002) Emerging global ecologies of production. In: Harries D (ed.) *The New Media Book*. London: BFI, 92–105.

Pennington A (2007) Specialized cameras for OB sports. *Broadcast Engineering* 49(11): 16, 18–21.

Rowe D (2004) *Sport, Culture and the Media*. 2nd ed. Maidenhead: Open University Press.

Rowe D (2011) Sports media: beyond broadcasting, beyond sports, beyond societies? In: Billings AC (ed.) *Sports Media: Transformation, Integration, Consumption*. Abingdon and New York: Routledge, 94–113.

Sigismondi P (2011) *The Digital Glocalization of Entertainment: New Paradigms in the 21st Century Global Mediascape*. New York: Springer.

Stauff M (2009) Sports on YouTube. In: Snickars P & Vonderau P (eds.) *The YouTube Reader*. Stockholm: National Library of Sweden, 236–51.

Surman P, Hopf K, Sexton I, Lee WK & Bates R (2008) Solving the 3D problem— The history and development of viable domestic 3DTV displays. In: Ozaktas HM & Onural L (eds.) *Three-Dimensional Television: Capture, Transmission, Display*. Berlin and New York: Springer, 471–503.

Thomas T (2006) Australian TV, fifty years on. *Media International Australia* 121: 188–98.

Whannel G (1990) Winner takes all: competition. In: Goodwin A & Whannel G (eds.) *Understanding Television*. London and New York: Routledge, 103–14.

Whannel G (1992) *Fields in Vision: Television Sport and Cultural Transformation*. London and New York: Routledge.

Witham J (2011) AFL's $1.25 billion broadcast deal. *afl.com.au*, 28 April. Online. Available from: www.afl.com.au/news/newsarticle/tabid/208/newsid/112560/default.aspx (Accessed 20 February 2012).

5 The Struggle for Platform Leadership in the European Sports Broadcasting Market

Tom Evens and Katrien Lefever

INTRODUCTION: THE TRANSITION OF POWER IN SPORTS BROADCASTING RIGHTS

The beginning of the courtship between sport and the media goes back to the nineteenth century, when newspapers began to cover sporting events. The evolution of this coverage created a mutually advantageous situation for both parties as they developed in parallel to become mass phenomena. While sporting organizations gained benefits from the extra media publicity that drove up stadium attendance, newspapers attracted additional readers through the insertion of sports sections and launched magazines specifically devoted to sports coverage (Helland, 2007). An historical example of this reciprocally beneficial situation is the Tour de France, which began as a small six-day race in 1903 and has since become one of the world's most watched sports events with more than two billion viewers. In an attempt to compete with its successful rival, "Le Vélo", the French sports newspaper *L'Auto* founded "La Grande Boucle" to increase the sales of the floundering newspaper (Dauncey & Hare, 2003).

With the breakthrough of television as a mass medium after World War II, television broadcasting started to take over as the leading sports medium. Since ticket sales represented the major revenue source for sporting organizations at that time, the rise of televised sports was originally thought to deplete stadium attendance because people could watch the events directly from their living room. For sports clubs, however, live televised sports helped to increase their fan base, and later, with the advent of pay television, proved to be a powerful financial engine (Buraimo, 2008). Whereas public service broadcasters pioneered sports coverage on the grounds of nation-building and cultural citizenship, commercial broadcasters also saw opportunities for high audience ratings and advertising sales. As technological innovation progressed over the years, pay television services and, then, vertically integrated digital television operators, started to play a major role in live sports. Sport has, then, become a strategic commodity in the battle for market share in the digital television and media industries (Evens & Lefever, 2011).

This chapter discusses the transition of power in the sports broadcasting rights marketplace. This "struggle" for platform leadership will be discussed within a broader European perspective and illustrated by means of a case study of Belgian soccer. Almost everywhere in Europe, free-to-air broadcasters have lost their leading position as providers of soccer games. Instead, pay television operators and telecommunications carriers are starting to claim leadership in this market. This chapter also identifies an interesting tension: the battle for strategic control has been fuelled by the deregulation and marketization of sport that has not always been in the public interest. This situation has seen the sports broadcasting market become increasingly re-regulated to preserve the social capital of sports and to guarantee fair competition in the marketplace (Lefever, 2012).

SPORTS RIGHTS AS A SITE OF STRUGGLE

Due to the commercial and strategic importance of coverage rights for popular sports, a struggle for platform leadership is taking place. In this "upstream" market, sports rights holders—usually represented by leagues or federations—and broadcasters negotiate over the terms for selling and buying sports rights. Typically, this market is characterized by intense competition for the acquisition of premium rights, which eventually produces inflated rights fees (Szymanski, 2006). To illustrate the enduring growth in live coverage rights prices, the amount of money the US broadcast network, NBC-Universal, paid for acquiring the summer Olympic television rights has tripled from US$456 million (in 1996) to US$1.418 billion (in 2020). This inflation has been largely caused by drastically increased competition in the programming market, where free-to-air broadcasters compete for audiences that can be sold to advertisers (Gaustad, 2000). For pay television and related service providers, programming live sports is also considered to be a successful strategy to build a subscriber base and create market share. As Boyle & Haynes (2004, p. 4) note, "football specifically has been viewed in the recent past as the cash cow of the new media sport economy and has driven by the rollout of cable, satellite and digital TV." Hence, television operators are increasingly involved in a struggle to control live sports rights that are used simultaneously to open and foreclose markets, thereby achieving platform leadership. By controlling premium sports rights, the ambition is to provide the most compelling content in order to extract value from a range of services and to gain the highest economic benefit. Sports markets thus have a multisided character and internalize the network externalities that are generated both by, and between, the supply and demand sides of sports broadcasting (Budzinski & Satzer, 2011).

This dependent relationship between sports organizations and media changed significantly following the introduction of broadcast technology in sport. First, the increased competition on the demand side has fundamentally changed the political economy of professional sports such as European club soccer. Television did not only gain increasing influence over the rules of the game itself, but helped to produce the current market structure that has seen clubs become heavily dependent on lucrative television income. On average, top European soccer clubs rely on broadcast rights for approximately thirty-five percent of their total income, with Italian clubs peaking at more than sixty percent (Deloitte, 2012). Secondly, the structure of media markets and traditional broadcast business models has been altered by the introduction of new technologies. The current struggle for platform leadership has been fuelled by technological developments, first with the entrance of multichannel, then digital and now multiplatform television, which have fundamentally affected the supply and exploitation of sports programming (Turner, 2007). As Hutchins and Rowe (2009, p. 354) argue, the Internet changes the:

> . . . long-established broadcast model characterized by scarcity, with high barriers of access and cost restricting the number of media companies and sports organizations able to create, control and distribute quality, popular sports content.

Sports rights are becoming a valuable strategic weapon for exerting market power and control in the online environment, as well as a possible acquisition target for leading social media platforms like Facebook and YouTube.

Against the background of these rapid technological developments, which could not have taken place without the deregulation of media and telecommunication markets, the battle for control over sports rights is paradoxically characterized by increased re-regulation (see Figure 5.1). Whereas deregulation and technological innovation have spurred convergence and

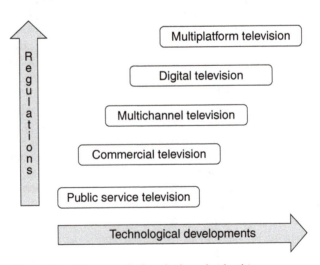

Figure 5.1   The struggle for platform leadership.

contributed to an abundance of distribution channels and consumer technologies, access to premium sports remains scarce and may eventually result in supply side monopolies. This eventuality could hurt not only the business of sport, but also the social capital generated by sporting activity. A tighter regulatory framework has been implemented in the European Union to preserve fair competition in the market and to protect the social and cultural role of sport. However, this increased regulation of the media sport market has been heavily opposed by commercial media companies, which argue for the dismantling of these regulations in favor of greater corporate control over the sale and exploitation of sports rights. Sports federations also, it should be noted, fear a devaluation of their sports rights packages by greater regulation.

THE BATTLE FOR CONTROL

Most public service broadcasters started to cover major sports events soon after World War II. In contrast to the United States, where public service television occupies a comparatively marginal position in the market, state-funded television played a foundational role in sports broadcasting in Europe (Hoehn & Lancefield, 2003). Public service broadcasters pioneered the live coverage of major sports events and thus the mediatized promotion of sports. In so doing, public service broadcasters helped to create the sports broadcasting market prior to the appearance of commercial television, which then paved the way for pay television. Rowe (2004) regards this pioneering role as a form of market research development. Public broadcasting accepted the risk and built up a business that was subsequently exploited by commercial free-to-air channels, and later by subscription-based platforms.

Early fears emerged that wealthy commercial channels would outbid public broadcasters and deprive viewers of events that they expected to see on "national" television services. The BBC, for instance, proposed a listed events policy in order to avoid "bidding wars" and to protect the "crown jewels". In 1954, the UK government listed events of national interest, which neither the BBC nor the commercial channels could broadcast on an exclusive basis. The regulation remained largely unchanged for many years until the rise of cable television prompted a reassessment (Smith, 2010). During the 1990s, this listed events mechanism moved back to the center of UK television policy. The commercial strategy of the new and wealthy satellite pay television provider, BSkyB, was based on the exclusive acquisition of premium sports rights. By programming live sports, BSkyB successfully broke into this burgeoning market and built up a substantial subscriber base. Other leading European pay television companies such as Canal+ and Mediaset used similar strategies. Following the migration of live sports coverage from free-to-air to subscription-based platforms, a harmonized listed events regulation was introduced at the European level (Evens & Lefever,

2011). To guarantee that the public would have access to events of "major importance for society", this list of major events was introduced in 1997 as part of the "Television Without Frontiers Directive."[1]

These policy developments did not prevent multichannel and, later, digital television operators attempting to acquire exclusive live sports rights to enhance their market position. Typically, most of these players transformed into vertically integrated operators, exploiting network infrastructure and managing subscription-based television services. In this context, exclusive live rights have become a crucial strategic weapon in the battle for market share, promising a substantial competitive advantage over rivals. Such exclusive dealing can, however, foreclose markets (Doganoglu & Wright, 2010). Hence, both national and European competition authorities monitor this widespread practice and regulate access to premium content. This situation partly explains the growing force of anti-trust and competition policy in European sports broadcasting markets.

In the European markets, the battle for premium rights has been fought largely between cable and satellite operators. Nikos Leandros and George Tsourvakas (2005) illustrate how this intense competition for premium rights has resulted in monopolistic pay television market structures and financial crisis, as pay television operators both overpaid for rights and overestimated consumer demand. A well-known example here is the collapse of the German media conglomerate, Kirch Group. The group went into administration in 2002 because of debts associated with a €315 million (US$411m) television deal to telecast Bundesliga matches. As a result, the German government had to provide a €200 million (US$261m) financial guarantee fund so that they could continue operating. Since the mid-2000s, satellite operators also began facing heavy competition from convergent media specialists, including cable and telephony operators. In Europe, cable companies Telenet (Belgium) and ZON (Portugal) play an important role in sports broadcasting, whereas Orange (France), Belgacom (Belgium), Deutsche Telekom (Germany) and Versatel/Tele2 (the Netherlands) use sports rights as part of their Internet Protocol television (IPTV) offerings. By attracting subscribers, these companies are able to sell bundled telecommunications services and increase the average revenue generated per user. In these markets, ownership of premium content rights, especially sport, is considered an important competitive advantage as it allows operators to lock-in subscribers.

The integration of traditional broadcast content with broadband delivery platforms creates opportunities for "over-the-top" services that bypass traditional network gatekeepers and access providers. This term relates to online platforms operated by third parties like Netflix, Hulu or YouTube that can be accessed through Internet-connected devices, including PCs, tablets, set-top boxes or gaming consoles. Further technological innovation could also trigger a new era for selling and exploiting sports media rights, and may pose heavy competition for the established providers of televised sport. To date, online and mobile rights have been considered a by-product of traditional "broadcasting" rights, but this situation may change in the future. If the centrality of the Internet in people's daily lives is reflected in the business of sports media, traditional locally operated television companies will suffer under the weight of increased competition and the spread of web-based and multiscreen viewing.

THE EUROPEAN SPORTS RIGHTS MARKET

Sports coverage rights represent an important dimension of the total sports market. Media rights make up about twenty percent of the global sports market, which was valued at US$118.7 billion in 2011 (PwC, 2010). On a global scale, the market for sports rights is worth an estimated US$23.1 billion. This value is, however, unequally distributed among the different continents and also within countries. North America, for example, comprises about seventy-six percent of the global sports market and generates thirty-eight percent of the value of sports rights. In Europe, eighty-eight percent of the value of soccer rights value is generated by the five major European leagues (in the UK, Italy, France, Spain and Germany). With a total value of €1.3 billion (US$1.7b), the EPL clearly generates the highest broadcast value, which is about three times the German Bundesliga's €440 million (US$574m) (for the 2009/2010 season).[2] The value of the broadcast deals in the top five European soccer competitions clearly exceeds those existing in the rest of Europe. Satellite provider Digiturk, for example, paid €260.3m (US$339.4m) annually as part of a current four-year-long deal with the Turkish Süper Lig, whereas the Polish League generates €33.8 million (US$44.1m) annually.[3] Although much depends on the size of the respective pay television markets, this unequal distribution creates competitive imbalance and is leading to a two-tiered European soccer landscape. Hence, discussions on financial fair play and competitive balance have been initiated by the Union of European Football Associations (UEFA).

The value of these sports rights markets is likely to expand in the coming years as a result of accelerating technological developments, although, as the next chapter by Kirton and David shows, the impact of online piracy is an unknown factor. As new players come into these markets, established sports broadcasters may eventually be pushed out. Table 5.1 presents an overview of selected broadcast deals for the major European soccer leagues and shows that, for the most prestigious competitions, a full migration from free-to-air to pay television has taken place. In the cases of the UEFA Champions League, FIFA World Cup and the national championships, subscription platforms have outbid public service and commercial broadcasters and placed these matches behind pay walls. The table also shows the European footprint of the leading pay television consortia, Canal+ and Sky. Sky is affiliated with satellite provider BSkyB, which not only provides television access but also sells broadband and phone services. The same arrangement exists for the French telecommunication company, Orange,

Table 5.1 Broadcasting rights in major European markets.

	National Championships	National Cup	National Team	Champions League	FIFA World Cup
France	*Live:* • Canal + • Orange *Highlights:* • France 2	FTA (*free-to-air*): • France Télévision • Eurosport	FTA: • TF1	*Pay:* • Canal+ FTA: • TF1	*Pay:* • Canal+ FTA: • TF1 • France Télévision
Germany	*Live:* • Sky *Highlights:* • ARD • Sport 1	*Pay:* • Sky FTA: • ARD • ZDF	FTA: • ARD • ZDF	*Pay:* • Sky FTA: • Sat.1	*Pay:* • Sky FTA: • ARD • ZDF • RTL
Italy	*Live:* • Sky *Highlights:* • RAI	FTA: • RAI	FTA: • RAI	*Pay:* • Sky FTA: • Mediaset	*Pay:* • Sky FTA: • RAI
Spain	*Live:* • Canal+ • Gol TV *Highlights:* • Cuatro • TVE	*Pay:* • Canal+ • GolTV FTA: • TVE • TV3	FTA: • TVE	*Pay:* • Gol TV FTA: • TVE • FORTA	*Pay:* • Canal+ FTA: • Telecinco • Cuatro
UK	*Live:* • Sky • ESPN *Highlights:* • BBC	FTA: • ITV	FTA: • ITV	*Pay:* • Sky FTA: • ITV	*Pay:* • Eurosport • ESPN FTA: • BBC • ITV

which also provides the French soccer league on the mobile platform. However, this dominance of Canal+ and Orange in the French market is now threatened by aggressive moves by the Qatar-based satellite channel, Al Jazeera, which is eager to expand its footprint in the European sports broadcasting market.

These developments indicate that the role of public service broadcasting in the sports market is increasingly contested all over Europe. Self-interested private television companies have claimed that state-funded public broadcasters distort the market, and should spend public money on programs that complement rather than compete with their commercial counterparts (like arts programming and documentaries). Widespread economic crises have also prompted public service broadcasters to employ cost-cutting and efficiency measures. Several public service broadcasters have announced that they will no longer bid for expensive live sports rights, including the UEFA Champions League and the FIFA World Cup. The BBC also now shares the rights for the Formula One World Championship with Sky Sports. Thanks to the EBU, most public service broadcasters could cover the 2012 Olympics in London, although this arrangement may change in the future.[4] Our attention now turns to a case study that highlights how competition policies and sector-specific media regulations influence the sale, acquisition and exploitation of sports broadcasting rights.

SOCCER RIGHTS IN BELGIUM

In the European context, Belgium acts as a "textbook" illustration of regulation and economic development in the sports broadcasting rights market. Not only has the Belgian Competition Council been busily shaping the conditions under which the Jupiler Pro League (the national league) sells and exploits its media rights, the major events list mechanism also guarantees free-to-air access to important sports events such as the Olympic Games and the FIFA World Cup.[5] In this section, we look closely at the structural transition of the Belgian sports broadcasting market and discuss how intervention by the competition authority has affected the operation of this sector. This detailed case study illustrates that, despite their opposition to regulatory intervention, Belgian sports associations have benefited from the increasing level of competition in the broadcast market, resulting in lucrative rights deals and an expanded amount of coverage.

The Analogue Era (1984–2004)

As in other countries, the mechanisms for the sale of media rights in Belgium developed roughly in parallel to the structural evolution of the television landscape. Soccer is by far the most popular sport on television, although coverage of the soccer league and Belgian Football Cup during this period remained limited to highlights in news programs or specific sports magazines. Only the matches of the Red Devils, the national soccer team, and some Belgian clubs in the European leagues, were shown live. In 1984, the Belgian Football Federation started to sell the rights to cover the national competition for the first time. Since the public service broadcasters, VRT (Flemish Community) and RTBF (French Community), enjoyed a *de jure* monopoly position at the time, they were granted the rights to broadcast the highlights of all matches. Due to a lack of competition in the market, the first contract (for the 1984–1987 period) was valued at only about €0.5 million (US$0.65m) per year. This amount then doubled to more than €1 million (US$1.3m) annually between 1986 and 1991. Beginning in 1987, the regional governments that were responsible for media policy began liberalizing the broadcast market in the northern and southern part of the country. Only a few years later, the Flemish private channel, VTM, had gained some forty percent market share and became a leading broadcaster. In 1994, VTM managed to convince RTBF, the public service broadcaster in South-Belgium, to offer a joint bid for the rights to Belgian soccer (valued at €5.12 million [US$6.67m] per year). As a result, the commercial broadcaster was able to acquire the rights to the highlights and became the leading sports outlet for many years. After paying €6.7 million (US$8.73m) per year, the joint arrangement between VTM and RTBF was renewed for the period 1997–2002. In exchange for this money, both channels were granted the right to show the highlights, as well as the live coverage of the Cup Final and matches featuring the national team. Belgium implemented the listed events mechanism partly as a result of this enduring market leadership, and also to prevent live sports migrating to pay television.

At the start of the 1990s, pay television channel FilmNet made its entrance into the Belgian market, launching the "24/7" sports channel, SuperSport. In 1996, the company was sold to the French Canal+ Group, one of the leading pay television operators in Europe. For weekly coverage of several live matches in the first division, Canal+ bid about €5.5 million (US$7.17m). This rights fee remained relatively stable over the following years. Since 2002, the Pro League, the organization that defends the interests of all professional soccer clubs in Belgium, has been selling and exploiting the broadcasting rights. For the 2002–2005 seasons, the league entered into an agreement with Canal+, which paid €9.8 million (US$13.01m) for live coverage of a limited number of games. VTM and RTBF each paid €2.8 million (US$3.65m) for the highlights. The cumulative value of the new Belgian broadcasting contract was €15.4 million (US$20.08m) (see Table 5.2). However, due to a disappointing consumer uptake of pay television subscriptions, the revenues generated failed to cover the significant investments in rights acquisition. As a result, Canal+ Belgium was split into two and sold to cable operator Telenet in the north and BeTV (later purchased by cable company VOO) in southern Belgium. Business analysts estimated that only 60,000 households subscribed to Canal+ at that time.

Table 5.2   Soccer rights valuation in Belgium (paid per season).[6]

	2002-2005	2005-2008	2009-2011	2011-2014
Live	Canal + €9.8m (US$13.01m)	Belgacom €36m[¥] (US$46.93m)	Belgacom €43m (US$56.06m)	Telenet (3 matches) €52.1m (US$67.92m) Sublicense VOO Belgacom (5 matches) €1m (US$1.3m)
Highlights Magazine	VTM/RTBF €5.6m (US$7.3m)	Sublicense VRT/RTBF	Sublicense VRT/RTBF	Sublicense VTM/ RTBF (Weekly magazine VRT)
Internet				
Mobile				
Total	€15.4m (US$20.08m)	€36m (US$46.93m)	€43m (US$56.06m)	€53.1m* (US$69.22m)

¥ Including €200,000 (US$260,728) for the highlights of the second soccer division.

* Telenet will cover all matches from the 2012-2013 season onwards. In return, the consortium annually pays an additional €1 million (US$1.3m).

The Digital Era (2005–2008)

The year 2005 was a milestone in the history of Belgian sports broadcasting. For the first time a company outside the television business was awarded the live rights to the Belgian soccer championship. Surprisingly, the telecommunications operator, Belgacom, outbid cable operator Telenet and acquired the exclusive rights for a record €36 million (US$46.93m). In order to position itself as an IPTV provider in the emerging digital television market, the company needed appealing content. This purchase saw Belgacom become a multimedia firm operating a digital television platform and a premium television channel covering live soccer. The rights had also moved from a traditional broadcaster to a telecommunications company for the first time, which raised competition policy issues.

Whilst launching the tender process, the Pro League claimed that it had considered the recommendations of the European Commission in the context of three competition cases. These cases, which concerned the selling of broadcasting rights to the UEFA Premier League, the EPL and the German Bundesliga, all dealt with the issue of joint selling. In such a scenario, the league collectively sells the rights to interested broadcasters on behalf of all its members. However, this joint selling practice attracted the attention of the European Commission in its role as a competition authority. The Commission acknowledged the potential foreclosing effects of a joint-sale mechanism, but still granted a conditional exemption. Four main amendments were stated:

1. Broadcasting rights should be held for a period of no longer than three years;
2. Sports rights should be traded through open and transparent tender procedures that give all interested parties equal opportunities;
3. Individual clubs should be granted the opportunity to sell rights that the league is unable to sell;
4. Broadcasting rights should be marketed in different packages to allow several competitors to acquire sports content.

The Belgian Competition Council used these conditions as a template when it ruled on the assignment of the broadcasting rights. For the 2005–2008 period, Belgacom made the highest bid for four of the six packages that were offered, whereas Telenet and RTBF submitted the highest offer for the two remaining packages. RTBF proposed a number of amendments to the contractual proposal that were sent to interested broadcasters before the tendering procedure. Given these amendments would fundamentally alter the principles included in the tender, the Pro League decided not to take its tender into account and awarded all rights to Belgacom.

Telenet, supported by pay television BeTV, filed a complaint against this Pro League decision claiming that the league violated competition rules when granting all rights to Belgacom. According to Telenet, the league was prohibited from granting all rights to a single party (even when that party made the highest bid on every package), and at least two parties should be granted access to rights packages. However, the Belgian Competition Council stated that it had no objection to the selling of all packages to one company. Furthermore, the claimants indicated that each package should be awarded to the highest bidder and that an exclusivity bonus, as offered by Belgacom, could not be accepted.

The Play-Offs (2008–2011)

Instead of carving up the broadcasting rights for different platforms, a new trend was that sports organizations, such as UEFA, decided to sell their broadcasting rights on a platform-neutral basis with packages distinguished by time window: live, near-live or deferred, highlight and clip rights. The idea here is that the owners of each package can exploit these rights across various platforms, including Internet and mobile media. Although the Belgian Pro League agreed to sell its rights on a platform-neutral basis, the Competition Council did not allow the joint selling of all live rights in a single package. The online and mobile rights were sold in separate packages and non-exclusively so that multiple companies could supply live sports on online and mobile platforms. The key outcome here was that no company was interested in these non-exclusive packages.

Belgacom maintained its leadership in the live soccer sports market over these years after a series of complex competition and policy decisions. In order to boost the value of the contract, the Pro League also decided to extend the regular competition with play-off matches between the six best ranked clubs from the 2009–2010 season onwards. This decision produced an unexpected sporting twist that matched the maneuverings in the media market. Two teams had finished on equal points at the end of the 2008–2009 season, and two additional matches were staged to decide the new champion. Since no one had ever planned for this dramatic outcome, the existing broadcasting contract with Belgacom did not include the live rights for these extra games. Although Belgacom had a first right of refusal for these matches, pay television BeTV outbid Belgacom and won the battle to show the games. Belgacom, which had invested several million in soccer, was obviously upset by this situation. The awarding of the nationwide rights to BeTV was also keenly debated in the Flemish Parliament, as the French-language broadcaster BeTV was not carried by Flemish cable company Telenet. More than half of Belgian soccer fans were, therefore, unable to watch these two important matches on a Flemish television channel. It was suggested that the Pro League sell its broadcasting rights to companies in each part of the country separately in the future. This plan could, however, have negative effects on the value of the future broadcasting contracts and might increase transaction costs for all negotiating parties.

Non-Exclusive Rights (2011–2014)

For the 2011–2014 seasons, and to everyone's surprise, no company acquired all the live rights to the Belgian soccer competition. Belgacom was unable to outbid Telenet for all live rights, so both operators each took a different rights package. Telenet outbid Belgacom for the three most attractive matches and acquired first choice of three live games each match day. Belgacom instead purchased the rights to broadcast the other five remaining matches. Whereas Belgacom offers its television services across the whole country, Telenet's activities are limited to the Flemish-speaking community. To remedy this situation, Telenet reached an agreement with Walloon cable operator, VOO, to broadcast the remaining matches in the southern part of the country, and also with Brussels-based cable company, Numéricable. In contrast to the previous contract, the new broadcasting deal also encompasses mobile and online media rights so that operators can serve their customers across different platforms. For the first time in six years, the commercial broadcaster VTM was also able to reposition itself in the sports broadcasting market by acquiring the highlight rights.

CONCLUSION: SHAPING A TRANSNATIONAL MEDIA SPORT ORDER

Reflecting the popularity of sports events, public service broadcasters were pioneers in the sports broadcasting market. Soon, private television companies were seduced by the commercial opportunities presented by sports coverage and started to outbid public service broadcasters for coverage rights. Later, commercial free-to-air television was dethroned by pay television as a migration from subscription platforms occurred. With the entrance of multichannel and later digital television, an increasing number of companies outside the established television business acknowledged the strategic power of live sports rights and joined the battle to control these rights. An interesting paradox is evident in this struggle for platform leadership. Whereas this battle was mainly driven by technological developments fuelled by a process of deregulation in European audiovisual markets, the sports broadcasting market has become increasingly regulated to guarantee fair competition and preserve the social role of sport in society.

This chapter mainly focused on the European sports arena and the Belgian television market in particular, which was used as a case study to illustrate the transition of power from traditional broadcasters to vertically integrated digital and telecommunications operators. This case also highlighted the increasing importance of sector-specific media and competition policies in the selling, buying and exploitation of media rights. As a result of this intensified battle for live sports rights, viewing opportunities for sports fans increased, and soccer clubs—which behave like supply side monopolists—have benefited from the increased competition on the demand side. Telecommunications operators have since become involved in an ongoing fight for rights acquisition, spending significant sums in the process. Compared to the 2005–2008 contract, the latest 2011–2014 Belgian broadcast deal increased in value quite considerably. Although this television income was distributed among all clubs, the bigger clubs benefited the most from this growth, which leaves open the possibility of them selling their rights on an individual basis.

Almost everywhere in Europe and elsewhere, broadcast deals have increased in value and competition for coverage rights is frequently tight and intense. Now that digital television is maturing in several large markets, it can be expected that telecommunications carriers will be reluctant to invest large amounts of money in the exclusive acquisition of live sports rights. This reluctance could ultimately produce a situation in which operators are willing to share rights in order to reduce capital expenses and focus on developing new, and probably less costly, competitive advantages. Alternatively, the rising popularity of online television services could trigger a new phase in the long-standing struggle for platform leadership and give another boost to the income flowing from "broadcasting" rights. However, this scenario also raises the question of whether the acquisition of national soccer rights by global technology firms such as Google or Apple would create the need for a new regulatory order, one that goes beyond the national and even European audiovisual policy frameworks. A transnational media sport order, rooted in national competitions and teams, is beginning to take shape, affecting the distribution of economic power in sports media markets and endangering the viewing rights of the general public. The consequences of these developments need to be closely watched and analyzed from social, market and access equality perspectives.

NOTES

1. After a revision of the Directive, this provision was renumbered to Article 14 of the Audiovisual Media Service Directive. This mechanism allows every member state to draw up a list of events that are of major interest for that society. According to the article, these events should be broadcast on "free-to-air" television ensuring that a "substantial proportion of the public" has the ability to watch those major events.
2. For more information, see http://www.ifm-sports.com/share/Fernsehen_in_Europa.pdf
3. For more information, see http://www.futebolfinance.com/ranking-de-direitos-de-transmissao-tv-2010
4. The EBU is a confederation of seventy-four (mainly, but not only, public service) broadcasting organizations from fifty-six countries. On behalf of its members, the EBU negotiates with rights holders. It is worth noting that the IOC has rejected the EBU's bid for the 2014 and 2016 Olympics in favor of a sports rights marketing agency, Sportfive. This decision may see the Olympics move to private subscription television for the first time in several western European countries. This tender did, however, specify that the rights holder is obliged to provide at least two hundred hours of free-to-air coverage of the summer Games and at least one hundred hours of free-to-air coverage of the winter Games. This stipulation means that Sportfive has to ensure that pay television operators will sublicense the free-to-air broadcasting rights.
5. The list, however, does not contain the Belgian soccer competition as an event of major importance to the Belgian population. Hence, the restrictions imposed on the listed events do not apply to the national soccer league.
6. Official figures provided by Pro League. Our thanks to Ludwig Sneyers, the CEO of the Jupiler Pro League Belgium.

REFERENCES

Boyle R & Haynes R (2004) *Football in the New Media Age*. London: Routledge.
Budzinski O & Satzer J (2011) Sports business and multisided markets: Towards a new analytical framework? *Sports, Business, Management: an International Journal* 1(2): 124–37.

Buraimo B (2008) Stadium attendance and television audience demand in English league football. *Managerial and Decision Economics* 29(6): 513–23.

Dauncey H & Hare G (2003) *Tour de France: 1903–2003*. New York: Routledge.

Deloitte (2012) *Fan Power: Football Money League*. Manchester, UK: Sport Business Group at Deloitte.

Doganoglu T & Wright J (2010) Exclusive dealing with network effects. *International Journal of Industrial Organization* 28(2): 145–54.

Evens T & Lefever K (2011) Playing the sports game: broadcasting rights in the digital television era. *Journal of Sport & Social Issues* 35(1): 33–49.

Gaustad T (2000) The economics of sports programming. *Nordicom Review* 21: 101–13.

Helland K (2007) Changing sports, changing media. Mass appeal, the sports/media complex and TV sports rights. *Nordicom Review* 28: 105–19.

Hoehn T & Lancefield D (2003) Broadcasting and sport. *Oxford Review of Economic Policy* 19(4): 552–68.

Hutchins B & Rowe D (2009) From broadcast scarcity to digital plenitude: the changing dynamics of the media sport content economy. *Television & New Media* 10(4): 354–70.

Leandros N & Tsourvakas G (2005) Intensive competition and company failures in subscription television: some European experiences. *International Journal on Media Management* 7(1–2): 24–38.

Lefever K (2012) *New Media and Sport: International Legal Aspects*. The Hague: T.M.C. Asser Press.

PwC (2010) *Back on Track? The Outlook for the Global Sports Market to 2013*. Online. Available from: http://www.pwc.com/gx/en/entertainment-media/pdf/Global-Sports-Outlook.pdf (Accessed 10 January 2012).

Rowe D (2004) Fulfilling the cultural mission: popular genre and public remit. *European Journal of Cultural Studies* 7(3): 381–400.

Smith P (2010) The politics of sports rights: the regulation of television sports rights in the UK. *Convergence: The International Journal of Research into New Media Technologies* 16(3): 316–33.

Szymanski S (2006) The economic evolution of sport and broadcasting. *The Australian Economic Review* 39(4): 428–34.

Turner P (2007) The impact of technology on the supply of sports broadcasting. *European Sports Management Quarterly* 7(4): 337–60.

6 The Challenge of Unauthorized Online Streaming to the English Premier League and Television Broadcasters

Andrew Kirton and Matthew David

INTRODUCTION: SOCCER'S EMERGENT ONLINE PRACTICES

As people appropriate the affordances of new technologies, we often see how emergent practices have the potential to disrupt established social, economic, political and cultural arrangements. This pattern has been particularly well illustrated in the digital age, as free online content reproduction and circulation have presented some significant challenges to the established systems and processes of media capital accumulation that developed in the pre-Internet era. The challenges of free online content circulation are now experienced in a range of industries, including the broadcasting industries to which sport became irrevocably bound in the second half of the twentieth century.

Richard Giulianotti and Roland Robertson (2009, p. 170) note the potential significance of the Internet for the future of soccer at the end of their book, *Globalization and Football*. They make reference to the erosion of national pay-television networks as individuals begin freely accessing live matches through Internet platforms. In this chapter we assert that such emergent online practices are indeed significant for soccer and for the precise reasons stated by Giulianotti and Robertson. Unauthorized "live-streaming"—an alternative form of online content distribution—threatens to disrupt a whole set of economic arrangements involving the broadcasting of soccer that developed during the pre-Internet era and upon which top-flight leagues and clubs have become heavily dependent. In this chapter we outline the challenge that live-streaming presents to the EPL and its broadcast partners.

The EPL is, according to Millward (2011), "the global football league." Clubs are owned, supported and played for by people from all corners of the world. The league has an estimated annual television audience of more than three billion people and generates cumulative revenues of around £2bn (US$3.21bn) per season. We focus on the EPL as a paradigmatic case of those "hyper-commoditized" (Giulianotti, 2002, 2005; Walsh & Giulianotti, 2007) sporting leagues that exist in today's global media sports cultural complex (Rowe, 2004). The challenges that live-streaming presents to this important league offer lessons of broad relevance to the whole domain of sport and media.

We first outline the economic relations involved in the live broadcasting of EPL matches and then discuss the emergence and nature of live-streaming as a challenge to these existing economic arrangements. We argue that this practice has the potential to exacerbate existing economic instability in the EPL. Our analysis shows how those with vested economic interests in maintaining existing arrangements have reacted and responded to live-streaming, and suggest that efforts to restrict it appear doomed to fail, especially given the apparent attitudes of many soccer fans. Finally, we consider what the future might hold for the EPL and its broadcasting partners.

THE BROADCASTING OF LIVE EPL SOCCER

Commercial television broadcasting has been a crucial factor in the development of soccer as a global industry. According to industry analysts Deloitte, broadcasting deals now represent "the greatest generator of total revenue" amongst the world's wealthiest clubs (2011, p. 36). In the 2009–2010 season, the money generated from broadcasting deals outstripped all other income streams at sixteen of the top twenty highest revenue generating clubs in world soccer, contributing to an average of forty-four percent of each club's total revenue. The EPL, as one of the first leagues in the world to seize upon the opportunities presented by commercial television broadcasting, has been at the forefront of these developments.[1] Since the EPL's formation in 1992, BSkyB has been the league's principal broadcaster and "marketing partner" (Boyle & Haynes, 2004; King, 2002 [1998]; Malcolm, Jones & Waddington, 2000; Sandvoss, 2003). In that year, BSkyB bought the exclusive rights to screen five seasons of live EPL matches to its paying subscribers for £191.5m (US$307.2m). This figure significantly outstripped the value of the previous broadcast contract held by the free-to-air commercial broadcaster ITV, which was worth £44m (US$70.6m) for four seasons from 1988. From this point onwards the amounts paid to the EPL for rights to live matches have risen at a substantial rate. In February 2009, BSkyB paid £1.6bn (US$2.57bn) to secure the rights to EPL matches for a three further seasons (2010–2013), whilst rival broadcasting company Setanta bid an additional £182m (US$292m) for rights to broadcast a much smaller number of live matches. In 2012, the EPL sold three further seasons (2013–2016) of domestic broadcast rights for just over £3bn (US$4.81bn)—an increase of £1.25bn (US$2bn) on the sum achieved in 2009 (BBC, 2012). Again, BSkyB secured the largest proportion of rights, paying £2.28bn (US$3.66bn) for the exclusive rights to broadcast 116 matches per season, whilst the leading telecommunications company, BT, committed £738m (US$1.184bn) for the rights to broadcast thirty-eight matches per season. In recent years, the number of territories in which EPL matches are broadcast has grown to 211 (more than the 193 member states of the United Nations), and the cumulative value of the EPL's overseas broadcasting deals have roughly doubled with each round of broadcasting rights negotiations (David & Millward, 2012).

The income generated by these various broadcasting deals is redistributed to EPL member clubs in a number of ways. First, an equal dividend from the sale of domestic broadcasting rights is released to all member clubs (£14.6m [US$23.4m] in 2009–2010 season, for instance). Second, a "facility payment" is made according to the number of times a club has been featured live on television in the UK. In 2009–2010, the lowest number of times a club featured live on television in the UK was ten, which translated into a facility payment of £6.3m (US$20.9m). Manchester United FC was screened twenty-four times, translating into a payment of £13m (US$20.85m). Third, clubs are awarded a payment based upon their final league placing. This meant that in the 2009–2010 season, Portsmouth FC—who finished bottom of the EPL—received £800,424 (US$1.28m), while champions Chelsea FC were awarded more than £16m (US$25.67m). Fourth, revenue from overseas television payments is divided and shared equally amongst clubs—in the 2009–2010 season, this contributed more than £10.1m (US$16.2m) to each club. These economic arrangements arguably benefit broadcasters and fans, as well as the EPL and its member clubs. Broadcasters such as BSkyB are able to secure exclusive rights to broadcast content that is in high demand and so attracts a significant number of subscribers. Exclusive EPL soccer coverage has been recognized as key to building BSkyB's subscription base and setting it on the road to success after uncertain—indeed, almost disastrous—beginnings in the 1980s (Douglas, 1999). BSkyB has, in turn, been credited with reviving English soccer after a period of economic "recession" in the 1980s (Taylor, 1984) and for helping the EPL to become the richest league in the world (Douglas, 1999). The partnership between the EPL and BSkyB has helped boost the profile and income of the league's clubs and allowed them to invest further in world-class players and facilities. Fans have, in turn, witnessed the outcomes of these economic arrangements through the increasing quality of the soccer spectacle made available each week. While these arrangements appear mutually beneficial for all those involved, they have not been universally praised, and there have been increasing signs of trouble in the EPL.

ECONOMIC UNCERTAINTY AND THE SPECTER OF LIVE-STREAMING

Despite an abundance of money flowing into the EPL, there are also ominous signs of economic uncertainty. Half of the current EPL clubs were, for example, *technically* insolvent in the middle of 2010 (Bose, 2010), while in February 2010, the then-EPL club Portsmouth FC entered into administration. In March 2011, Bloomberg revealed a report by Wigan Athletic FC's auditors stating that there was "material uncertainty which may cast significant doubt about the company's [Wigan Athletic] ability to continue as a going concern" (Panja, 2011). With cumulative club debt in the EPL reaching £2.6bn (US$4.17bn) in 2010–2011 (Deloitte, 2011), many people, including politicians, academics and supporters, have begun asking questions about the sustainability of the current economic arrangements (see, for instance, Culture Media & Sport Select Committee, 2011; Hamil & Walters, 2010). One issue coming into sharp focus in this regard is the amount of money spent on player wages. Deloitte (2011) reported that, in the 2009–2010 season, EPL clubs spent on average sixty-eight percent of their income on player wages. Manchester City FC reportedly spent 107 percent of its income on wages, with Chelsea FC recording the highest wage bill of £147m (US$236m). Both teams reported significant losses for the season. The EPL is currently considering the implementation of UEFA's new "financial fair play" rules, which would impose limits on club's spending in this area. The EPL might worry about excessive spending among its member clubs, but it may soon have to deal with a reduction in income as its broadcasting partners confront the challenge of live-streaming.

Live-streaming can be summarized as a process whereby a legitimate digital television broadcast is retrieved and then, simultaneously, made available to view online. It essentially allows anyone with access to the Internet to view content free-of-charge for which they would otherwise have to pay to access, especially if a subscription television provider controls the content. In recent years, the number of people viewing all manner of streamed content on the Internet has exploded. The technologies that enable the process have been developing since the mid-1990s. However, the expansion of bandwidth and advances in programming and software has seen these streams become more widely available. Today, any number of websites offering free live-streaming software and services can be found. Until relatively recently, the most active of these websites and services were based in China, where a rising number of people were using them to watch subscription satellite television channels such as HBO, ESPN and MTV online for free. Geoffrey Fowler and Sarah McBride reported in 2005 that live-streaming was spreading to Europe, with users beginning to tap into Chinese services to watch European soccer matches (Fowler & McBride, 2005). They noted that these services quickly gained a substantial following when they emerged online, referring to one piece of free live-streaming software downloaded 1.5 million times in 2005 alone and to a particular NBA game that drew about 50,000 simultaneous peer-to-peer viewers. Programmers around the world have since been recreating and advancing the necessary technology, as is evidenced by the sheer volume of live-streaming websites that have emerged in the last five years. Growing demand for live-streaming services has also led to numerous technical innovations that have improved quality, accessibility, simplicity of use and reliability of live-streaming. Examining the live-streaming portal Justin. tv, Jack Birmingham and Matthew David (2011) report that 90,690 channels were created in the thirty-one days of July 2008 alone.

The uptake of live-streaming technologies among soccer fans in particular is evidenced by the appearance of dedicated live-streaming portals such as livesoccertv.com, livefootballol.com and freefootball.org. Currently, on match-days, numerous streams for every single EPL game can be found. Supporters on every EPL club-specific "e-zine" and message-board discuss where the best quality live-streams of matches can be found (David & Millward, 2012). The game played between Chelsea FC and Liverpool FC on 26 October 2008 gained more than 574,000 individual "hits" during the course of the ninety minutes, and the 6 September 2008 England away game versus Croatia had six separate streams available, with the most popular gaining just over 30,000 viewers at any one time (Birmingham & David, 2011). Copyright monitoring and enforcement agency, NetResult, has identified games with more than one million users (Smith, 2009).[2] In the case of EPL matches, it seems that the vast majority of live-streams consist of content being broadcast legitimately overseas. The EPL prohibits some games from being shown *live* in the UK on the premise that such live broadcasts might impact on match-day attendances. However, these matches *are* often shown live and legally in other countries by foreign broadcast partners. Users then capture this broadcast footage and simultaneously reproduce it online, making it available for anyone in the world with access to the Internet to watch free of charge, including EPL fans in the UK. David and Millward (2012) thus argue that the increased availability of digital television coverage of the EPL overseas is linked directly to an increased number of unauthorized live-streams and their subsequent take-up in the UK.[3]

These developments in digital and networking technology are helping to expose commercial television broadcasters to the same kinds of challenges plaguing the music, film, games and software industries for the last decade or so. As with *all* commercial enterprises whose business models involve providing access to content in return for payment, commercial broadcasters of television rely upon a certain level of "scarcity" in terms of access. In other words, in order to make money from content distribution, the content that broadcasters effectively sell access to must not be freely or more cheaply accessible elsewhere. In the last twenty years, though, we have moved rapidly from a situation of "broadcast scarcity" to "digital plenitude" (Hutchins & Rowe, 2012). As we know from the experiences of the music, film, book, games and software industries, digital and networking technologies have been crucial in affording people alternative means of accessing content that would otherwise be "rationed" or restricted.[4]

Current claims about the impact of live-streaming on television broadcasters are largely speculative and unsubstantiated, but there are signs of turbulence that have been cautiously construed as suggestive of an impact. Birmingham and David (2011) argue that the commercial broadcaster Setanta's failure to secure an adequate number of subscribers to cover its investments in EPL broadcasting rights was, in part, a reflection of people switching to free access by means of live-streaming over the Internet. The failure of ESPN to profit from its European sports broadcasting operations after having secured the rights to broadcast some live EPL games after Setanta's demise could be seen in a similar light—as partially the result of large numbers of people choosing to watch games online for free, rather than investing in television broadcast subscriptions. As David (2011) has acknowledged elsewhere, until the emergence of live-streaming, it had been difficult for fans to separate following their team from paying for expensive broadcast television subscription packages, meaning that clubs were, in turn, being *guaranteed* an important extra source of income. But with cheaper alternatives now emerging and developing online, fewer fans may decide to invest in broadcast television subscriptions. The EPL and its broadcasters are understandably becoming anxious about the rise in unauthorized online broadcasts of its matches and the potential financial implications. In 2009, the EPL's Chief Executive, Richard Scudamore, described live-streaming as a "very real threat". The fear is that as live-streaming capacities develop, millions will cancel expensive broadcast subscriptions to watch games online for free. This outcome would translate into lower income for the EPL and its member clubs. Given the financial turmoil in which the EPL currently finds itself, the result could be a full blown financial crisis:

> . . . the current threat to future revenues posed by the free-to-access broadcast of Premiership matches on live-streaming websites over the Internet may be the last straw in tipping most clubs in the EPL into bankruptcy. (David, 2011, p. 95)

In light of these potential implications and consequences, the EPL and its broadcasters have been moving to tackle alternative points of online access to live matches.

THE EPL AND ITS BROADCASTERS FIGHT BACK

As has already been acknowledged, commercial television broadcasters are by no means the first content "owning" and "distributing" companies to face the challenges presented by free online content circulation and access. The computer games, software, film, book and music industries have all been dealing with the same challenge of "digital plenitude". In these other content industries, companies have typically embarked on aggressive ideological, legal and political campaigns against the free digital reproduction and distribution of "their" content. These campaigns have been ideological in the sense that they involve attempts to persuade consumers to shun what the established industry defines as "illegitimate" access points and to appreciate the value of "officially" endorsed arrangements. Legal efforts have involved action against those involved the in unauthorized content distribution, while political campaigning has involved lobbying of governments in an attempt to induce quick legislative reactions. The EPL, the Sports Rights Owners Coalition (SROC) (of which the EPL is a leading member) and BSkyB have all embarked on campaigns against live-streaming that look very similar in this regard.

Attempts by people to evade the requirement to pay for access content have typically and frequently been branded by content owners as acts of disloyalty, selfishness and ignorance in the sense that they endanger the *future* of content provision (see David [2010] and Kirton [2010] for examples taken from the music industry). BSkyB, SROC, the EPL and its clubs are now deploying such rhetoric in relation to fans viewing free live EPL matches online. For instance, Oliver Weingarten, the EPL's lawyer and author of a SROC submission to a recent UK Government consultation on Intellectual Property and Growth, has stated:

> The long term consequences [of live-streaming] for the game are that it has the potential to devalue or dilute the rights value, and in turn that will dilute the product that we are able to turn out and the quality of player coming to the league. (quoted in Football Supporters' Federation, 2009a)

Similarly, Sunderland FC manager Niall Quinn has argued that, in accessing cheaper foreign broadcasts, fans were "damaging the progress of their clubs" (Quinn, quoted by Taylor, 2011). The extent to which such rhetoric might resonate with soccer fans remains to be seen, but *alone* it is unlikely to stop fans seeking cheaper points of access to EPL games.[5]

Like companies in other popular media content industries, the EPL has turned to its lawyers to stem the free distribution of "its" content online. The relevant legal frameworks in this regard are those of intellectual property rights. Within most legal territories, broadcasts are legally recognized as a form of intellectual property, and thus are protected by copyright laws, which essentially provide defined parties with the *exclusive* legal right to reproduce and distribute certain kinds of intangible goods such as broadcasts. In bidding for contracts with the EPL, broadcasters such as BSkyB are attempting to purchase the exclusive right to broadcast EPL matches—those broadcasts effectively then become the property of the broadcasting company. To reproduce and/or distribute a legitimately broadcast EPL match without the broadcaster's permission (as copyright holder) is considered a form of copyright infringement. It is according to these principles that live-streamers of EPL matches, and websites providing the space to do so, face the prospect of litigation. The EPL's Chief Executive, Scudamore, revealed in 2009 that the EPL had sent more than 700 "cease and desist" letters to live-streaming websites, mainly in China, informing them of the illegality of their activities (Football Supporters' Federation, 2009b). The EPL claimed an eighty-seven percent "success rate," yet none of these letters resulted in actual legal proceedings, only the voluntary removal of infringing content (streams) from a website. Actually litigating against those involved in live-streaming is likely to prove difficult within existing legal frameworks, stemming partly from the issue of defining who precisely should be legally liable for copyright infringement (David, 2011). The question of whether a website and streaming service such as Justin.tv is responsible for what users upload and stream live relates to a debate that has been raging over the last ten years in relation to peer-to-peer file sharing sites. Used to distribute music and video files, such sites simply claim that they provide a service that has legitimate uses, and they themselves cannot be held responsible for what users upload and offer to other users. Such a "dual-use" defense on the part of file sharing service providers has proved successful in some cases (file sharing platforms Grokster and Morpheus used it successfully in the US courts, for example), although this claim has been unsuccessful in other instances. Napster in the US was closed on grounds of contributory infringement because exchanges passed through a central server over which the company had control. Similarly, the individuals behind The Pirate Bay in Sweden were found to be actively *promoting* the use of the service for the purpose of copyright infringement.

Live-streaming services and websites may evade legal action by agreeing to remove streams or links to streams identified as infringing copyright. Thus, in 2008 the EPL claimed that the operators of Justin.tv were aware of the unauthorized match streams via their website, but were doing nothing to prevent them, thereby effectively "contributing" to copyright infringement. Justin.tv's Chief Executive Officer, Michael Siebel, responded to these claims by stating that he "does not anticipate any (legal) action" and that Justin. tv "follow the guidelines set out by the DMCA [Digital Millennium Copyright Act] and takes content off the website when requested by a copyright holder" (Birmingham & David, 2011, p. 74). As long as Justin.tv works with copyright holders in this way, enabling them to report infringements and seeking to act on such reports, it remains legally immune to liability. The problem with this system for copyright holders and content owners is that the time taken to contact the streaming portal, and for a stream to be investigated and removed, is far longer than the duration of the event being streamed—EPL matches last only ninety minutes. Websites such as Justin. tv are likely to come under increasing pressure to monitor and restrict usage via legislative responses that place legal obligations on Internet Service Providers (ISPs) and websites to cooperate with content owners' attempts to curb unauthorized online distribution. Content owning and distributing companies have been, as noted earlier, involved in aggressive lobbying campaigns in this regard.[6] Such mooted extensions of copyright law and their enforcement via legislative action are, of course, extremely controversial. It is highly questionable whether legislation and policy should seek to protect existing copyright monopolies from technical innovation and the choices that such innovations enable (David, 2010, 2011). Prohibitions of this kind rarely work (increased restriction simply results in online traffic displacement and increased technological adaptation and innovation), and the successful clamping down on Internet distribution has no overall social benefits. In other words, such legislative actions do not generate any *additional* wealth or advantage. At the same time, they might have very significant negative implications in terms of technological innovation, privacy, freedom of expression and freedom of access to valuable content.

THE VIEW FROM THE TERRACES

We noted earlier that it has been difficult for soccer fans to disentangle supporting their club from investing in expensive broadcast television subscriptions. With the emergence and continuing development of live-streaming as a cheaper alternative, we might, then, expect to see fewer fans taking out expensive subscriptions to Sky Television and its competitors. However, this scenario involves an assumption that reignites debates about the nature of soccer fandom and support. Should we understand fans and supporters simply as economically rational "customers" looking for the cheapest way to practice fandom, or as consumers somehow obliged to engage in seemingly less economically rational practices? There have been some useful debates in the sociology of sport about the ways in which fans "consume" soccer and how this activity might connect to their levels of commitment and support (Crawford, 2004; Giulianotti, 2002; King, 1997; Sandvoss, 2003). The views of fans about live-streaming have not been explored in any serious or systematic way, but we can draw on some useful examples from the public domain to highlight some important points here.

First, it *is* well understood that fans are unlikely to see themselves only as conventional customers/consumers. Indeed, following Giulianotti (2002), King (1997) and others, in consuming live soccer fans are more likely to see themselves as "members" of a club/community and so to display signs of a deeper sense of brand loyalty in this regard. Whether this identification translates into a willingness to pay for expensive broadcast subscriptions when there are cheaper alternatives on offer is uncertain. Yet, despite retaining a deep sense of loyalty to their clubs, many fans have become deeply dissatisfied with the increasing expense of being a supporter. Ian Taylor (1971a, 1971b) argued forty years ago that some soccer fans felt disenfranchised by its increasing commercialization. The reaction of some Sunderland FC supporters to Quinn's above-quoted comments about fans endangering the future of their club by seeking out cheaper broadcasts (via "parallel imports" in this case) revealed some evidence of such disenfranchisement. In responding, supporters frequently argued that players are "paid too much," and that ticket prices are too high for "ordinary fans" (David & Millward, 2012). A story attributed to the Football Supporters' Federation, and that appeared on most EPL club news pages in 2009, is also revealing in this regard:

The Premier League will huff and puff because they stand to lose billions in television deals. But the Internet is a system developed to allow the US Government to communicate in the event of a nuclear holocaust. It's pretty Richard Scudamore proof. Clubs are getting worried but it's a problem of their own making. Extortionate prices mean the next generation has (largely) turned their back on the live game. A lot of younger fans today don't need the live fix. They think football's watched on television anyway and the average Premier League crowd is now in its mid-40's and rising in age year-on-year. But what happens when the masses realise they can watch—for nothing—live games on the Internet? Television revenue disappears and clubs go bust . . . Clubs have to drop prices and win back the next generation who aren't currently hooked on the live game. Relying on the Russian Roulette of television revenue will cost them in the end. (Football Supporters' Federation, 2009c)

As this quotation indicates, the ultra-commercialization of elite soccer, and the increasing mediatization of fandom, may be eroding the bonds between fan and club. Average admission prices have risen by more than 200 percent since the creation of the EPL in 1992 (Birmingham & David, 2011). There has also been an increase over time in the subscription rates for live broadcasts of EPL matches, with access to Sky Sports channels currently costing more than £50 (US$80) per month (as part of its "bundled" service). An inexorable rise in the cost of watching soccer has led some fans to seek out cheaper access points such as live-streams. As the Football Supporters' Federation suggests above, this phenomenon looks set to intensify as the next generation of fans is socialized into an environment in which sports fandom is *predominantly* a mediated phenomenon and where alternative points of access proliferate online. With alternative means of watching live EPL soccer developing online and the scarcity of access upon which broadcasters have relied now being eroded, broadcasters may well begin to reconsider their current levels of investment in rights to broadcast the EPL. In this sense, the EPL and its member clubs face a potential reduction in income that could tip them into a full-blown economic crisis, the implications of which for this global league could be far reaching.

CONCLUSION: CONTROLLED SCARCITY AND THE CHALLENGE OF LIVE-STREAMING

The emergence of live-streaming, and the challenges that it poses to current arrangements for the broadcasting of EPL soccer, illustrate a process that is becoming familiar in the digital age. Technological developments afford the emergence and development of practices that have the potential to undermine existing economic arrangements. Nowhere is this pattern more visible than in the global media content and copyright industries, to which soccer became irrevocably bound in the pre-Internet era. Commercial television broadcasting has for a long time relied upon the presence and maintenance of a controlled scarcity in terms of access to the content that it distributes. In an age when digital networked technologies make the widespread reproduction and circulation of content relatively easy for users, maintaining such scarcity is a major challenge for such companies. This industry must necessarily adapt to the new technological environment and deal with the challenges that are posed, meaning that the relationships it developed with content providers like the EPL will also likely change. What the future might look like in this regard is uncertain, but we offer the following general comments and thoughts based on what has been presented in this chapter.

With a customer base of more than ten million subscribers and an operating profit of more than £1bn (US$1.6bn) (British Sky Broadcasting Group Plc, 2011), BSkyB is not about to collapse as a result of the live-streaming of EPL matches. Yet, the free online circulation of content may well see BSkyB reconsider current levels of investment in EPL broadcast rights. It would also be naive for the EPL to rely on a continuing rise in broadcasting income, which is what ongoing debt accumulation practices among EPL clubs appear to presume will occur. The consequences of a contraction in broadcasting income for EPL clubs could be significant given that it currently represents a significant proportion of their total income, and around half of those clubs are already technically insolvent. We are not suggesting that a number of EPL clubs are about to be declared bankrupt and disappear because of live-streaming. Rather, we propose that the business models that they rely on for current income levels will need to be reconfigured in order to deal with the parameters of the new environment.

The digital "revolution" has so far revealed a high level of resistance to change on the part of established corporate content providers and distributors. This pattern has been true of the recorded music industry, and it looks to be the case with the sports broadcasting industry. There will be continued attempts by those who principally benefit from existing economic arrangements to sustain them for as long as possible, but they look doomed to failure. Fans have become increasingly dissatisfied with the expense of supporting a soccer team. Many soccer followers are finding cheaper alternatives to expensive television subscriptions and are unconcerned about the supposed implications for the future of their clubs. Litigation to stop live-streaming is also proving ineffective so far. The EPL is likely to put further pressure on the government to modify legislation to make it easier for them to take legal action against these services and their users. However, the extension of copyright laws and enforcement regimes has already been met with significant public and political resistance. Furthermore, the experience of the music industry tells us that increased litigation and user restrictions are actually a catalyst for innovation in the technologies and techniques used for free online content distribution.

The EPL and its broadcasters could choose to make legitimate content offerings more attractive than the free alternatives. The EPL may draw selectively on approaches taken by leagues and clubs in some other countries, such as MLB in the US (see Chapter 3) and cricket leagues in India that offer comparatively low-cost, legal live-streaming services (Birmingham & David, 2011; Hutchins & Rowe, 2012).[7] The introduction of a reasonably priced or advertising funded online service, providing high image quality streams and "on-demand" viewing capabilities, might attract many fans in the UK. BSkyB has already made some moves to adapt to the new environment by including access to online content as part of its television subscription packages. However, given that a subscription to Sky Television is still necessary in order to access this online content, it seems unlikely that fans will move away from *free* live-streams. How the EPL and its broadcasting partners ultimately deal with the challenge of live-streaming will be an important issue to follow in the coming years. Meanwhile, every passing month is likely to see live-streaming services developing further and becoming increasingly popular. Far from reflecting a simple economic rationalism among soccer fans, the popularity of live-streaming reflects an enduring desire to witness live sports events and to practice fandom in ways that resist the commercial imperatives that have come to dominate contemporary sport. The EPL and its broadcasting partners risk alienating fans further in their attempts to resist change. With technical capacities and competencies constantly developing, free content reproduction and circulation looks set to become a growing challenge for those clinging to the broadcasting arrangements of the past in soccer and in elite sport as a whole.

NOTES

1. It has been widely acknowledged that the driving force behind the creation of the EPL was a thirst for increasing revenues and profitability among the directors of top-flight English clubs (see Conn, 2002 [1997]; Fynn and Guest, 1994, p. 25; King, 2002 [1998]). Believing that they could generate higher broadcasting rights revenues—in the context of the increasing popularity of subscription-based television broadcasting and a simultaneous resurgence of interest in English soccer after the national team's performance in the 1990 World Cup—these clubs moved to create a more exclusive league in which income from broadcasters would be retained by member clubs, rather than distributed across several divisions as had happened in the past.
2. As with other forms of illicit online content distribution, and other forms of illicit cultural practice more broadly, it is inherently difficult to derive any accurate total figure for live-streaming practices.
3. David & Millward (2012) note the dynamic relationship between live-streaming and the legitimate parallel importing of broadcasts from overseas broadcasting companies. They concentrate upon parallel importing in the light of the 2011 ruling of the European Court of Justice that declared national broadcast monopolies within the European Union to be unlawful.

4. The exact nature of the relationship between file sharing and music industry revenues has been fiercely debated, but the convergence and appropriation of digital and networking technologies is bound up with the declining revenues observed in some areas of the music industry in the last ten years.
5. Such rhetoric was clearly unsuccessful when deployed by music recording companies in relation to online music file sharing.
6. See Kirton (2010) for a discussion of the development of the UK's *Digital Economy Act 2010* and the involvement of music record companies in this process.
7. It should also be noted that these leagues can also take a highly punitive approach to alleged copyright infringement.

REFERENCES

Birmingham J & David M (2011) Live-streaming: will football fans continue to be more law abiding than music fans? *Sport in Society* 14(1): 69–81.
Bose M (2010) The deflating world of English football. *The Spectator*, 20 February, 14–15.
Boyle R & Haynes R (2004) *Football in the New Media Age*. London: Routledge.
BBC (British Broadcasting Corporation) (2012) Premier League rights sold to BT and BSkyB for £3bn. Online. Available from: http://www.bbc.co.uk/news/business-18430036 (Accessed 5 July 2012).
British Sky Broadcasting Group Plc (2011) *Annual Review 2011*. Isleworth: BSkyB.
Conn D (2002 [1997]) *The Football Business: The Modern Football Classic*. London: Mainstream.
Crawford G (2004) *Consuming Sport*. London: Routledge.
Culture, Media & Sport Select Committee (2011) *Football Governance* [HC 792–1]. London: The Stationary Office.
David M (2010) *Peer to Peer and the Music Industry: The Criminalization of Sharing*. London: Sage.
David M (2011) Music lessons: football finance and live-streaming. *Journal of Policy Research in Tourism, Leisure & Events* 3(1): 95–8.
David M & Millward P (2012) Football's coming home? Digital de-territorialisation and the contradictions of transnational sports coverage. *British Journal of Sociology* 63(2): 349–69.
Deloitte (2011) *The Untouchables: The Football Money League 2011*. Manchester: Deloitte.
Douglas T (1999) Murdoch's rise to the top. *BBC News*, 12 March. Online. Available from: http://news.bbc.co.uk/1/hi/special_report/1999/03/99/murdochs_big_match/167937.stm (Accessed 30 June 2012).
Football Supporters' Federation (2009a) Premier League fears over Internet streaming. *The Football Supporters' Federation*, 23 February. Online. Available from: http://www.fsf.org.uk/news/Premier-League-fears-over-Internet-streaming.php?id=added|desc|360| (Accessed 30 June 2012).
Football Supporters' Federation (2009b) Premier League urge crackdown on illegal websites. *The Football Supporters' Federation*, 22nd January. Online. Available from: http://www.fsf.org.uk/news/Premier-League-urge-crackdown-on-illegal-websites.php (Accessed 30 June 2012).
Football Supporters' Federation (2009c) FSF on net loss of football's bumper television deal. *Vital Football*, 31 March. Online. Available from: http://www.astonvilla.vitalfootball.co.uk/article.asp?a=7500636 (Accessed 30 June 2012).

Fowler GA & McBride S (2005) Newest export from China: pirated pay television. *Wall Street Journal*, 2 September, B1.

Fynn A & Guest L (1994) *Out of Time: Why Football Isn't Working!* London: Simon & Schuster.

Giulianotti R (2002) Supporters, Followers, Fans and Flâneurs: a taxonomy of spectator identities in football. *Journal of Sport and Social Issues* 26(1): 25–46.

Giulianotti R (2005) *Sport: A Critical Sociology*. Cambridge: Polity.

Giulianotti R & Robertson R (2009) *Globalization and Football*. London: Sage.

Hamil S & Walters G (2010) Financial performance in English professional football: "an inconvenient truth". *Soccer & Society* 11(4): 354–72.

Hutchins B & Rowe D (2012) *Sport Beyond Television: The Internet, Digital Media and the Rise of Networked Media Sport*. New York: Routledge.

King A (1997) New directors, customers and fans: the transformation of English football in the 1990s. *Sociology of Sport Journal* 14(3): 224–40.

King A (2002 [1998]) *The End of the Terraces: The Transformation of English Football in the 1990's*. London: Leicester University Press.

Kirton A (2010) *Discourse and Power in the Formulation of UK Anti-File-Sharing Legislation: The Place of Recording Company and Creator Interests*. PhD Thesis, University of Liverpool, UK.

Malcolm D, Jones I & Waddington I (2000) The people's game? Football spectatorship and demographic change. In: Garland J, Malcolm D & Rowe M (eds.) *The Future of Football: Challenges For The Twenty-First Century*. London: Frank Cass. 129–43.

Millward P (2011) *The Global Football League*. Basingstoke: Palgrave.

Panja T (2011) Wigan auditor says soccer club would be at risk without owner's millions. *Bloomberg*, 2 March. Online. Available from: http://www.bloomberg.com/news/2011-03-02/wigan-auditor-says-soccer-club-would-be-at-risk-without-owner-s-millions.html (Accessed 30 June 2012).

Rowe D (2004) *Sport, Culture, and the Media*. 2nd ed. Maidenhead, Berkshire: Open University Press.

Sandvoss C (2003) *A Game of Two Halves: Football, Television and Globalization*. London: Routledge.

Scudamore R (2009) Call it by its name—this is theft. *The Guardian*, 23 November, G2: 4.

Smith P (2009) Interview: NetResult CEO Christopher Stokes on tackling football television pirates. *PaidContent: UK*, 22 September. Online. Available from: http://paidcontent.co.uk/article/419-interview-netresult-ceo-christopher-stokes-on-tackling-football-television-pira/ (Accessed 30 June 2012).

Taylor I (1971a) Soccer consciousness and soccer hooliganism. In: Cohen S (ed.) *Images of Deviance*. Middlesex: Harmondsworth, 134–64.

Taylor I (1971b) Football mad: a speculative sociology of football hooliganism. In: Dunning E (ed.) *The Sociology of Sport: A Selection of Readings*. London: Frank Cass, 352–77.

Taylor I (1984) Professional sport and the recession: the case of British soccer. *International Review for the Sociology of Sport* 19: 7–30.

Taylor L (2011) Niall Quinn "despises" Sunderland fans who watch foreign broadcasts. *The Guardian*, 4 February. Online. Available from: http://www.guardian.co.uk/football/2011/feb/04/niall-quinn-sunderland-overseas-broadcasts?INTCMP=SRCH (Accessed 30 June 2012).

Walsh A J & Giulianotti R (2007) *Ethics, Money and Sport*. Abingdon: Routledge.

Part II
Users, Audiences and Identities

7 Online Belongings
Female Fan Experiences in Online Soccer Forums

Deirdre Hynes and Ann-Marie Cook

INTRODUCTION: THE PARADOX AT THE HEART OF ONLINE INTERACTION

From early radio commentaries and sports reports to illegal Internet streams, the soccer *fan* has enjoyed a mediated relationship with the game from the late 1940s. More recently, however, soccer and the culture of soccer fandom have undergone radical changes with the introduction of digital and new media technologies that have transformed the ways in which the game is experienced, from attendance at live matches to televised spectacles with live social media commentary via Twitter and Facebook. The development of Web 2.0 technologies has facilitated the emergence of shared community spaces, such as the plethora of message boards and online forums created by soccer clubs, supporters' organizations and fans themselves. Within these networks, the act of following and supporting a chosen team fosters interaction and promotes a sense of belonging that transcends the spatial and temporal constraints that regulate offline and physical interactions (boyd, 2011; Livingstone, 2005; Rheingold, 1993; Song, 2009; Wellman & Gulia, 1999). Traditionally, communalism was underpinned by activities that were centered on pubs, stadiums, offline social networks and fanzines. Now, online soccer forums offer new platforms for dynamic engagement that take advantage of the Internet's capacity to disseminate information widely and instantly, and function as social and symbolic meeting places where online and offline activities, such as boycotts, petitions, rallies and supporters' unions, can be organized. Buoyed by the increased social and sociological relevance of communication flows and the use and ownership of new media technologies, the semiotic expression of social identity via soccer fandom is now possible in the information age (Castells, 1996, 1997).

The term "fan" has generated considerable discussion, particularly around the contested issue of spectator identities (Giulianotti, 2002). In his seminal work on the subject, Giulianotti defines four ideal types of spectator identity: supporters, followers, fans and flâneurs. By enabling the support of soccer clubs from a geographical and temporal distance, and promoting the cultivation of relationships with clubs and players built upon the consumption of club-related products (pay-per-view subscriptions, merchandise, shares, etc.), the Internet facilitates the *follower* type and the cool *fan* typology described by Giulianotti. This development has significant ramifications for the ongoing debates and conflicts between authentic *supporters/fans* and *Johnny-come-latelys/plastics/bandwagon jumpers*. Status in this context is defined on the basis of factors like geography, match day attendance, ties to the club (familial or otherwise), duration of support for the club, and the possession of subcultural capital that enables claims to greater levels of status vis-à-vis other supporters (Giulianotti, 2002, p. 34). As spaces that facilitate interaction, engagement and identity formation, online soccer forums have the potential—at least in theory—to foster greater levels of participation and inclusiveness as they expand the scope of activities and influence available to fans. In practice, however, life in online forums foments an experience of discontinuity, where activities are compartmentalized within a series of fleeting textual encounters of brief temporal duration.

Indeed, there is a great paradox at the heart of online interaction. The Internet facilitates unprecedented levels of participation and fosters communal bonds that reach around the globe, but the values of inclusivity and community cohesion are ultimately undermined when the ideologies, power structures and social scripts that govern offline living condition the terms of online engagement. The position of women within the male-dominated world (both real and virtual) of soccer is a case in point. On one hand, the participation of female fans in forums is indicative of shifts taking place within soccer culture as efforts by governing bodies to make the game more inclusive by appealing to women, ethnic minorities and families disrupt the tradition of privileging white, working-class males. On the other hand, online forums (like their real-life counterparts) can be seen to operate in ways that marginalize women within the discourses of fandom, regulate the performance of their identities as fans and diminish the feeling of belonging to a group.

The heavily masculinized character of soccer and soccer culture informs the dynamics of fan websites, which are populated primarily by men. For example, based on usage figures from August 2012, male posters on the popular Liverpool FC[1] supporters' forum, RAWK (Red and White Kop), outnumbered female posters by nearly thirteen to one. This figure reflects the overall state of scholarship on soccer fan communities that, while growing in volume, continues to consistently overlook the position and experience of women. Even literature that deals with the experiences of female fans tends to focus on "real-world" engagement, rather than on online communities. This research is relevant, though, to conversations about online forums, in part because it offers a useful springboard for thinking about critical issues pertaining to gender dynamics in a predominantly masculine environment. Also, the empirical data presented in this chapter reveals the existence of a close relationship between offline and virtual expressions of fandom.

This is an opportune moment to bring into sharp relief what often remains invisible in other studies of sport and online communities: the ways in which women experience, negotiate and articulate their identities as fans in the technologically mediated, gendered space of online forums. We situate the analysis of female fans' online experiences at the intersection of discourses concerning digital technologies that mediate the relationships between fans and clubs, historical and contemporary perspectives on the position of women within soccer culture, and theoretical conceptualizations of identity formation. Discussion of empirical data collected through interviews with fans is framed in relation to Judith Butler's (1993, 1999, 2004) scholarship on the body and gender, Erving Goffman's (1959) writings on the presentation of the self in everyday life and Pierre Bourdieu's concept of "habitus" (1984). This chapter seeks, then, not only to expose the means by which identity is constructed, maintained and mediated by information and communication technologies, but to shed light on its implications for the cultural politics of sports fandom.

WOMEN AND SOCCER: A BRIEF OVERVIEW

Social reality is not a given, but is instead continually created and recreated through language, symbols and signs. Through ongoing repetition and reproduction, conventions that structure perceptions of reality become so ingrained in culture that their artificiality (or "constructedness") is virtually erased. It was through this process that the marginalization of women became embedded within the social fabric of soccer as both a game and as a cultural milieu. Following the work of Foucault, Todd Crosset (1990) situates the rise of sport in the nineteenth century as a response to the erosion of men's power and privilege over women. Physical performance offered a means of promoting dominant heteronormative masculinities (Sabo & Panepinto, 1990) and naturalizing ideological conceptions that affirmed the superiority of male sexuality over female sexuality. David Whitson (1990, p. 20) furthers this argument in two ways: first, through his discussion of sport as a male institution in both the numerical sense and in terms of the values and behavioral norms that it promotes; and second, through analysis of how sport and male attributes (i.e., aggressiveness, competitiveness, etc.) confirm patterns of male privilege and female subordination that exist outside sport within society as a whole. Drawing upon the arguments of Eric Dunning, Whitson (1990, pp. 24–25) then explains that not only is male hegemony strengthened by practices that honor physical prowess and skills such as fighting, but male advantages are also eroded when society is pacified and the segregation of the sexes breaks down. In the name of preserving the "proving" ground of sport as a thoroughly masculine domain, the inclusion of women came to be viewed as a challenge and threat to masculinity (Connell, 2005). As a consequence, female participation and membership in sporting communities was either discouraged or prohibited outright. These developments have fostered a general acceptance of soccer as exclusively masculine—a man's game (Harris, 2004; Jeanes & Kay, 2007; Robson, 2000; Whannel, 1992). It is not, however, a game for just *any* sort of man. As Garry Robson (2000, p. x) explains, soccer remained the:

> . . . practical medium par excellence of the continuing expression and celebration of the core practices and concerns of embodied masculinity in a specifically *working class* variant. (our emphasis)

The male-dominated, homosocial space associated with soccer is inextricably tied to conceptualizations of identity. Thus, much is at stake when the dynamics and conventions that have historically defined the soccer experience give way to new trends in identity brought about by the increasing corporatization and excessive commodification of the game.

The financial success of recent EURO Championships and FIFA World Cup competitions suggests that soccer is doing a good job of selling and corporatizing itself. In a move to attract *new* fans, governing bodies have attempted to open up soccer—on the terraces as well as on the pitch (Selmer & Sülzle, 2010)[2]—by actively promoting the attendance of ethnic minorities, *women*, families and a more middle-class type of fan. FIFA president Sepp Blatter even went as far as to declare that the future of soccer is feminine (Williams, 2003, p. 1). The widespread recognition that the global institution of soccer is winning the battle to rebrand itself as welcoming and inclusive has prompted questions about how the influx of "new" fans changes the game. Phasing out the "pot-bellied, chair throwing English man" has cleared the way for affluent middle-class *families* (who can afford the ever-increasing costs of ticket prices and club merchandise) for whom attendance at games sometimes serves as a status symbol rather than as an expression of true loyalty to a club. Meanwhile, the presence of women, ethnic minorities and children in FIFA's "family" has served the dual purpose of demonstrating a commitment to inclusion, and introducing a level of civility that checks the anti-social behavior that has tainted the game's image in the past. The corporatization of the game has been accompanied by a globalization of its market base, thus displacing young, working-class males from the privileged position that they once occupied as the game's "preferred" audience (Crabbe & Brown, 2004). The hyper-commodification of the game has taken the form of all-seater stadiums, increased policing, economic "squeezing" of fans and the emergence of the "day tripper". This "opening up" of soccer "culture" addresses many people who wish to "witness" a spectacle, as opposed to those who emotionally invest in a meaningful, ritualistic and highly charged event. These factors have worked in concert to sanitize and, therefore, to diminish what traditional, male fans understand as an authentic match day experience (Crabbe & Brown, 2004). The impact of this sanitization can be observed to full effect among male fans in the 30–40 age bracket, for whom the soccer ground has often represented an accessible site for the public display of highly charged feeling and that stood in contrast to experiences of mundane "everyday" life (Crabbe & Brown, 2004).

The research that underpins this chapter sits within the context of the transformation of soccer and the explicit efforts to "de-masculinize" the game. Although the changing face of the soccer fan has been a topic of much discussion and analysis (Brimson & Brimson, 1996; Crabbe & Brown, 2004; Robson, 2000; Selmer & Sülzle, 2010; Slaughter, 2004), studies seldom address the issues vis-à-vis female fans. The existing literature on women and soccer traverses the playing pitch to the stands, engaging with issues and tensions in ways that highlight the extent to which gender is bound up with the identity of soccer fandom. Female players contest labels of lesbianism in a sport associated primarily with men (Caudwell, 1999). Katharine W. Jones (2008), on the other hand, argues that women sometimes downplay their gender identities in order to reinforce their fan identities. Working from data collected over the course of thirty-eight interviews, Jones highlights three strategies employed by women in response to sexism and homophobia at soccer matches. First, some women displayed disgust at other fans for making sexist and homophobic remarks at the game. These female fans tended to redefine fandom to exclude abusers. Second, some women downplayed sexism, and third, some women embraced gender stereotypes. These female fans accepted the traditional ideas about gender within soccer and, in doing so, reconfirmed the notion that femininity is inconsistent with "authentic" fandom, and that abuse is part of the game. These responses are hardly indicative of the sense of investment and belonging that soccer institutions seek to promote by pushing for greater female participation. However, the fact that all of these data concern real-life interactions raises questions about whether similar dynamics exist in online fan spaces where the markers of gender identity can be masked to create a more equal "playing field" between male and female posters.

The online (virtual) experience is worthy of attention because it changes and challenges the traditional environment of soccer fandom in two crucial ways. The first fundamental challenge lies in the fact that the online self can be presented as a bodiless, genderless construct, thereby bringing a new dimension to an area of study where much analysis hinges upon the gendered, corporeal female body. The second challenge stems from the fact that the self is constructed from a position of safety behind the screen, where spatial and temporal constraints are largely irrelevant. The absence of the symbolic, corporeal, physical and locational markers that shape offline identity adds new dimensions to soccer fandom that need to be unpacked and analyzed. The research object in this case did not fit with traditional modes of data collection (Jones, 1999), because this exploratory study draws on the online and offline experiences of sixteen female fans. The empirical data were gathered by way of online interviews and observations of participant interaction in online forums. The respondents were members of online forums that were set up by clubs, fans and corporate interests to promote discussion and analysis of soccer and other, unrelated topics.[3]

ONLINE SOCCER FORUM EXPERIENCES: PERSPECTIVES AND IMPLICATIONS

One of the key ideas to emerge from the data was a preference for online interaction over offline gatherings:

> It was cheaper and healthier talking about the game I'd just been to on Internet forums than it was staying an extra 3 hours in the pub. Also, you can participate in discussions any time you like and not have to shout to be heard. It seemed more civilized, sometimes. SD

However, online engagement in soccer Internet forums involved a number of challenges stemming from participation in the forum becoming more problematic once a poster is known to be female. Respondents spoke of the extra attention paid to them because of their status as women and their expressed femininity:

> I didn't thoroughly consider its consequences when I signed up. In retrospect, I'd rather be "neuter". With reference to my "main forum", it was some kind of sensation. I got lots of attention—but less respect at times. KL

Sometimes, identification as a woman resulted in unwelcome advances, suggestive language and sexist remarks intended to undermine the credibility and validity of comments made by female posters:

> The usual humorous "chat up", innuendos, the clearly tongue in cheek responses about women and football and/or women should be at home etc., etc. None of which I took seriously. KH

There is also a sense among respondents that the treatment they received online was made possible because male posters had a level of freedom to be more patronizing and arrogant in a virtual environment than they would be in real life. As JT explains:

> I think males don't think they have to behave as well as they would if they were talking to you face-to-face. I'm sure that none of them would dream of saying, "What's your problem love, time of the month?" in person to a woman who was getting wound up, but it happens on the forum and nothing is said. To me, that is the same as saying to someone you know to be say, Asian, "What's up, too much spice in your curry?" or similar, which would rightly be deleted and the person infracted

straightaway. It can cut dead what you were contributing to the discussion and make you feel you have to justify your presence—even if said jokingly. I think a certain type of poster can take males expressing anger or irritation, but not females and they will be less tolerant of it.

In this way, the network itself becomes an instrument of power that enables the males who dominate the space to use language to alienate, demean and generally to "put women in their place".

Participants developed a range of tactics to combat the sexism that they experienced online. At the margins, the appropriation of male gender markers, male language styles, reluctance to assert one's femininity through visible markers (verbal, textual or other) and the inclination to protect one's forum persona all combined to shape the online experience of female fans. Some women attempted to gain credibility and to "compensate for their femininity" by reinforcing their affiliation with the club and brandishing their knowledge of the game. Others refused to reveal their gender in the hope of being judged on the content of their posts rather than on the basis of physical attributes.[4] Contributors spoke of actively seeking to mask their identity by adopting non-gender specific communication styles. AK observed, for example, "I've been told many times that I talk (type) like a bloke". The assumption that a poster is male is not surprising as the online forum population is male-dominated. In fact, there appears to be a default position that posters are male unless proven otherwise:

Most people initially thought I was a bloke, and it was kinda funny seeing the reaction when they realized I wasn't. And I guess most people who don't know me would think I'm a bloke due to the fact that people tend to take it for granted that people there are blokes—old fashioned as that may seem. BM

The general sense of ownership of the forum space is also male-dominated, as witnessed by the attempts of female posters to fit in and pose as little disruption to the male status quo as possible:

After somebody recently referred to me as "she" indirectly, one poster replied to him "Jaysus! Is jannno a bird?" Poster replied he didn't know for sure but had always assumed so and put out an apology for any embarrassment he may have caused. I ignored the whole conversation . . . (I) wouldn't lie directly. I avoid any questions—of which there have been half a dozen or so, and one direct "outing" attempt, which I found intimidating and I didn't answer it. Nobody on the forum (except Admins) could know for a fact. JT

Even when female posters attempt to work within the "rules" of the male-dominated discursive space, they are constantly faced with the challenge of fending off efforts to "out" them as women. As such, females can find themselves positioned as enablers whose silence allows male posters to maintain their dominance in the forum:

> I have been in discussions where it (the question of "what do women know about football?") has been said to another female, but as I am trying to protect my own "identity" and because I think some suspect, I have resisted jumping in to defend them or put down the sexist. I suppose I am trying to avoid the label of "uptight woman" that some unreasonable people might express if my gender was known and I objected to sexist comments. I find myself aware of this concern and it inhibits my posting. JT

Such self-regulation means that mounting a concerted resistance aimed at changing the dynamics of the community is out of the question. Consequently, unless women opt to leave the forum altogether, they are faced with dilemmas about whether to make a conscious decision to identify openly as a woman or not; to assume *feminine* or *masculine* attributes (such as astrological gender symbols for female/male); and to choose not to display gender markers such as usernames, avatars and general profile settings. The decisions that are reached are significant because they ultimately determine the course of the poster's experience in the forum.

The flexibility that posters have to project a gender identity that may or may not coincide with their physical body invites a consideration of respondents' experiences in the context of Butler's critique of gender (1999, 1993, 2004). Gender "is not a singular act", she argues, "but a repetition and a ritual, which achieves its effects through its naturalization in the context of a body" (1999, p. xv). The physical body itself does not determine gender; rather, it is the site upon which the repetitive acts, gestures, movements, styles and desires that formulate gender identity play out. The body is a corporeal theater in which identity is performatively constituted by the very expressions that are said to be its results (Butler, 1999) and subsequently sustained through corporeal signs and discursive means. Despite the centrality of the physical body to Butler's thought, her notion of performativity offers valuable insights into the implications of female fan experiences in online forums.

The interplay between offline and online fan activities, particularly the negative responses to hyperfemininity regardless of whether it is observed at matches or on message boards, indicates that considerations of the gendered, physical body are still pertinent to the conversation. However, the key issue here is how the construction of gender takes place within a virtual terrain where the physical cues and markers (i.e., body shape, face, hair, clothing) that condition offline gender performance simply do not exist—or at least not in the same way as they do during offline interactions. Because forums are structured around the act of posting, language assumes a greater level of significance as the locus of identity formation and interaction. Reality in this virtual world is increasingly imagined and performed through linguistic acts that reveal and conceal, to varying degrees, information about a poster's identity. The strength, aggression and competitiveness that secure the supremacy of the male body on the pitch find textual corollaries in the demonstration of statistical and historical knowledge, rhetorical skill and the ability to use wit and even verbal cruelty to undermine an opponent. Although the study's participants flagged a sense of discomfort at the way male fans employed these rhetorical weapons, the shift from the realm of the physical to the realm of the linguistic means that female fans have a greater opportunity to engage with existing power hierarchies.

By interacting in a virtual world that is distinct from—but influenced by—the physical world, online fans occupy a position that is informed by the same sort of spatial breakdown that Goffman (1959) identifies in his work on the theatrical and performative nature of everyday life. The public performance, he argues, is built around face-work in the presentation of self in everyday life. As social data are communicated through the body, we gather information about those we meet through appearances, cues, expressive gestures and status symbols. In keeping with the theatrical metaphor, he asserts the symbolic existence of front and back regions or stages. The front region is the public sphere in which appearance is predicated upon employing fixed props; the back region is the private sphere where the public persona is constructed. For females in online forums, the backstage area is constituted as the realm of everyday life, where gender and femininity gets drawn back to the body. The front stage exists as a virtual world wherein the newly constructed persona emerges and engages with others. The act of "performing" online allows for new identities to be managed, modified and manipulated. We understand our *Self* only in relation to the *Other* in a dialogic process of negotiation that produces a sense of shared meanings and tacit knowledge via the exchange of information. Participants in Internet forums, then, construct and maintain what Goffman terms the presentation of self in mediated, digital space, the opportunities and rules of which dictate the negotiation process.

The respondents in this study found their femininity to be an integral part of their online persona, regardless of whether it was openly known or "closeted". Even though forums constitute a space in which the body as a physical entity is replaced by a bodiless virtual self that can be (re) constructed in any way that the fan chooses, performance is still subject to conditions and constraints that create a range of acceptable beliefs and practices within the virtual community. The Bourdieusian concept of "habitus" (Bourdieu, 1984) offers a useful framework for thinking about the shared dispositions of the group community described by the participants in this study. According to Bourdieu, fields have particular rules and customs, as well as forms of authority that impose themselves on those who participate. As individuals interact they engage with these fields, thus producing a particular habitus. In online forums, the development of a discreet, distinct "habitus" hinges on the masculinization of soccer in general and on the particular ways in which female posters negotiate the dual identities of "fan" and "female." The desire to assimilate into the masculine territory of the soccer forum—or soccer *habitus*—necessitates stifling characteristics of femininity (and, to a certain extent, of feminism). The online environment offers an additional line of cover, or camouflage, which enables women to either present themselves as gender neutral or to "pass" as male in order to participate and be taken seriously in forum discussions. Similarly, conflicts among female posters over acceptable behavior are driven by the normative, masculinized conditions of a culture in which hyper- or extreme-femininity is regarded as the antithesis of a *true* and *authentic* fan identity.

Indeed, the most significant theme to emerge from the interviews was not the conflict between male fans and female fans, but rather the existence of exclusionary boundaries created by female fans to define what sort of women are *welcome* at soccer matches and forums. The criteria applied to females who seek acceptance as fans are strict. The interrogation of soccer knowledge and statistical information—the "gold standard" of authentic fandom—is a common litmus test applied by females and males alike:

> Depends on their knowledge, if their [sic] clueless and just want to talk about someone's hair or cute face then I would rather they stay away. CA

Respondents were highly critical of so-called hyperfemininity and sought to distance themselves from displays of what Jones (2008) calls "emphasized" femininity by rejecting women "who didn't do fandom properly":

> But one thing that does get on my tits is when I see a girl walking to the game in her 6-inch stilettos, her Armani handbag and Gucci jeans, arm in arm with her similarly affected boyfriend, and I'm thinking, "Christ, someone who actually wants to watch the game could have had your ticket". SD

Beliefs about what constitutes an *acceptable* female fan at matches finds an online corollary in negative reactions directed toward female posters who seem more interested in finding a date than discussing soccer:

> Sometimes you'll get a thread started by some 18 year old wannabe WAG, saying "Hiya, boys, I'm new here . . ." and she'll get 350 replies from would-be Casanovas wanking over their keyboard. That really annoys me. Some girls treat football forums like a dating site and it's pathetic. SD

Objections to hyperfemininity and affluence, along with the notion that these attributes signify an inauthentic fan, are very much in keeping with the broader themes that shape discourses around the game: masculinization, working-class identity and general fears about threats to the authenticity of the match experience. However, in the context of online forums, the negative reaction to hyperfemininity acquires additional meaning as an expression of female fans' ongoing efforts to fight the perception that women are principally interested in matches—just not the sort that take place on the pitch.

Sport is an institution where the physical body features most crucially, with the strong, fit masculine body recognized as a powerful weapon in the sporting arena. The weakened, vulnerable female body is deemed inferior and, therefore, discouraged from engaging in sporting activities. Whereas actual game play stresses the centrality of the body, sports fandom emphasizes social interactions predicated upon thoughts and emotions rather than corporeal physicality. The disembodiment that accompanies online participation should, in theory, facilitate engagements that are not subject to the constraints of gendered space that exist offline. The hyperbole surrounding the Internet as a site of liberation from fixed identity categories promises a utopian, boundless sphere. In fact, for many commentators, a crucial aspect of virtual communities is the potential to produce social spaces in which " 'unfreedoms' such as gender, race, ethnicity and class are left behind" (Seidler cited in Ferreday, 2009, p. 20). When the masculine sphere of sport and the body are separated in soccer forums, female inclusion remains deeply problematic because fans exhibit a reluctance to advertise, celebrate, negotiate or perform femininity, as femininity is linked to the sexualized, hyperfeminine female body. However, as Debra Ferreday (2009, pp. 20–21) concedes, online belonging is dependent upon the ability to produce an *"unmarked"* self that bears no trace of the racial and gender markings that shape offline identities and prejudices. Yet, as the responses to this study demonstrate, the creation of an unmarked self is often difficult to achieve in soccer forums where members appear intent on outing the females in their midst. This pattern is compounded by the fact that forum participation is very much loaded with offline baggage and social constructs that reproduce and reconstruct offline "unfreedoms" in a virtual setting.

CONCLUSION: MASCULINIZATION OFFLINE AND ONLINE

Despite the enormous popularity of soccer among females as both a spectator and participation sport, the men's game remains the preserve of popular media attention and corporate investment. More importantly, it remains ideologically masculine[5] in character, bolstered by a sense of nostalgia for a "glorious past" in which the game was played by "real men" in vibrant, lively stadiums filled with boys and men whose allegiance to the club ran strong and deep. Women may be overtly welcomed in highly stylized and mediatized arenas, but their accounts of match day experiences, physically based fan communities and online forums reveal an ongoing struggle for respect, acceptance and ownership of the masculinized game. Chief among the sources of conflict are the internal struggles over what it means to be female and the pervasiveness of both heteronormative femininity and hegemonic masculine sensibilities. These factors impede the process of universal acceptance by prescribing what *sort* of woman constitutes a "proper" fan. The popular, heteronormative notions of manliness that drive the masculinization of soccer *offline* as a game and cultural milieu also shape the contours of the game's *online* forums, creating an environment in which women must regulate the expression of their gender identity in order to feel comfortable.

Performances of the role of female fan are achieved through association, dedication, conformity, concealment, non-engagement and active withdrawal via textual discourse. The results bring varying degrees of success and raise a host of questions about communal dynamics, the capability of online networks to realize their potential as catalysts for participation, the possibilities of greater social and cultural inclusion in soccer, and the ontological and epistemological foundations of gender identities. More research is needed to promote a better understanding of these issues and the data collected through this study will be employed in further investigations aimed at generating a more complete picture of female fans' experiences. Research and scholarly analysis are also not the only areas in need of more attention. The strides that have been taken by soccer's institutions and others to promote greater participation by women are welcome, but there is still much work to be done before the vice-like grip of masculinity and patriarchy can be sufficiently loosened to give female fans a genuine sense of belonging.

NOTES

1. Liverpool FC competes in the EPL.
2. The success of such campaigns varies. On the terraces the visibility of female and non-White male faces is increasingly apparent. On the pitch, the numbers of female players and teams annually increase. Furthermore, we have recently seen the presence of female officials in English league games.
3. In an attempt to reach a specific and targeted sample population, participants were contacted by email and asked to participate in the study. Although some participants were known to the researcher personally, others were "snowballed"/named (Mann & Stewart, 2000, p. 79). The interview document was sent via email and returned with responses. Anonymity as well as the right to withdraw participation was assured. General online contributions to discussions have not been included in the study unless the respondent in the interview referenced them. All participants were informed about the reasons for the study and the potential uses of the information. There was excellent rapport between the researcher and the respondents. Respondents were also so enthusiastic about topic that it didn't "require any selling at all" (Mann

& Stewart, 2000, p. 131) to secure participation. The interview document was standardized, with different sections comprised of questions designed to tap various aspects of the soccer experience. It invited open-ended responses that provided focused, specific contextual information (given the limitations of cost, time, reach) (Mann & Stewart, 2000, pp. 71–75). Responses were analyzed and placed into groups where categories were defined on the basis of themes addressed, including the formation and development of the early relationship with the club, the role of the mother in the relationship, the relationship to the game and club, and past and contemporary online and offline match experiences.

4. Genderless here could also be considered as "nominally" male since the majority of forum members are male and, unless it is explicitly stated in one's member profile, it is generally assumed that one is male.

5. Masculinity here is understood as the popular and universal "deep" or "true" masculine stereotype upheld and celebrated in popular culture. The masculinity in question is that of hegemonic forms of masculinity—the most honored and desired—where muscular male sporting heroes are shining exemplars. Of course, we agree with Connell's claim that there is no one pattern of masculinity, and that we should speak of multiple masculinities shaped by culture and history, and separated by social relations and diversified by relations of hierarchy.

REFERENCES

Bourdieu P (1984) *Distinction: A Social Critique of the Judgement of Taste*. London: Routledge.

boyd d (2011) Social network sites as networked publics: affordances, dynamics, and implications. In: Papacharissi Z (ed.) *Networked Self: Identity, Community, and Culture on Social Network Sites*. NY: Routledge, 39–58.

Brimson D & Brimson E (1996) *Everywhere We Go: Behind the Matchday Madness*. London: Headline Book Publishing.

Butler J (1993) *Bodies that Matter*. New York: Routledge.

Butler J (1999) [1990] *Gender Trouble*. London: Routledge.

Butler J (2004) *Undoing Gender*. New York: Routledge.

Castells M (1996) *The Rise of the Network Society*. Cambridge, MA: Oxford, UK: Blackwell.

Castells M (1997) *The Power of Identity*. Cambridge, MA: Oxford, UK: Blackwell.

Caudwell J (1999) Women's football in the United Kingdom: theorizing gender and unpacking the butch lesbian image. *Journal of Sport & Social Issues* 23(4): 390–402.

Connell RW (2005) *Masculinities*. Cambridge, UK: Polity Press.

Crabbe T & Brown A (2004) "You're not welcome anymore": the football crowd, class and social exclusion. In: Wagg S (ed.) *British Football and Social Exclusion*. London Routledge, 21–38.

Crosset T (1990) Masculinity, sexuality, and the development of early modern sport. In: Messner M & Sabo D (eds.) *Sport, Men and the Gender Order: Critical Feminist Perspectives*. Champaign, IL: Human Kinetics Publishers, 45–54.

Ferreday D (2009) *Online Belongings: Fantasy, Virtuality, Community*. Oxford: Peter Lang.

Giulianotti R (2002) Supporters, Followers, Fans and Flâneurs: a taxonomy of spectator identities in football. *Journal of Sport and Social Issues* 26(1): 25–46.

Goffman E (1959) *The Presentation of Self in Everyday Life*. New York: Doubleday Anchor Books.

Harris J (2004) Still a man's game? Women footballers, personal experience and tabloid myth. In: Wagg S (ed.) *British Football and Social Exclusion*. London Routledge, 89–104.

Jeanes R & Kay T (2007) Can football be a female game? An examination of girls' perceptions of football and gender identity. In: Magee J, Caudwell J, Liston K & Scraton S (eds.) *Women and Football in Europe: Histories, Equity and Experience*. Vol. 1. Oxford: Meyer and Meyer Sport, 105–30.

Jones KW (2008) Female fandom: identity, sexism, and men's professional football in England. *Sociology of Sport Journal* 25(4): 516–37.

Jones S (ed.) (1999) *Doing Internet Research*. London: Sage.

Livingstone S (ed.) (2005) *Audiences and Publics: When Cultural Engagement Matters for the Public Sphere*. Bristol, UK: Intellect Press.

Mann C & Stewart F (2000) *Internet Communication and Qualitative Research: A Handbook for Researching Online*. Sage: London.

Rheingold H (1993) *The Virtual Community: Homesteading on the Electronic Frontier*. New York: Harper Perennial Paperback.

Robson G (2000) *"No One Likes Us, We Don't Care": The Myth and Reality of Millwall Fandom*. Oxford: Berg.

Sabo D & Panepinto J (1990) Football ritual and the social reproduction of masculinity. In: Messner M & Sabo D (eds.) *Sports, Men and the Gender Order: Critical Feminist Perspectives*. Champaign, IL: Human Kinetics Publishers, 115–26.

Selmer N & Sülzle A (2010) (En-)gendering the European football family: the changing discourse on women and gender at EURO 2008. *Soccer & Society* 11(6): 803–14.

Slaughter P (2004) A day out with the "old boys". In: Wagg S (ed.) *British Football and Social Exclusion*. London: Routledge, 55–72.

Song FW (2009) *Virtual Communities: Bowling Alone, Online Together*. New York: Peter Lang Publishing.

Wellman B & Gulia M (1999). Virtual communities as communities: net Surfers don't ride alone. In: Smith M & Kollock P (eds.) *Communities in Cyberspace*. Berkeley, CA: Routledge, 167–94.

Whannel G (1992) *Fields in Vision: Television, Sport and Cultural Transformation*. London: Routledge.

Whitson D (1990) Sport in the social construction of masculinity. In: Messner M & Sabo D (eds.) *Sport, Men and the Gender Order: Critical Feminist Perspectives*. Champaign, IL: Human Kinetics Publishers, 19–29.

Williams J (2003) *A Game for Rough Girls? A History of Women's Football in Britain*. London: Routledge.

8 Eye Candy and Sex Objects
Gender, Race and Sport on YouTube

David J. Leonard[1]

INTRODUCTION: THE INTRANSIGENT POWER OF STEREOTYPES

Title IX of the Education Amendments of 1972 is a landmark piece of federal legislation signed into US law four decades ago. Its passing granted women equal access to education programs, including high school and college athletics. Following from this advance, it seems plausible to claim victory in the fight against sexism in sport given that the 2012 US Olympic Team was the first in history to boast more female athletes than male. In a recent column about Title IX and international tennis champion, Serena Williams, Dave Zirin (2012) reflected on the importance of this legislation:

> There is arguably no piece of progressive legislation that's touched more people's lives than Title IX, which allowed young women equal opportunity in education and sports. According to the Women's Sports Foundation, one in thirty-five high school girls played sports forty years ago; one in three do today. Before Title IX, fewer than 16,000 women participated in college sports; today that number exceeds 200,000. All stereotypes about women being too "emotional" to handle sports were answered when the gyms were unlocked, and they arrived in droves. It is a reform that has improved the quality of life for tens of millions of women around the country.

Despite the promised transformation of sporting landscapes throughout the US, Zirin also outlines the persistence of sexism in sports culture evident through inequity in pay rates, coaching and resource disparities, differential treatment from the press and the intransigent power of stereotypes. These problems reflect the condition of women's sporting competition in many other countries. Recognizing this incomplete transformation and the need for persistent agitation in order to realize gender equality, sport remains a place where dreams of social justice are deferred.

One has to look no further than media platforms and online communities to illustrate the ways that gender, sexuality and "race" constrain and contain female athletes, and the ways that racism, sexism and homophobia exist as prisms and prisons of sporting consumption. For instance, it is difficult to find significant and sustained coverage of women's sports on ESPN, ESPN.com, Fox Sports or SI-CNN.com. A recent study by Michael Messner and Cheryl Cooky (2010, p. 8) found that network television coverage of women's sports actually declined from 5 percent to 1.6 percent between 1989 and 2009. This coverage has been in free fall even with the ascendance of the Women's National Basketball Association (WNBA), the popularity of the women's soccer World Cup and women's tennis, and the dramatic growth of collegiate female basketball competition.

Female athletes have not, however, been excluded from public screens and consumption, as they are increasingly visible on sports-related websites and user-generated content sites such as YouTube. These online spaces are bypassing the traditional "gatekeeping" mechanisms performed by television networks and professional journalists that have long excluded women from the sports media sphere (Rowe, 2004). The problem is that many of these online spaces rapidly circulate the types of representation already available in the commercial news media, often reducing female athletes to sexual objects for male consumption. This chapter examines the profound impact of the Internet—and YouTube in particular—on the consumption and representation of female athletes. Exploring the ways in which race, gender and sexuality operate in these settings, it is argued that digital media are fostering the dissemination of sexist tropes and hyper-sexualized representations. While focusing on gender and sexuality, the question of how race complicates this situation is also discussed. The limited attention afforded to female athletes, particularly those of color, reflects the barriers that prevent the fulfillment of the ambitions of Title IX. Unable to appeal to male viewers, female athletes who do not meet hegemonic expectations of femininity and sexuality remain excluded from the few available media narratives that celebrate women's sporting achievements.

The substantive coverage and national attention achieved by female athletes is often achieved through sex and sex appeal. Women athletes who are successful *and* elicit pleasure from male viewers garner the vast majority of coverage. As Matthew Syed (2008) observes about women's tennis:

> There has always been a soft-porn dimension to women's tennis, but with the progression of Maria Sharapova, Ana Ivanovic, Jelena Jankovic and Daniela Hantuchova to the semi-finals of the Australian Open, this has been into the realms of adolescent (and non-adolescent) male fantasy. (Cited in McKay & Johnson, 2008, p. 495)

This situation contributes to the relative invisibility of certain athletes and the high profile of others in the media landscape. Moreover, I argue that the relative "openness" of the Internet has not diversified the representations of female athletes or the discourses that surround them.

In examining the discursive, representational and textual utterances relating to several US female athletes—Serena Williams (tennis), Brittney Griner (basketball), Allison Stokke (track and field), Alex Morgan (soccer) and Hope Solo (soccer)—I reflect on the power and agency denied to female athletes online. In looking at various YouTube videos involving these women, ranging from clips of athletic performances to media interviews, I seek to understand the ways in which race, gender and sexuality operate in this online space. Particular attention is given to how user comments define and constrain female athletic bodies. In examining these comments, I highlight how they illustrate the power of "gender and heterosexist logic" and the "White racial framing" in which this logic sits. This chapter examines these overarching patterns, and the ways in which fans engage with and interpret race, gender and sexuality in sport. While focusing on the US, the discussion here is also relevant to many other national cultures characterized by corporate media regimes, routine sporting spectacle and widespread consumer access to social software tools such as YouTube.

A BRIEF NOTE ON DIGITAL MEDIA

Each day, sports fans visit various sports websites, participate in fantasy sports, celebrate and criticize teams, players and sporting cultures on blogs, in discussion groups, and on listserves, and gain joyful pleasure in playing sports video games. Each of these media, to varying degrees, embody what has come to be known as new media, a catch-all phrase that includes everything from the Internet and e-commerce, to the Blogosphere, video games, virtual reality, and other examples in which media technologies are defined by increased accessibility, fluidity, and interactivity (Crosbie, 2006; Jenkins, 2006; Silver & Massanari, 2006). New media are not simply a constellation of new tools and technologies but rather a changing contextual landscape, a cultural terrain facilitated 'by the television, the telephone, the telecommunications networks crisscrossing the globe' (Wark, 1994, p. vii).

(quoted in Leonard, 2009, p. 2)

This statement from a previous work of mine provides the context from which this analysis proceeds and builds on the work of other scholars in the field of sport and new media (including Ferriter, 2009; Hutchins & Rowe, 2012; Sanderson, 2011), as well as research centered on gender and sexuality in sport (Douglas, 2005; Kane, 2011; McKay & Johnson, 2008; Schultz, 2005; Spencer, 2004). Focusing specifically on user-generated content in the form of YouTube comments, this chapter shows how this space intersects with surveillance, branding and representational confinement. This online video platform is significant in the context of sport (cf. Stauff, 2009; Burgess & Green, 2009), allowing fans and nonparticipants to define, consume and deploy sports content. YouTube provides people with "a built-in audience for self-expression . . . you are not just expressing yourself, you're performing for an audience, often an audience of complete strangers" (Cross, 2011, p. 4).

Despite optimistic claims about new media and the democratization of sport in digital environments, the evidence presented here suggests that online media contribute to the recapitulation of dominant gendered ideologies and power relations. In some ways, online spaces are regressive and entrench social injustice. The ability to define the parameters of widely disseminated debate, to comment, and to otherwise circulate narratives and tropes on YouTube, Facebook and Twitter highlight an important change in how cultural and social power functions:

> The Internet makes it temptingly easy, effortless even, to publish your thoughts, whether in a blog, through a tweet, or on a Facebook wall [or on a YouTube comment section]. What's going on line is a gigantic power shift away from established authorities like editors, publishers, and media elite into unchartered realms of individualized expression. People can present themselves and their ideas in their own way, perhaps even assuming a new identity in the process. (Cross, 2011, p. 5)

The characteristics of interactivity, performativity and anonymity, as well as the centrality of images to online media, have produced a space ripe for rhetorical violence. As will be shown, these spaces advance the sexual commodification and degradation of both White and African-American female athletes. In fact, the dynamics of user engagement in selected online contexts contribute to frequent incidents of racism, sexism and homophobia.

THE AUDACITY OF WHITE ATHLETIC SEXUALITY

Typing the names of Allison Stokke, Alex Morgan or Hope Solo into a search engine offers access to a range of web pages that document and comment on their bodies, sexuality and sex appeal. Three websites mention Solo posing nude for ESPN on the first results page of Google, while Stokke generates five websites that mention her body, her "hotness" and appeal as "eye candy". Clicking through takes the user to endless photos of their athletic performances, and images of bikinis and sexualized frames. On YouTube, there are many videos of each athlete. Yet, irrespective of whether the video focuses on their sporting performance or physical attractiveness, user comments almost invariably reduce these athletic women to sexual objects. For instance, a video interview with Morgan elicited the following responses among the list of comments:

> Damn she's FLAT (Lists YouTube ID)
>
> hmm . . . must be a childrens sports bra :D_(Lists YouTube ID)
>
> Under her sports bra_ fucker (Lists YouTube ID)
>
> i would_ tap tha (Lists YouTube ID)
>
> I mean. . . . . I mean. . . . . . I mean #LesbiHonest. . . . ohh_ yeaHHH (Lists YouTube ID)
>
> Big nose. . . . flat chest . . . nasty smokers voice. . . . . . . BUT,_ I'd eat her pussy at least (Lists YouTube ID)[2]

Reflecting a pattern in user behavior, a YouTube post of soccer's Solo and Morgan from ESPN prompted the following puerile responses:

> I? WANT TO HAVE A THREESOME WITH THEM (Lists YouTube ID)
>
> Massive lulz were had. Hope is too awesome for girly crap like heels and dancing XD (Lists YouTube ID)
>
> i wanna ride? her solo. . . . . . . giggity (Lists YouTube ID)
>
> alex morgan is literally a goddess? (Lists YouTube ID)
>
> Never? in my life ah seen such beauty (Lists YouTube ID)
>
> funny? ESPN chose the 2 hottest players from the team (Lists YouTube ID)
>
> Was a great final and great advertisement for the? women games (Lists YouTube ID)[3]

Pole-vaulter Stokke has also spoken in the news about the unwanted attention that her looks and body receive on the Web. YouTube users responded to her concern by intensifying the offensive sexualizing frame that the story sought to reveal and problematize:

> so what? happens with male athletes? 100 times more. . . . shes lying because she loves the attention (Lists YouTube ID)
>
> Damn, that? must suck for Allison. Getting unwanted attention (Lists YouTube ID)
>
> Here people, you see your typical american overreacted reaction to these sorts of things. Whats wrong with admiring a beauty? i mean cmon, shes not just hot, shes a friggin pole vaulter with BOOBS, thats unheard? of lol (Lists YouTube ID)
>
> Degrading my fuckin dick. She's? a fuckin angel. People get mad cause we say she's gorgeous? Haters! (Lists YouTube ID)
>
> i? wanna sex her. (Lists YouTube ID)
>
> She can vault my pole ;) . . . on second thought, ? scratch that. That sounds painful (Lists YouTube ID)[4]

Often blaming the women for the sexualizing process, these online exchanges naturalize the placement of female athletes as sexual commodities. User comments rehash sexualizing stereotypes and consume women as little more than objects. Considered alongside user-generated content that is sometimes little more than a quasi-pornographic slideshow, this combination prevents the entry of women into specifically *sporting* discourses where their athletic achievements are acknowledged. As is argued below, other discourses also come into play that continue to place women outside sport *per se*.

BLACK AIN'T BEAUTIFUL IN SPORTS: THE CASE OF THE WILLIAMS SISTERS

Compared to track and field's Stokke, motor racing's Danica Patrick, tennis' Sharapova and even the WNBA's Candace Parker (Leonard, 2011), the Williams sisters have been subjected to repeated racist and sexist taunts about their bodies and physical appearance. The Williams sisters are thought to compare poorly with the idealized and authentically rendered feminine images that exist inside and outside of sports culture. Parker, Sharapova and Patrick are represented as athletic, but also as "girly" and sexual. In contrast, the Williams sisters have been constructed as muscular, aggressive and man-like in many sections of the sports media. For example, the way in which tennis' "glamour girl" Anna Kournikova compares herself to the Williams sisters highlights how the tripartite combination of Whiteness/femininity/heterosexuality operates in opposition to Blackness/masculinity/asexuality in popular sporting grammar:

> I hate my muscles. I'm not Venus Williams. I'm not Serena Williams. I'm feminine. I don't want to look like they do. I'm not masculine like they are. (Cited in Schultz, 2005, p. 346)

The Williams sisters are seen as Black athletes who, because of their Blackness, physicality and strength, are treated differently from many other sportswomen and positioned in relation to other Black male athletes. As Jaime Schultz (2005) outlines, the ridicule of the Williams sisters occurs through sexualizing tropes that emphasize hegemonic standards of beauty. Jim Rome, a nationally syndicated radio talk-show host, has consistently referred to them as Predator 1 and Predator 2. Likewise, Sid Rosenberg, another radio presenter, has described the Williams sisters as unattractive:

> I can't even watch them play anymore. I find it disgusting. I find both of those, what do you want to call them—they're just too muscular. They're boys. (Cited in Schultz, 2005, p. 346).

This rhetoric fits within a larger context of White supremacy in the history of the US:

The dominant male, white culture drew a direct correspondence between stereotyped depictions of black womanhood and 'manly' athletic and physically gifted females. Their racialized notions of the virile or mannish black female athlete stemmed from a number of persistent historical myths: the linking of African American women's work history as slaves, their supposedly "natural" brute strength and endurance inherited from their African origins, and the notion that vigorous or competitive sport masculinized women physically and sexually. (Vertinsky & Captain, 1998, cited in Schultz, 2005, p. 347).

James McKay and Helen Johnson (2008) also identify a telling historical parallel between the treatment of Serena Williams in particular, and Althea Gibson, an African-American tennis star from the 1950s and 1960s:

> Go Back To The Cotten [sic] Plantation Nigger. (Banner in the stands when Althea Gibson walked on court to defend her US Open title in 1958)
>
> That's the way to do it! Hit the net like any Negro would! (Male heckling Serena Williams before she served at the 2007 Sony Ericsson Championships in Miami)

The fraught and conflicted history of race and sport is perpetuated on the Internet. The abuse of the Williams sisters continues in comment sections and blogs that play upon and disseminate longstanding stereotypes about Blackness. However, these online spaces also illustrate a level of sexualization of the Williams sisters only occasionally evident in mainstream sports news and websites. On YouTube, female athletes of color can be subjected to a sexualizing gaze that, in a familiar pattern, reduces their significance to male sexual pleasure. In other words, whereas female athletes of color are largely absent from a sexualizing gaze in many commercial news media reports, fan- and user-generated content perpetuates this process. In a discussion that followed a video showing Venus Williams's newest outfit, respondents focused on her sexuality, beauty and body:

> So if she plays in Amsterdam, she should wear nothing (Lists YouTube ID)
>
> Just play nekkid. Don't beat around yer bush (Lists YouTube ID)
>
> UGLY IS AS UGLY_ DOES (Lists YouTube ID)
>
> NO MATTER HOW YU DRESS AN UGLY_ DUCK,..IT'S STILL AN UGLY DUCK. . . . SIGH (Lists YouTube ID)
>
> How about tell it like it really is she has skills not lucky_ out fits (Lists YouTube ID)
>
> Dang wear_ the right size (Lists YouTube ID)[5]

Serena Williams's presence on YouTube is defined by the fetishization of her body. For instance, following a match where Serena Williams did the "splits" when playing a point, YouTube comments exploded in number:

> Dayummmmmmmmmmmmm . . . Now hop_ up on my dick and do a full split! (Lists YouTube ID)
> exactly shit she split on me anytime lmfao (Lists YouTube ID)
> This girl is more talented than meets_ the eye! (Lists YouTube ID)
> Dammmmmmmmmmmmmmmnnnnn_ mmmmmmhmmmmm: (Lists YouTube ID)
> Serena so damn fine. . . . . Make a nigga wanna lick the sweat off ha? (Lists YouTube ID)
> Damn, ? she is so fine in an Amazonian/will-crush-your-puny-ass kind of way. . . (Lists YouTube ID)
> All that junk in the trunk and pack in the rack, and she still can do a_ split? Works for me! (Lists YouTube ID)
> Sounds like_ porn if you just close your eyes and listen (Lists YouTube ID)[6]

Similarly, responding to a commercial for beauty products that featured Serena and Venus Williams, users expressed excitement and pleasure in "consuming" their bodies. Their sexual appeal and body parts—breasts and bottoms, for instance—become the focus of user comments and exchanges, as well as representing them in racial terms:

> I like Venus better I'm not? really mezmorized by that ass of Serena sorry (Lists YouTube ID)
> You both in my? bed, loving you down, my wifes,, (Lists YouTube ID)
> beautiful? women. (Lists YouTube ID)
> more like drag? queens (Lists YouTube ID)
> Talk? about sumbluminal messages?! I felt like i was just mind raped! (Lists YouTube ID)
> Aaaaaaw,they? are transgender. (Lists YouTube ID)
> Serena's? boobs are epic. (Lists YouTube ID)[7]

My discussion so far indicates that White female athletes are popularly consumed through sexuality and sexual appeal. This treatment contrasts with female athletes of color, such as the Williams sisters, who face a sexualization based upon racial logics. The next section discusses All-American champion basketball player, Britney Griner, who adds further complexity to this picture.

BASKETBALL'S BRITNEY GRINER

Griner's sporting performance is outstanding. Using the jargon of basketball, she averages 22.7 points/game, sixty percent from field and more than eighty percent from line, almost ten rebounds each game, and 155 blocks after thirty games in the season. Her team is undefeated and ranked number one, outscoring opponents by 30+ points per game. With outstanding performance statistics like these, Griner should be celebrated on magazine covers and in lengthy biographical pieces broadcast on ESPN. But her on-court success has not translated into widespread attention. Unable to embody traditional notions of feminine beauty, there is little space for Griner in the national imagination. Her athletic greatness is, therefore, relatively invisible to all but regular followers of the game.

Griner emerged on the US national scene in 2009. The limited amount of media coverage that she received identified her as a player who challenged the expectations of female athletes. Unlike the vast majority of celebrated female athletes, she was, according to the narrative, an "androgynous female" who challenged the "rigidity of sex roles" (Trebay, 2010). Often comparing her to men, stories consistently positioned Griner as an aberration. For example, in the opinion of Lyndsey D'Arcangelo (2010):

> The world of women's basketball has never seen a player like this before. Griner has the athletic skills and build of any budding male college basketball star, which has brought her gender into question.

Guy Trebay (2010) also highlights the ways in which the dominant narrative of Griner figures her not as a basketball player, but as a signifier of gender and sexuality:

> Feminine beauty ideals have shifted with amazing velocity over the last several decades, in no realm more starkly than sports. Muscular athleticism of a sort that once raised eyebrows is now commonplace. Partly this can be credited to the presence on the sports scene of Amazonian wonders like the Williams sisters, statuesque goddesses like Maria Sharapova, Misty May Treanor and Kerri Walsh, sinewy running machines like Paula Radcliffe or thick-thighed soccer dynamos like Mia Hamm.

In apparently breaking the feminine "box" that confines female athletes in sports cultures, Griner is a potentially ground-breaking female athlete because of her exceptional performances. However, the response to Griner evident on YouTube and other online platforms like Twitter recycle longstanding racial stereotypes, gendered/sexist language and homophobic tropes. The sight of Griner dunking a basketball—a skill presumably reserved for men—prompted the following types of response:

> Whats up, Im brittney? Griner, and I have bigger balls than you!
> (Lists YouTube ID)
> That's a? man! (Lists YouTube ID)

> When did the NCAA start letting dudes? play on the girls teams??
> (Lists YouTube ID)
> That's a big bitch! -? duece bigalow (Lists YouTube ID)
> Sorry but 'she' has a Y chromosome. It is? at least a hermaphrodite
> (Lists YouTube ID)
> Brittney is a weird name for a guy? (Lists YouTube ID)
> Sex change, or what? What is up with that? She not only sounds
> like a man, she talks like a man. And apparently fights like one,
> too. Although? that cold-cock on the Texas Tech gal was strictly a
> punk move: (Lists YouTube ID)[8]

In preserving the hegemonic logic and structure of race, gender and sexuality, this video of Griner's dunk is used to reassert and maintain these power structures.

User-generated online media are operating here to reaffirm dominant ideologies and narratives. Griner's lack of sexual appeal, her "masculine ways" and her "thug demeanor" are used to demonize her (and, on occasion, to offer an unconvincing explanation of a more generalized lack of interest in women's sport). The media's inattention to Griner's on-court performance illustrates how her incompatibility with a desired feminine subjectivity limits her presence in the popular sporting imagination. One has to look no further than YouTube comments to see the interconnection between the perceived masculinity of Griner and her erasure from the sporting landscape. She is commonly dismissed as a "male" or a "freak" or used as an aberrant example that helps stabilize the cultural and sexual norms embodied by female athletes who fulfill male expectations (such as the aforementioned Kournikova).

As highlighted by the previous section, the treatment both of Griner and the Williams sisters fits into a broader historical pattern where African-American female athletes are either framed as masculine by the news media or trivialized and then ignored (Cooky, Wachs, Messner & Dworkin, 2010). The efforts made to describe, contain and represent Griner are consistent with this history. Athletes such as Griner find themselves stuck on the "outside looking in", unable to access the few commercial opportunities available to female athletes because they are unable or unwilling to satisfy the sexualized aesthetics of heterosexual male pleasure.

CONCLUSION: THE ONLINE "BACKSTAGE"

As the examples presented throughout this chapter demonstrate, the anonymity afforded by online environments offers a platform for people to disseminate their views, ideologies and worldview, irrespective of how offensive they may be. Racism, sexism and homophobia are, therefore, given full-throated voice through widely available communications technologies and online platforms. As Pablo Boczkowski explains:

We always had people shouting on the street. It was a handful of people, and the sender of the message could be clearly identified. Now the audience is much bigger, it's more unknown, it's more diverse potentially, and this has changed the dynamics of the game. (quoted in NewsOne Staff, 2010)

The existence of avatars, online "handles" and anonymous user accounts that can be quickly and easily deleted, fosters a culture where epithets and sexist/racist pronouncements are seemingly detached from the physical body that gives them voice. These characteristics increase the likelihood of racist and sexist expression in online environments. This argument is supported by a range of examples and evidence, including a study of 264 US high school students by Brendesha Tines from the University of Illinois. She found that twenty-nine percent of African-Americans and forty-two percent of those identifying as "other" or mixed race experienced racial epithets or other forms of racism online (Washington, 2010). It would, therefore, be a mistake to conclude that offensive YouTube comments directed at the Williams sisters, Griner, Stokke, Solo or Morgan are atypical. Rather, they are a visible manifestation of routine online sexism and racism.

Leslie Picca and Joe Feagin (2007) identify two forms of conversation and linguistic choices exhibited by White people when talking about race. Drawing upon Goffman, they identify dialogue that occurs on the "front stage"—those open and often public spaces. Then there is the "backstage," which are private and exclusively or predominantly White spaces. The backstage has been a place rife with racial epithets, jokes, stereotypes and other White racial frames that do not mesh with "postracial" and politically progressive narratives. The advent of the Internet and platforms such as YouTube now provide glimpses of these backstage conversations, which sometimes reveal ugly and unedifying evidence. This conclusion is summarized by Feagin in direct terms, offering little comfort for women's sport and African-American athletes forced to cope with this situation:

> Like the loudest ambulance siren you've ever heard . . . All this stuff was already there. It's just the Internet has opened a window into it that we normally would not have had. (Cited in Fox News Latino, 2010)

NOTES

1. This chapter was developed from arguments presented in several previously published pieces by David J. Leonard: 1. (2012) Violence on and off the ice: Twitter racism and the NHL. *Racialicous*, 16 May. Online. Available from: http://www.racialicious.com/2012/05/16/violence-on-and-off-the-ice-twitter-racism-and-the-nhl/ (Accessed 16 May 2012); 2. (2012) Not entertained? Brittney Griner continues to challenge expectations. *Slam Online*, 29 February. Online. Available from: http://www.slamonline

.com/online/college-hs/college/2012/02/not-entertained (Accessed 29 February 2012); 3. (2012) Serena Williams and the politics of hate(rs). *NewBlackMan (in Exile)*, 11 January. Online. Available from: http://newblackman.blogspot.com/2012/01/serena-williams-and-politics-of-haters.html (Accessed 11 January 2012); 4. (forthcoming) Dilemmas and contradictions: black female athletes. In: Lori Martin (ed.) *Racism and Sport*. Praeger Publisher; 5. (2012) Brittney Griner, women athletes and the erotic gaze. *NewBlackMan (in Exile)*, 12 July. Online. Available from: http://newblackman.blogspot.com/2012/07/britney-griner-women-athletes-and.html (Accessed 12 July 2012); 6. (2012) Serena Williams: "Ain't I a champion?" 8 July. Online. Available from: http://newblackman.blogspot.com/2012/07/serena-williams-aint-i-champion.html (Accessed 6 March 2013).

2. http://www.youtube.com/watch?v=XIRMpRBab-Q (Accessed 6 March 2013).
3. http://www.youtube.com/watch?v=GwrwWtGVblw&feature=related (Accessed 6 March 2013).
4. http://www.youtube.com/watch?v=YXqmQdHdRck (Accessed 6 March 2013).
5. http://www.youtube.com/watch?NR=1&feature=endscreen&v=hU4L6-4A0rY (Accessed 6 March 2013).
6. http://www.youtube.com/watch?v=tZj4KdK91OA (Accessed 6 March 2013); http://www.youtube.com/watch?v=EAZLBI4Rxqg&feature=related (Accessed 6 March 2013).
7. http://www.youtube.com/watch?v=deGBIHWE150&feature=related (Accessed 6 March 2013).
8. http://www.youtube.com/watch?v=Mx8ktfa0nLA (Accessed 6 March 2013).

REFERENCES

Burgess J & Green J (2009) *YouTube: Online Video and Participatory Culture.* Cambridge, UK: Polity Press.

Cooky C, Wachs FL, Messner MA & Dworkin SL (2010) It's not about the game: Don Imus, race, class, gender and sexuality in contemporary media. *Sociology of Sport Journal* 27(2): 139–59.

Crosbie V (2006) What is new media? *Corante*, 27 April. Online. Available from: http://rebuildingmedia.corante.com/archives/2006_04.php (Accessed 28 October 2008).

Cross M (2011) *Bloggerati, Twitterati: How Blogs and Twitter are Transforming Popular Culture.* Santa Barbara: Praeger.

D'Arcangelo L (2010) Brittney Griner may push gender boundaries, but not on purpose. *Curve*, 19 February. Online. Available from: http://www.curvemag.com/Blogs/Playing-for-Our-Team/Web-Articles-2010/Brittney-Griner-May-Push-Gender-Boundaries-But-Not-on-Purpose/ (Accessed 26 July 2012).

Douglas DD (2005) Venus, Serena and the Women's Tennis Association: when and where race enters. *Sociology of Sport Journal* 22(3): 256–82.

Ferriter M (2009) "Arguably the greatest": sport fans and communities at work on Wikipedia. *Sociology of Sport Journal* 26(1): 127–54.

Fox News Latino (2010) Bigotry against hispanics finds an open forum: the internet. 29 September. Online. Available from: http://latino.foxnews.com/latino/lifestyle/2010/09/29/bigotry-hispanics-finds-open-forum-internet/#ixzz21lLrlnWm (Accessed 26 July 2012).

Hutchins B & Rowe D (2012) *Sport Beyond Television: The Internet, Digital Media and the Rise of Networked Media.* London: Routledge.

Jenkins H (2006) *Convergence Culture: Where Old and New Media Collide.* New York: New York University Press.

Kane MJ (2011) Sex sells sex, not women's sports. *The Nation,* 27 July. Online. Available from: http://www.thenation.com/article/162390/sex-sells-sex-not-womens-sports (Accessed 23 September 2011).

Leonard DJ (2009) New media and global sporting cultures: moving beyond the clichés and binaries. *Sociology of Sport Journal* 26(1): 1–16.

Leonard DJ (2011) The "selling of Candace Parker" and the diminishment of women's sports. *NewBlackMan (in Exile),* 1 September. Online. Available from: http://newblackman.blogspot.com/2011/09/selling-of-candace-parker-and.html (Accessed 26 July 2012).

McKay J & Johnson H (2008) Pornographic eroticism and sexual grotesquerie in representations of African-American sportswomen. *Social Identities* 14(4): 491–504.

Messner M & Cooky C (2010) *Gender in Televised Sports: News and Highlight Shows, 1989–2009.* Los Angeles: Centre for Feminist Research, University of Southern California.

NewsOne staff (2010) Racism is still alive and well in online comment sections. *NewsOne,* 24 September. Online. Available from: newsone.com/777255/racism-is-still-alive-and-well-in-online-comment-sections/ (Accessed 26 July 2012).

Picca LH & Feagin J (2007). *Two-Faced Racism: Whites in the Backstage and Frontstage.* New York: Routledge.

Rowe D (2004) *Sport, Culture, and the Media.* 2nd ed. Maidenhead, Berkshire: Open University Press.

Sanderson J (2011) *How Social Media is Changing Sports: It's a Whole New Ballgame.* New York: Hamilton Press.

Schultz J (2005) Reading the catsuit: Serena Williams and the production of blackness at the 2002 U.S. Open. *Journal of Sport and Social Issues* 29(3): 338–57.

Silver D & Massanari A (eds.) (2006) *Critical Cyberculture Studies.* New York: New York University Press.

Spencer N (2004) Sister Act VI: Venus and Serena Williams at Indian Wells: "Sincere fictions" and white racism. *Journal of Sport and Social Issues* 28(2): 115–35.

Stauff M (2009) Sports on YouTube. In: Snickars P & Vonderau P (eds.) *The YouTube Reader.* Stockholm, Sweden: National Library of Sweden, 236–52.

Trebay G (2010) Brittney Griner, basketball star, helps redefine beauty. *The New York Times.* 5 April. Online. Available from: http://www.nytimes.com/2010/04/08/fashion/08Brittney.html (Accessed 26 July 2012).

Washington J (2010) Racist messages pose quandary for Internet sites. *The Bay State Banner,* 30 September. Online. Available from: http://www.baystatebanner.com/natl16-2010-09-30 (Accessed 1 November 2010).

Zirin D (2012) Serena Williams and getting "emotional" for Title IX. *The Nation,* 9 July. Online. Available from: www.thenation.com/blog/168793/serena-williams-and-getting-emotional-title-ix# (Accessed 26 July 2012).

9 Facebook, Twitter and Sports Fans

Identity Protection and Social Network Sites in US Sports

Jimmy Sanderson

INTRODUCTION: DIGITAL MEDIA AND THE AMPLIFICATION OF IDENTITY

The advent of digital technologies has significantly increased the ability of sports fans to openly express their identity (McCarthy, 2011; Sanderson, 2011a; Spinda, 2011). As digital technologies have advanced and become more collaborative, the audience for identity expression has exponentially increased. In the early days of the Internet, fan identity expressions were asynchronously expressed via message boards, with limited opportunities for simultaneous engagement with others (End, 2001; End et al., 2003). However, social networking sites offer sports fans the capability to concomitantly interact with other sports fans *and* athletes and sports personalities. The integration and community building facilitated on social networking sites expose people to vast social networks that enable them to forge connections in ways that would be unlikely to occur elsewhere (boyd & Ellison, 2007). This unprecedented digital access stimulates behavior such as parasocial interaction (Kassing & Sanderson, 2009; Sanderson, 2010a) as fans communicate comments directly to athletes and sports figures. Accordingly, when athletes and sports figures undertake an action that threatens fan identity, social networking sites are natural mechanisms to manage social identity threats. These domains, which provide access to supportive and sympathetic others, serve as convenient communicative platforms where fans can be rallied quickly (Sanderson, 2011b). For example, fans in the US used Facebook to promote rallies held to persuade University of Southern California head football coach, Pete Carroll, and Michigan State University head basketball coach, Tom Izzo, to rebuff offers to coach professional franchises (Carroll left, Izzo stayed).

This chapter explores how US sports fans use social networking sites to protect their individual and collective identities when they are under threat. When sports teams announce unpopular decisions, athletes voluntarily leave teams or beloved sports figures are the subject of unfavorable media reports, social networking sites are abuzz as fans collectively strive to make sense of these events and to defend their "fractured" identities. Sporting events, pubs and other physical contexts where sport is consumed face-to-face will clearly continue to host manifestations of fan identity. Nevertheless, digital media have amplified opportunities for identity expression, and fans are increasingly using these channels to bolster and promulgate various identities to wide audiences, including to athletes and sports figures. A case in point concerns San Francisco 49ers gridiron player, Kyle Williams. On 22 January 2012, the 49ers played the New York Giants for the right to represent the National Football Conference in the Super Bowl. The 49ers lost a close game in overtime, 20–17, and Williams fumbled two punts during the game—mistakes that were widely framed as the reason for the 49ers' defeat. The team's fans were understandably upset at the loss, but some took their frustration to an alarming level by sending death threats to Williams via his Twitter account. A sample of these messages included, "@KyleWilliams_10. I hope you, your wife, kids and family die, you deserve it", "I hope you get aids and die" and "If you died tomorrow, no one would attend your funeral. I hope your parents disown you" (Heck, 2012). While troubling, comments of this nature are frequent on social networking sites—vividly depicting the strength and potential toxicity of fan identity.

Why would a person wish death on an athlete whose mistakes result in a disappointing result? One answer lies in social identity theory (SIT) (Tajfel & Turner, 1986). SIT provides an optimal framework from which to interpret fan behavior, positing that individuals have both personal and social identities, the latter based on demographic classifications or organizational memberships that are quite salient (Turner, 1982). People tend to gravitate towards social groups whose attributes align with their self-concept (Fink, Parker, Martin & Higgins, 2009), and group membership becomes a source of self-esteem that is bolstered by negatively labeling divergent or "out" groups (Turner, 1975). Considering these concepts, it is unsurprising that sports fandom is an important component of social identity (Fink et al., 2009; Wann, Royal & Roberts, 2000). Strong reactions occur when a sports team or athlete engages in behavior that threatens social identity. Social identity is intricately linked to sport, so when teams or athletes undertake an action that diminishes the team's likelihood of success, fans perceive this behavior to be a personal affront.

Although this chapter centers on sports in the US, the trends discussed herein possess international applicability. Sports fans in many countries across the globe employ social media to protect their identity. Consider, for example, the case of Ariane Friedrich, a German pole-vaulter. After receiving a sexually explicit message from a fan via Facebook, she publicly posted the man's name and contact information on Facebook. Her action prompted more than 10,000 comments from fans debating the appropriateness of her actions (Kelly, 2012). Another incident involved Australian swimmer Stephanie Rice, who tweeted a picture of herself wearing a low-cut bikini in July 2012. This action prompted fans to voice their displeasure via Twitter, including calling for Rice to be removed from the Olympic team (Smith, 2012). Fans' propensity to engage in this behavior is facilitated by the telepresence of the Internet (Hutchins, 2011), as fans can easily and conveniently dispatch these comments to athletes. Indeed, with the capability to dispense these comments from devices ranging from a cellular phone to a tablet, this behavior is important for athletes and sports teams to consider when using social media. My attention now turns to discussion of two factors that lead to fans enacting identity protection: (a) athletes and sports figures voluntarily leaving a team and; (b) expressions by athletes and sports figures that conflict with the identity of fans.

THE VOLUNTARY DEPARTURE

Many fans correlate their self-esteem with the success of a sports team. This relationship is evidenced by language such as "we" when describing the team (Cialdini et al., 1976). Thus, when a key contributor to the team's success voluntarily leaves the team, fans may sustain a fall in self-esteem, as an integral component to potential team success is lost. I explored how University of Cincinnati football fans used Facebook after head coach Brian Kelly left the school to take up the same position at the University of Notre Dame (Sanderson, 2011b). Kelly's departure occurred immediately after an exceptionally successful season, and he announced his departure at the team's annual end-of-season awards banquet. Although many outsiders considered his move to Notre Dame as a step up the career ladder, Cincinnati fans perceived it as evidence that their football program was not of "elite" quality. Efforts were made by fans to combat this affront to their identity. Some sought to motivate and rally others by conveying messages such as, "We Will Replace BK And Continue Where We Ended . . . Winning Big East Cha[m]pionship Year In and Year Out". Other individuals were more inflammatory in their remarks. Examples here include: "Brian Kelly can eat shit and die", "Im burning down this motherfuckers house", "I hope he and the Irish die in a fiery plane crash on their way the flight out to get their asses kicked by USC [University of Southern California] this season", and "HEY BRIAN KELLY EAT A BAG OF DICKS AND CHOKE ON A GIANT BLACK DILDO YOU PIECE OF SHIT" (Sanderson, in press).

Fans who were upset that Kelly had left Cincinnati found a supportive community on Facebook where their feelings and emotions were validated and encouraged. Sanderson noted that there was an abundance of information shared in this Facebook community, including Kelly's residential address. As this case demonstrates, social networking sites provide a convenient, accessible gathering place for aggrieved fans whose collective identity has been threatened. Within these domains, fans work together to reconfigure their social identity by degrading and humiliating a once-beloved figure who is felt to have betrayed them. Players and coaches commonly leave sports teams for "greener pastures". However, social networking sites offer fans the ability to connect and interact with others who not only feel their loss, but also "understand" the hurt that is felt. Yet, the interaction in these communities can also foster and promote aggressive and, in extreme circumstances, criminal behavior. Many Facebook participants openly encouraged others to deface Kelly's residence, and Kelly did, in fact, report that his house had been vandalized (Sanderson, 2011b). In an effort to remediate damage to social identity, inappropriate behavior may escalate and emerge as a response that requires law enforcement if criminal acts occur. Identity protection is not limited to a player or coach willingly leaving the team. In some instances, fans may disagree with an athlete's behavior or public comments, perceiving them to reflect negatively upon the team and fan base. Social media platforms offer a prime avenue to express these sentiments directly to sports organizations and athletes.

IDENTITY EXPRESSION AT VARIANCE WITH FAN IDENTITY

Digital technology has flattened media hierarchies, including through athletes using social networking sites to break news and to offer commentary (Sanderson, 2011a). However, athletes have experienced a host of public relations issues when using social media (primarily Twitter) for this purpose. For example, in May 2011, Pittsburgh Steelers running back, Rashard Mendenhall, posted commentary on Twitter that questioned people's celebration of Osama bin Laden's death (Florio, 2011). These tweets generated a storm of controversy, and many irate Steelers' fans posted comments to Mendenhall via Twitter and to the Steelers via Facebook.

Mendenhall is far from the only athlete to express public commentary that has drawn the ire of fans. Sanderson (2008, pp. 349–51) explored "parasocial interaction" occurring on Boston Red Sox pitcher Curt Schilling's blog after he publicly rebuked the sports news media and fellow baseball player, Barry Bonds. One fan took Schilling to task for his comments:

> In any situation where you represent my baseball team (and yes a sports-talk radio show about baseball issues qualifies), I would greatly appreciate it if you would please stop the jousting and running battle with the media, avoid loaded questions, and keep your non-baseball opinions to yourself during the baseball season. You're a veteran, not a rookie. (9 May 2007)

Another fan rebuked Schilling for his open expression of a Christian religious faith:

> Reporters roll their eyes at your faith? Maybe because you are hypocritical in your bashing of others and your judging and bitching. You also shove it down people's throats, just as you do your politics. Not everyone feels the need to wear their religion on their sleeve. When the Red Sox won the

World Series in 2004, (yes thanks to your heroics which you deserve a permanent place in every Red Sox fan's heart for, and that of many others on the team too), you couldn't wait to pollute my voicemail with your political hucksterism. PLEASE spare me the whining!!!! Just try to ask yourself when you are tempted to bash others or blow off your mouth and offend others who don't necessarily all think like you do: What would Jesus do? I believe in Him too, and I seriously doubt he would act like you. You are so self righteous and holier than thou. (27 April 2007)

Still others castigated Schilling for his affiliation with the US Republican Party and support for [then] President George W. Bush. For instance, "Hey Curt, if you care so much about 'integrity,' then why in God's name are you a Republican?" Another response reads:

You've got the blood of 3373 (and counting) decent, dead American soldiers on your hands through your shilling for George Bush and Dick Cheney and their useless war. These deaths, and those of tens of thousands of other innocents in this war are what you should be talking about, not some silly news report about a bloody sock. Shame on you. Have some integrity and Christian decency admit you made a mistake. Gary Thorne sure did. Apologize to the families who suffer their loss quietly. Jesus will forgive you. (9 May 2007)

Fan commentary directed at Schilling demonstrated a conflict between athlete identity and fan identity. That is, when athletes express their identity (as Schilling did) some vocal fans may perceive these statements to reflect poorly on the team and, therefore, on themselves. Fans then protect their identity by rebuking athletes for their public disclosures.

Another telling example of this pattern occurred in January 2012. The Boston Bruins captured the NHL's Stanley Cup during the 2011 season. As a result, and as part of cultural tradition, the team was scheduled to visit the White House to be congratulated by President Barack Obama. However, on 24 January 2012, goalie Tim Thomas—one of the integral players in the Bruins championship run—posted on his Facebook page that he would not be attending the White House with the team:

I believe the Federal government has grown out of control, threatening the Rights, Liberties, and Property of the People. This is being done at the Executive, Legislative, and Judicial level. This is in direct opposition to the Constitution and the Founding Fathers vision for the Federal government. Because I believe this, today I exercised my right as a Free Citizen, and did not visit the White House. This was not about politics or party, as in my opinion both parties are responsible for the situation we are in as a country. This was about a choice I had to make as an INDIVIDUAL. This is the only public statement I will be making on this topic. TT

Thomas's decision prompted a huge reaction from both sports reporters and fans. Given that Thomas posted his intentions on Facebook, fans could respond to his post and communicate their feelings directly to him. Whereas Thomas received some support from fans, many others criticized him. Some of the more vitriolic comments included, "You are an embarrassment to the United States of America!" and:

> The best way to stop this so-called threat (which is simple-minded bullshit) is to not visit one of the most iconic places in the world and not meet the leader of the free world. You embarrassed your team and the NHL and made yourself look like an idiot teabagger—which I guess you are, actually. What a douchebag. (23 January 2012)

Another person "shared":

> Clearly this WAS motivated by politics, Tim. Have some respect for your fans and at least be honest with them about the fact you're a teabaggin' republican. I still love the Bruins and will continue to support them but can no longer wear my Tim Thomas jersey in good conscience (Obama's name will be covering yours). I'll also be donating $1 to ActBlue, the nation's largest source of funds for Democratic campaigns, for every save you make for the remainder of the season! GO BRUINS! (24 January 2012)

Interestingly, both Schilling and Thomas played in the same geographic market (Boston) and both received considerable rebuke from fans for their political affiliation and commentary. Social networking sites provide outlets for fans to convey their contempt for an athlete's actions and (potentially) converse with them. A fan could certainly write a letter to an athlete to express similar sentiments, but social networking sites create a digital proximity that fans are unlikely to experience face-to-face.

Identity protection is not solely tied to professional athletes, and the prevalence and adoption of social networking sites has also given fans unprecedented access to amateur athletes. American college football arguably provides the most convincing example of this trend, with its recruiting coverage experiencing tremendous growth over the past decade. Recruitment is now a year-round process, which is a visible consequence of the Internet's growth as a dominant sports media and news platform. There are many computer-mediated outlets that fans can access about football recruitment information. The most prominent sites are Scout.com, Rivals.com, and the ESPN College Sports Network, a partnership between ESPN and popular team-dedicated sites for large football programs such as the University of Alabama, the University of Texas and the University of Southern California (Lemke, 2008). The popularity of Scout.com and Rivals.com has resulted in the purchase of these sites by larger corporations. In 2005, News Corporation purchased Scout.com for US$50 million, and just two years later Yahoo! acquired Rivals.com for approximately

US$100 million (Rovell, 2007). Rivals.com has actually branched into satellite radio, and now has a daily morning show on SiriusXM, providing fans with another media outlet for recruiting information.

Recruiting sites offer fans a plethora of information about high school football players, enabling them to access rankings of the top players overall, the best players in each position and a list of the universities that athletes are considering. These sites also contain video highlights of players' on-field performances, video interviews with them and articles by site personnel reporting news about various athletes. User participation is also a popular activity on recruiting sites. There are opportunities for fans to participate in forums open to the general public and premium or "insider" forums that claim to offer access to high quality recruiting information for a monthly or yearly fee. Given the amount of coverage, fans develop attachments to players as they progress through high school. As these high school players are linked to various college football programs, fans develop expectations that the player will attend a particular school. Fans eagerly await the first Wednesday in February, now known as "Signing Day". On this day, high school and junior college recruits sign letters-of-intent that commit them to attending the school. The recruiting process is fickle and, as one might expect from 17- and 18-year-old young men, decisions can be changed for a variety of reasons. A player may change his mind at the last minute, simultaneously elevating the identity of one school's fan-base while deflating the identity of another. Social media, in turn, provide an outlet for fans to react and respond to the highs and lows of the recruitment process.

A notable example of this pattern occurred during Signing Day on 1 February 2012. It involved Deontay Greenberry, a wide receiver from Fresno in California. Greenberry had verbally committed to the University of Notre Dame, but then signed unexpectedly with the University of Houston. While it has recently experienced success, Houston is not widely viewed as an elite program of the same standard as Notre Dame. Accordingly, Greenberry's decision bewildered Notre Dame fans, who gathered in discussion forums to manage collectively this affront to their pride. In one domain (www.irishenvy.com), fans shared sentiments such as:

> Blew my mind for sure. F*cking Houston???? I mean Houston?? I'm typing this with one hand due to the fact that I'm holding a trash bin in the other and dry heaving, Houston??? (1 February 2012)

Another fan reasoned:

> Notre Dame is bigger than one recruit, life will go on without him. If he was scared of competition he won't need to worry about it at Houston, i prefer recruits who are willing to compete and push themselves everyday to be better. Houston=easywayout. (1 February 2012)

This opinion was mirrored in the following comment:

> Absolute poop. There is no rationale that would justify picking Houston over ND. If he were a 2-star WR with no major offers, absolutely jump at the chance to play in an air raid offense. When you are an elite WR with pro potential, it makes no sense whatsoever. (1 February 2012)

Notre Dame fans clearly did not expect Greenberry to change his mind and commit to another school. Amplifying their angst was his commitment to a school perceived to be below the status of Notre Dame. Thus, the identity of Notre Dame fans took a perceived hit as an elite athlete willingly shunned them to join a less prestigious school. Fans needed to make sense of Greenberry's move, and social media provided them with an opportunity collectively to come to terms with what had just occurred. One way of mitigating this identity threat was to frame Greenberry as "afraid" of competition and lacking the intellectual ability to succeed at Notre Dame.

Social networking sites help fans perpetuate narratives that demean those who threaten their identity, thereby bolstering the self-esteem of the fanbase. But identity protection need not be limited to negative situations and, indeed, an advantage of social networking sites is that athletes can encourage fans—both directly and indirectly—to support them when *their* reputations "take a hit". This trend is now discussed.

PROTECTING ATHLETES' IDENTITIES

Social networking sites constitute a tremendous resource for athletes to employ when their identities have been challenged, as they can rally fans quickly and "outsource" the work of identity protection to them. A compelling example of this trend occurred with professional golfer John Daly. He asked his Twitter followers to harass sports journalist Gary Smits. Smits wrote an article disclosing disciplinary issues in Daly's PGA Tour file. Daly tweeted on 2 March 2010, "here's the JERK who writes NON-NEWS article on debut of my show—CALL & FLOOD his line and let's tell him how WE feel." The telephone calls to Smits started around midnight—minutes after Daly sent the tweet (Gola, 2010, p. 73). Although most callers hung up, Smits reported that approximately twenty-five percent left messages, some of which were quite abusive. It is unclear how many of the callers were following Daly on Twitter, but it is noteworthy that calls began pouring into Smits's office moments after Daly posted his request.

In another study, I noted how fans validated the identity of the aforementioned Boston Red Sox pitcher, Schilling, via his blog (Sanderson, 2010b, pp. 198–200). The prominence of these postings transformed Schilling's blog into a space where fans mobilized to support and defend him against what they saw as unwarranted attacks on his reputation. In 2007, Schilling was criticized by members of the media for using his blog to rebuke the news and journalism industry. Baltimore Orioles play-by-play commentator, Gary Thorne, alleged that Schilling had faked an injury during the 2004 American League Championship Series. Fans overwhelmingly supported Schilling's use of his blog to chastise journalists and commentators. Examples included, "It is a good thing you created this blog to speak directly with the fans of MLB, without having the media sully your message", and "it is so refreshing to hear things directly from an athlete instead of it being manipulated by the press". Others defended Schilling by expressing empathy, acknowledging that they would have reacted in a similar fashion. These messages included, "If I was in your position I would tell all the critics and so called experts to go to hell (which you probably do anyways)", "I don't blame you for reacting like this. I'd be calling for the man's job if I'd been Swift Boated in the same way", and "Curt, as a person who also says what he thinks, often times to a fault, I can sympathize with you here".

Fans also emphatically reminded Schilling of his identity as a heroic figure in Red Sox history, their feelings stemming from his pivotal role in ending the Red Sox's eighty-six-year World Series championship drought. There messages included, "All of us longtime fans in Red Sox Nation will be forever grateful to the gutsy effort displayed by Schilling during the incredible championship run" and:

> Thanks for coming to Boston, thanks for being a tremendous and historic part of Red Sox baseball, thanks for not being so worried about what your marketing agents say to talk straight with the fans and community, thanks for not just paying lip service to history and fans of the Sox but actually immersing yourself, in both, thanks for the WORLD SERIES, and thanks in advance for just continuing to be yourself for as long as you're here. (27 April 2007)

Fans also suggested that those people who disparaged Schilling were merely masquerading as Red Sox fans. These offerings were typified by commentary such as, "TRUE Red Sox fans support who you are, and what you do" and "Your true fans know that you didn't fake the sock". Some fans offered support through commitments to tangible action:

> Curt, I know you are telling the truth, and the Nation stands behind you. I, and thousands of others, are more than willing to testify to that under oath. (27 April 2007)

Fans' protection of athlete identity also encompasses off-the-field behavior. Sanderson (2010a) contrasted how the marital infidelities of golf's Tiger Woods were framed by the news media and fan postings on Woods's

Facebook page. While mainstream news media accounts focused on the salacious nature of Woods's extramarital activity and relished his fall from grace, fans defended Woods and framed his infidelity as a manifestation of human weakness—a trait that made Woods similar to them. For example, "Shame on all you people casting stones at Tiger! We are not here to judge him or anyone else for that matter". Others stated, "We are all sinners, and he who is without sin is a liar" and "get a grip, you have sinned, i have sinned, tiger has sinned, everyone has sinned". Other comments included:

> Its easy for you or I to sit back and say these things but YOU walk in [his] shoes for a week or even one day and go through what he does and has done for so long and see if you make the same JUDGEMENT you are so willingly making right now. (Sanderson, 2010a, pp. 446–47)

As is evidenced by this case, social media enable fans to participate in the framing of athlete identity, a capability that historically rested in the hands of the mass media. However, with the ability to generate and disseminate content, fans now play a role in creating the narratives that contribute to athlete identities. This is an important mechanism that athletes can use to promote favorable public representations.

IMPLICATIONS

Fans protect their own identities as well as those of athletes through social media. These practices have many implications, several of which are now discussed. First, social networking sites create opportunities for increased surveillance of athletes and sports figures. With compact cellular phones that possess advanced photographic, audio and video technology, fans who encounter athletes can document and broadcast information and pictures that can find and place athletes in compromising positions. For instance, Sanderson (2009) profiled three instances where professional athletes' off-the-field activities were captured by fans and transmitted via the Internet. Each of these athletes received a public rebuke from the sports organization for which they played, and fan agreement with these sanctions was overwhelming. Perhaps the most vivid account chronicled involved Matt Leinart, who at the time played quarterback for the Arizona Cardinals. In April 2008, photos taken at a party at Leinart's home were posted on the-dirty.com (a site that openly asks for people to send them photos of celebrities that depict them partying, drunk or involved in unflattering behavior). These photos included Leinart in a hot tub with several young women, as well as holding a beer bong, the contents of which the women were consuming. The Cardinals issued a stern rebuke to Leinart and sports journalists questioned how seriously he took his "vocation". Comments posted on the

Arizona Republic's website indicated that a number of fans supported the censure of Leinart, including:

> When you are paid tens of millions to do a job, you had better be working on it year round. His work ethic has always been questioned, and his constant pics on the Hollywood/Scottsdale scene prove his ethics. I don't care if he is 25, I don't care if he is single-he is paid to be a professional. You don't see Manning doing this, Brady, etc-why? They take their profession serious. (Sanderson, 2009, p. 250)

Leinart's case typifies how fan identity protection reinforces organizational surveillance and monitoring—a benefit that sports organizations receive free-of-charge and a service that fans willingly provide. With advances in digital technology and mobile media, it is quite easy for athletes' behavior to be documented and transmitted, particularly when a fan perceives that athlete behavior is detracting from the team's success. Social networking sites are a convenient mechanism for fans to easily broadcast athletes' private behavior, as well as a domain where organizational discipline can be reinforced through fan commentary. The advent of social networking sites has expanded the ability of employers to monitor employees, and fans can magnify the scope of this practice in the sports world.

Another implication arising from these trends is the increasing prevalence of scathing commentary by fans about athletes and sports figures. The correlation between fan expression and team success is so significant that hostile reactions appear to be almost instinctual. Problematic online behavior, such as "trolling" and "flaming" (Herring, Job-Sluder, Schekler & Barab, 2002; Lee, 2005; Turnage, 2007), are not new, but inflammatory commentary appears to be the default response when fans' pride has been hurt. The fact that some athletes then respond to hurtful comments intensifies rather than defuses the situation. An exchange between Kansas City Chiefs running back, Larry Johnson, and fans on Twitter demonstrates this point. In October 2009, after a loss against the San Diego Chargers, Johnson used Twitter to voice his displeasure with head coach Todd Haley. Fans then responded with tweets that included, "Interesting comments by Larry Johnson (@toonlcon) about 'coaches.' Hey LJ, is it Haley's fault you fall when D-Linemen blow on you?" Another tweet soon referenced a previous allegation of wrongdoing by Johnson, "Apologies. His Twitter alias is @ toonicon whatever the hell that means. Probably something about spitting in women's faces". The proverbial "floodgates" then opened and others began condemning Johnson, who then launched a barrage of tweets in response to his attackers:

> @[Lists Twitter ID] Make me regret it. Lmao. U don't stop my checks. Lmao. So 'tweet' away.
>
> @[Lists Twitter ID] then don't reply then. Still richer then u. Keep goin. Come play our game ooops forgot u can't.

@[Lists Twitter ID] got nuthn to do wit hiring my father. But u wouldn't know cuz u don't play either so keep on the sideline lil gril n cheer.

@[Lists Twitter ID] sorry to tell u ur the reason y ur broke n dissn on twitter lmao.

@[Lists Twitter ID] think bout a clever diss then wit ur fag pic. Christopher street boy. Is what us east coast cats call u.

@[Lists Twitter ID] Sorry ur a cornball n ur mom birthed u broke. But I'm cakn patna. While u work or school for 5 dollas n hour. Ha! (Sanderson, 2011a, pp. 50–51)

The next day reporters questioned Johnson about his tweets and he refused to retract or apologize for them. Based on these actions, the Chiefs suspended him for two weeks for "conduct detrimental to the team", a disciplinary action that cost him almost US$300,000 (Battista, 2009). The Chiefs released Johnson on 9 November 2009.

A similar situation occurred in March 2010 when news reports surfaced indicating that Pittsburgh Steelers wide receiver Santonio Holmes had been accused of assaulting a woman in a Florida nightclub. Some fans were apparently upset by these reports and began directing criticism at Holmes for his alleged actions—via his Twitter account. On 29 March 2010, Holmes appeared to grow tired of these messages and tweeted to a fan, "y u tryna make me look like the bad guy. U shud try finding the worst thing that you could drink n kill urself". This message further worsened Holmes's difficult relationship with the Steelers and the NFL (he was suspended for the first four games of the 2010–2011 season for violating the league's substance abuse policy). Holmes was subsequently traded to the New York Jets on 11 April 2010 (Sanderson, 2011a, p. 5).

In both situations, while arguably provoked, the athlete suffered adverse consequences for his online activities. There is no indication that fans will cease directing hostile commentary at athletes. However, some athletes have become more strategic when receiving these messages, particularly via Twitter. For example, Baltimore Ravens running back Ray Rice re-tweeted the following message that he received from a fan:

@RayRice27 rice u fucking pussy, how about u become a real RB and stop being ur teams leading WR every week??? Just lost fantasy cuz of u. (19 December 2011)

Apparently, Rice's performance on that weekend had cost this fan a victory in fantasy football. Via Twitter, the fan saw fit to express his discontent and frustration directly at Rice. Retransmitting messages gives athletes the opportunity to address critics and enables other followers to notify the offending user that such messages are inappropriate (i.e., to engage in-group policing practices). This outcome may help stem the prevalence of hostile fan expressions, but athletes must proceed cautiously as the cases of Johnson and Holmes plainly testify.

CONCLUSION: MEDIATING THE FAN BEHAVIOR OF THE FUTURE

Social networking sites have proliferated throughout the sports world in a relatively short period of time (Hutchins, 2011; Sanderson, 2011a; Sanderson & Kassing, 2011). Consequently, fans now have an unprecedented ability to defend their individual and collective identity in public when they perceive that they have been threatened. While protecting fan identity can be done positively, there appears to be an overwhelming display of inflammatory and highly critical behavior. Certainly, such behavior is not new—attendance at any sporting event bears witness to fans engaging in practices such as those mentioned in this chapter. However, social networking sites extend the boundaries of this behavior and pull athletes and sports figures into the fray.

It will be instructive to observe how fan behavior is expressed and mediated in the future. Fandom maintains a strong hold on people and the lack of accountability that accompanies often-anonymous online postings elevates the willingness of fans to express and protect identity in this manner. Indeed, communication can now happen almost instantaneously while consuming sport. A fan watching a telecast observes an athlete commit an error and can immediately take to Twitter or Facebook to voice their displeasure directly to the athlete, and join with other fans in expressing disillusionment. Sports communication and media scholars are well positioned to shed light on the behavior that is occurring in these digital domains. As this book highlights, there is no shortage of opportunities for scholars to research how "game-changing" social networking sites and digital technologies are influencing fandom.

REFERENCES

Battista J (2009) As Johnson's suspension ends, so does his time with the Chiefs. *The New York Times*, 9 November. Online. Available from: http://www.nytimes.com/2009/11/10/sports/football/10chiefs.html (Accessed 9 November 2009).

boyd D & Ellison NB (2007) Social network sites: definition, history, and scholarship. *Journal of Computer-Mediated Communication* 13(1): 210–30.

Cialdini RB, Borden RJ, Thorne A, Walker MR, Freeman S & Sloan L R (1976) Basking in reflected glory: three (football) studies. *Journal of Personality and Social Psychology* 34(3): 366–75.

End CM (2001) An examination of NFL fans' computer mediated BIRGing. *Journal of Sport Behavior* 24(2): 162–81.

End CM, Campbell J, Kretschmar JM, Mueller D & Dietz-Uhler B (2003) Outcome's influence on sports fans' computer-mediated attributions. *International Sports Journal* 7(2): 128–39.

Fink JS, Parker HM, Martin B & Higgins J (2009) Off-field behavior of athletes and team identification: using social identity theory and balance theory to explain fan reactions. *Journal of Sport Management* 23(2): 142–55.

Florio M (2011) Rashard Mendenhall raises eyebrows with bin Laden tweets. *NBC Sports* 2 May. Online. Available from: http://profootballtalk.nbc-sports.com/2011/05/02/rashard-mendenhall-raises-eyebrows-with-bin-laden-tweets (Accessed 2 May 2011).

Gola H (2010) Daly's tweet revenge. In snit, puts writer's cell number on the web. *New York Daily News*, 4 March.

Heck, J (2012). San Francisco receiver Kyle Williams receives death threats on Twitter. *Bleacher Report*, 23 January. Online. Available from: http://bleacherreport.com/articles/1034961-san-francisco-receiver-kyle-williams-receivers-death-threats-on-twitter (Accessed 23 January 2012).

Herring, Job-Sluder K, Schekler R & Barab S (2002) Searching for safety online: managing "trolling" in a feminist forum. *Information Society* 18(5): 371–84.

Hutchins B (2011) The acceleration of media sport culture. *Information, Communication, & Society* 14(2): 237–57.

Kassing JW & Sanderson J (2009) "You're the kind of guy that we all want for a drinking buddy": expressions of parasocial interaction on Floydlandis.com. *Western Journal of Communication* 73(2): 182–203.

Kelly T (2012) Ariane Freidrich, German high jumper, outs stalker on Facebook. *Huff Post Women*, 24 April. Online. Available from: http://www.huffingtonpost.com/2012/04/24/ariane-friedrich-german-high-jumper_n_1449001.html (Accessed 24 April 2012).

Lee H (2005) Behavioral strategies for dealing with flaming in an online forum. *Sociological Quarterly* 46(5): 385–403.

Lemke T (2008) ESPN, college sites forming partnerships. *The Washington Times*, 31 July. Online. Available from: http://www.washingtontimes.com/news/2008/jul/31/espn-college-sites-forming-partnerships/?page=all (Accessed 2 May 2011).

McCarthy B (2011) From shanfan to gymnastlike: how online fan texts are affecting access to gymnastics media coverage. *International Journal of Sport Communication* 4(3): 265–83.

Rovell D (2007) Yahoo buys Rivals.com: is the deal worth it? *CNBC*, 21 June. Online. Available from: http://www.cnbc.com/id/19340539/Yahoo_Buys_Rivalscom_Is_The_Deal_Worth_It (Accessed 1 December 2012).

Sanderson J (2008) "You are the type of person that children should look up to as a hero": parasocial interaction on 38pitches.com. *International Journal of Sport Communication* 1(3): 337–60.

Sanderson J (2009) Professional athletes' shrinking privacy boundaries: fans, information and communication technologies, and athlete monitoring. *International Journal of Sport Communication* 2(2): 240–56.

Sanderson J (2010a) Framing tiger's troubles: comparing traditional and social media. *International Journal of Sport Communication* 3(4): 438–53.

Sanderson J (2010b) "The Nation stands behind you": mobilizing social support on 38pitches.com. *Communication Quarterly* 58(2): 188–206.

Sanderson J (2011a) *It's a Whole New Ballgame: How Social Media is Changing Sports*. New York: Hampton Press.

Sanderson J (2011b) From loving the hero to despising the villain: Exploring sports fans social identity management on Facebook. Paper presented at the *97th Annual Conference of the National Communication Association*, New Orleans, LA, 15–18 November 2011.

Sanderson J (in press) From loving the hero to despising the villain: Exploring sports fans social identity management on Facebook. *Mass Communication and Society*.

Sanderson J & Kassing JW (2011) Tweets and blogs: transformative, adversarial, and integrative developments in sports media. In: Billings AC (ed.) *Sports Media: Transformation, Integration, Consumption*. New York: Routledge, 114–27.

Smith E (2012). From triumph to scandal: Olympians in the social media spotlight. *CNN Living*, 2 July. Online. Available from: http://articles.cnn.com/2012-07-02/living/living_olympics-scandal-twitter-photos_1_social-media-olympic-team-photos?_s=PM:LIVING (Accessed 2 July 2012).

Spinda JSW (2011) The development of basking in reflected glory (BIRGing) and cutting off reflected failure (CORFing) measures. *Journal of Sport Behavior* 34(4): 392–420.

Tajfel H & Turner JC (1986) Social identity theory of intergroup behavior. In: Austin W & Worchel S (eds.) *Psychology of intergroup relations*. Chicago: Nelson-Hall, 33–47.

Turnage AK (2007) Email flaming behaviors and organizational conflict. *Journal of Computer-Mediated Communication* 13(1): 43–59.

Turner JC (1975) Social comparisons and social identity: some prospects for intergroup behavior. *European Journal of Social Psychology* 5(1): 5–34.

Turner JC (1982) Towards a cognitive redefinition of the social group. In: Tajfel H (ed.) *Self, Identity, and Intergroup Relations*. Cambridge: University Press, 15–40.

Wann DL, Royalty J & Roberts A (2000) The self-presentation of sports fans: investigating the importance of team identification and self-esteem. *Journal of Sport Behavior* 23(2): 198–201.

10 Fan Movements in the Network Society

Project, Resistance and Legitimizing Identities among Manchester United Supporters

Peter Millward

INTRODUCTION: SPORT SUPPORTERS AND THE "SPACE OF FLOWS"

This chapter explores the emergence of "project", "resistance" and "legitimizing" identities among supporters of Manchester United, one of the largest sporting clubs and brands in the world. These issues are connected to the private ownership of the club and consider the role of social interaction and networked communications in the development, articulation and maintenance of fan cultures in "the network society" (Castells, 2000). In setting the scene for my analysis, it is necessary to note that the American businessman, Malcolm Glazer, and his family bought Manchester United with a £790m (US$1.267bn) takeover bid in May 2005. Prior to the takeover, the Glazer family had initially purchased a 2.9 percent stake in the club in March 2003, but by 28 June 2005, the family owned a ninety-eight percent shareholding and delisted it from the London stock exchange. Under Glazer's ownership, Manchester United's on-field performance has been strong, winning both the EPL titles and the UEFA Champions League. However, various fan-diaries clearly show that supporters' concerns about the Glazer buyout are not principally related to the team's success (see Brady, 2006; Crowther, 2006; Wood, 2008). Instead, a major concern is the amount of debt that the family has loaded onto the club, which is viewed by some as morally out-of-step with the "spirit of football" (as well as needing to be serviced by annual interest repayments of around £60m (US$96m)—see Conn 2010).[1] The following sections explore the responses of Manchester United fans to the commercialization of the game and, in particular, the Glazer family's purchase of the club. This chapter tells the story of the fan identities that have emerged in response to these developments, including the establishment of a new club FC United of Manchester (hereafter FC United), and the rise of the "Green and Gold" social movement in 2010.

The sociological scholarship of Castells provides the theoretical framework for the analysis presented here. His empirical project focuses on the transnational flows of informational capital—encompassing people, money and information—in the network society. Emphasizing that the Internet increasingly mediates social relations, he argues that the capitalist "mode of production" underwent deep changes in the 1980s as the "the mode of development" moved from an industrial and mainly nationally-based footing to an informational and transnational structure. This transformation was driven by the development of a new technological paradigm that allowed information and capital to move instantaneously across the globe. According to Castells (2000), networks are now the primary form of social organization throughout the world and, emphasizing the transnational socio-cultural and economic values generated by networked connections, have made established national boundaries and regulatory frameworks porous or "lighter" compared to previous eras. In this account, capital is largely synonymous with power, taking mobile informational forms, as well as material and "traditional" symbolic forms. Communication and collective action are also included in this model of power (Castells, 2004). Castells (2009) has recently argued that new digitally networked technologies have expanded the ability of social actors to change the relationship between media and power, thereby providing avenues for the initiation of political action and social mobilization.

As the "network league" (Millward, 2011), the EPL forges transnational connections around the world through flows of capital, people and images. Many dimensions of the EPL are part of a transnational space of flows, which was not the case twenty-five years ago. It is widely acknowledged that elite professional soccer in England reached its *nadir* at the end of the 1980s, as fan support became popularly conflated with "violence". In the light of various "hooligan" disasters, a moral panic erupted that saw government proposals for fans to carry identity cards. Indeed, Taylor's (1984) description of soccer in the 1980s as a sport in "recession" is accurate. The EPL was subsequently born as the Football Association (FA) Premiership in August 1992, and its new broadcasters, BSkyB, seized the opportunity to rebrand the sport. The broadcaster's billboard adverts described the new league as "A Whole New Ball Game", and the EPL's partnership with BSkyB was central to the recovery of English soccer from "recession".

A key argument of Castells (1998, 2000, 2009) is that the agents in the "space of flows" settle in the most lucrative space, which is often global in scope. This outcome has proven to be the case with the EPL, which, although nationally organized, has become transnational in terms of its fans, players and team managers, as well by investments in individual clubs by "foreign" investors. There have also been discussions about playing an extra round of competitive matches in overseas locations. In recent years, the number of territories in which it is possible to subscribe to digital broadcasts of matches has grown to 211 worldwide (personal interview, EPL senior financial director, 29 January 2009). The cumulative value of the EPL's overseas broadcasting contracts has roughly doubled with each new negotiation in the twenty-first century (see Harris, 2010; Wilson, J 2007). As capital is power in the network society, the value of overseas markets is growing apace with the three-season overseas contracts signed in 2010 worth £1.4bn (US$2.25bn). This figure sits alongside domestic broadcasting rights valued at £1.782bn (US$2.86bn) for the same period.

IDENTITIES

In the *Power of Identity,* Castells (2004) positions social movements as the product of personal and collective identities. These identities emerge in relation to changing state and market conditions that are external to movement members, but shape their everyday lived practices. Structural changes, such as those shaped by the economic base of society, prompt subjects to respond in one of three ways. These are described as legitimizing, resistance and project identities. First, Castells (2004, p. 8) postulates that a legitimizing identity helps to generate a civil society, which he understands to be individual responses (or non-responses) that do not challenge existing structural conditions. Thus, the legitimizing identity could be one of agreement or apathy, but is largely formed and expressed at the level of the individual. Second, he discusses the emergence of resistance identities, understood in terms of social actors whose position in society is weakened by structural changes. He argues that under such conditions, actors often come together to form defensive "communes or communities" as group members seek solace in each other (sometimes even subverting their shared oppression to make it seem subjectively favorable). Locally-based communal bonds between members are strong and "refuse to be flushed away by global flows and radical individualism" (Castells, 2004, p. 9). Such values are based on traditional sources of collective identity, such as religion, nationhood or the family, or non-traditional values that are based on proactive social movement goals (Castells, 2004, p. 356). Third, Castells (2004, p. 8) suggests that social actors may choose to mobilize:

> . . . on the basis of whatever cultural materials are available to them, build a new identity that redefines their position in society and, by doing so, seek the transformation of overall structure.

This process involves the collective development of a project identity or an alternative vision of a civil society (see also Freeman, 1973, pp. 794–95, 805). If such identities are to develop, Castells argues that they are likely to emerge from communal resistance identities. He stresses, however, that not all communal resistance identities change prevailing social conditions (Castells, 2004, p. 357).[2] Nonetheless, the emergence of a project identity represents a group's vision of a new reality that may seek to revolutionize or reform the conditions of the world.

The various ways in which the Internet is used have affected how collective and individual identities are formed, and how fans talk about soccer. There are also an increasing number of social media platforms such as Facebook and Twitter. Castells (2009) and Leah Lievrouw (2011) discuss the possibility that these services help to generate chains of transnational connection that play a role in shaping and expressing social identities. As such, social networking media—while often connecting people in localized communities—alter the ways in which fans engage with soccer across the world. These conditions also create the possibility that the Internet can be used as a tool for organizing and developing grassroots collective action (Castells, 2009).

Renowned Manchester United fan blogger and online "opinion leader" (see Chapter 10), Rob Blanchette,[3] has demonstrated how fans are able communicate with each other, making in excess of 50,000 soccer related tweets to a community of followers of more than 5,000 fans. Discussing the power of Twitter in the long-established Manchester United fanzine, *Red News*, he states:

> The Internet has brought us into uncharted territory, regarding how we watch and view our club, and how we connect with these players. We are yet to see what impact in the long term our collective voice of individual nuggets of tweets has. Social media has helped topple governments and dictators, and it has contributed to national rioting in our streets . . . Social media is a tremendous form of communication for us that walk this planet at the moment. But let us hope it doesn't become the terminal disease that it also threatens to mutate in to. (Blanchette, 2012a)

Blanchette highlights how supporter communities can engage with soccer players through social media services such as Twitter. The same "citizen journalist" presented a similar case several months later on a Manchester United themed blog, *The Faithful*, arguing, "I think social media has created a monster. The way people congregate has changed. The way people act as a collective has also changed" (Blanchette, 2012b). As far back as 1971, Taylor stated that a sub-cultural rump of fans felt alienated from players on account of wealth differentials. From the vantage point of the twenty-first century, Blanchette believes that Twitter has the power to bring fans and players together and, as a result, has both subjectively positive and negative effects on soccer and society. Attention now turns to the emergence of project identities in this context.

PROJECT IDENTITIES

As noted earlier, Castells (2004) argues that project identities are proactive movements aimed at transforming society, rather than merely establishing the conditions for their own survival in opposition to the dominant actors. Environmental, feminist and gay/lesbian movements are, he proposes, some of the most typical examples of this identity. The formation of FC United of Manchester by disenchanted Manchester United fans at the start of the 2005–2006 season arguably represents the manifestation of a project identity in the context of soccer. Across the 1990s, a sizable number of Manchester United supporters claimed to be disengaged from the hyper-commercial practices of the club, believing that they had sanitized the atmosphere at club home matches (King, 2002). Adam Brown and Andy Walsh (1999) show how a group of like-minded Manchester United fans expressed their concerns. Connected to either the Independent Manchester United Supporters Association (IMUSA) or Shareholders Unite Against Murdoch (SUAM),[4] they came together successfully in opposing the proposed purchase of the club by BSkyB majority shareholder, Murdoch, in 1998. Castells (2004, p. 8) suggests that a project identity becomes real:

> When social actors, on the basis of whatever cultural materials are available to them, build a new identity that redefines their position in society and, by so doing, seek the transformation of overall social structure [and emerge from] . . . current resistance identities.

In response to Glazer's later purchase of the club, some fans mobilized against its detachment from local supporter communities. Their response was to set up an entirely new club, FC United (see Brown, 2007, 2008; Millward, 2011). Understood as the product of a project identity, FC United was not solely about opposing the Glazer's purchase of Manchester United. The new club claimed to be "a broad church" where:

> There's a home there for the most rabid anti-Glazer protester who out of principle will not give him a penny of their money; there's a home there for those people who can't afford to go to Old Trafford; there's a home there for people who want to watch Manchester United and just see it as an extension of the United family—first team, reserve team, supporters' team. (FC United board member, Jules Spencer, speaking on "Inside Out—North West", BBC, 26 September 2005)

Organized as an Industrial and Provident Society, the club is led by fans that include Brown and Walsh and many other former members of IMUSA. It is run on a semi-professional basis and, although currently based at Bury FC's stadium (Gigg Lane), has raised the finances to build its own ground in the Moston district of the city. FC United staged its first game on 16 July 2005 and was promoted in each of its first three seasons, and currently plays in the seventh tier of English soccer, the Northern Premier League Premier Division. This club did not form in the virtual space of social networks, but in the "space of places" (Castells, 2000). This process took the form of, first, a small meeting of Manchester United supporters connected to the fan groups and fanzines around the time of the Glazer takeover. A meeting was held "in the curry house in Rusholme [a district of Manchester]" (Walsh speaking on "Choices", BBC Radio Four, 13 December 2005), where the idea of a new club was floated. A public meeting was then held at the Apollo Theatre on the fringes of Manchester city center on 30 May 2005.

Online communication has played a role in the subsequent development of the club and what it stands for in a number of ways. Indeed, in the immediate aftermath of the meeting at the Apollo Theatre, the Manchester United *Red Issue* Internet forum[5] buzzed with debate about the prospect of creating a new club (virtual fieldnotes, 1 June 2005). However, there was little consensus in the views offered on this idea, as not all supporters believed it to be a good idea. Just as Brown (2008) had argued that FC United split the Manchester United fan communities in offline settings, it also had a similar effect in *Red Issue's* Internet forum in that period. FC United has a lively unofficial online message board and, given the vibrancy of this forum, it is tempting to follow Habermas's theoretical framework (1986, 1989) and to assert that the forum is a "public sphere" where decisions about the club's future are made. However, whilst FC United institutionalizes some elements of a "participatory democracy" (Taylor, 1971a, 1971b), the connection between the views of fans and decision-making processes is unclear. Club decisions are made largely by team managers and board members, rather than by supporters. Nonetheless, Pete Crowther's fan diary about the club's first season reveals affinities within the message board community that appear to renew his faith in FC United's mission. This belief underlines the power of communicative media forms in the maintenance of the fan-driven project identities:

> The unofficial site is the nervous system of the club and is visited on a daily basis by hundreds of FC fans. If something FC-related is happening, then you can find it advertised, described, analysed and criticised on the unofficial site . . . If you want to be challenged, provoked and exhilarated, then put on your tin helmet and visit the main FC United forum. (Crowther, 2006, pp. 62–63)

Nick Crossley (1999) found that some social movements prosper from the existence of "working utopias" that members can visit to "top up" their beliefs in movement aims. Discussions on this forum reinforce the aims that define FC United. Working utopias are spaces where a movement's culture is reformed and/or reproduced, and "people visit them in order to learn how to practice differently; how to perceive, think and act in different ways" (Crossley, 1999, p. 817). This notion resonates with the case of FC United, where fans believe that they are being indoctrinated in, and/or reintroduced to, "traditional" ways of supporting a soccer club, as the following exchange evidences:

FC UNITED FAN 1: One of the best things about this thing we have is this forum. This is where FC happens, we make the rules and we make friends. Whenever I doubt what we did in 2005, I just come on here, have a chat and I know I made the right decision

FC UNITED FAN 2: Internet mong alert :P ["emoticon" language for a tongue sticking out]

FC UNITED FAN 3: There's no need to doubt the walkaway, we have OUR club. But you're probably right that this is the best place to come in those moments of weakness. It's a special place— I'll grant you that! (Comments from 11 October 2008)[6]

FC United's Internet forum differs from Crossley's (1999) typical working utopia as it exists in a virtual space, as opposed to an identifiably physical place. However, along with match-day attendance, this forum bolsters the group's motives for collective action. The project identity in evidence here is a cross-fertilization of fandom and activism, with websites serving as meeting places for group members to discuss tactical repertoires. Such websites carry a heavy symbolic value that serves to renew political attitudes and to allow people to debate club strategies.

RESISTANCE IDENTITIES

Locality continues to be an important consideration for many fans of clubs, despite the emergence of the EPL as a globally integrated network league and the presentation of leading clubs such as Manchester United as global brands (Bridgewater, 2010; Millward, 2011). Indeed, this issue is important for those fans claiming fealty towards a club on the grounds of locality above all else (see, for instance, King, 1997; Robson, 2000; Taylor, 1971a; 1971b). The subjective assertion that localized association with a club should be highly valued is unsurprising in a global age. Castells explains that social experiences in the transnational "spaces of flows" can be disorienting for those people inhabiting locally rooted "places" who forge strong locally based communal bonds (Castells, 2004, p. 356). Deploying social movement strategies, some "local" fans, then, express defensive attitudes toward the globalization of the EPL and resist the overseas ownership of clubs. The global reach of the EPL's broadcasting deals also means that local fan protests can gain purchase on the global stage.

The pattern described here is evident in the case of the Green and Gold protest by Manchester United supporters. Castells (2004, p. 8) states that a resistance identity is:

generated by those actors who are in positions/conditions devalued and/ or stigmatized by the logic of domination. These actors build trenches of resistance and survival on the basis of principles different from, or opposed to, those permeating the institutions of society.

This is a form of resistance that seeks to reform the existing conditions, not create a new environment (as happens with the development of a project identity). Manifestations of resistance identities have developed among Manchester United supporters, ranging, as observed earlier, from complaints about the loss of a vibrant atmosphere at home matches to organized resistance to Murdoch's proposed takeover of the club. In 2005, a "fight from within" protest emerged at Manchester United and announced itself on many online fan sites, including the *Red Issue* forum after the fans' public meeting on 30 May. The constituents of the "fight from within" resistance movement included those members of IMUSA who felt that they could not replace their principal support for Manchester United with that for FC United. These supporters largely pledged to continue supporting Manchester United, but would alter their ways of doing so. Most obviously, they boycotted the club's official merchandise and thus sought to lower the profitability of the club, thereby making the club less attractive to the Glazer family (see Friedman, 1999, for more on consumer boycotts).

Following reports that the Glazer family was trying to restructure the club's debt in 2010, the Red Knights were formed and asked for fan support through television and Internet channels. This group was led by Jim O'Neill, the Head of Global Economic Research at Goldman Sachs, and aimed to buy the club from the Glazers. The group liaised with the Manchester United Supporters' Trust (MUST) Chief Executive, Duncan Drasdo, and asked fans who carried the "fight from within" to pledge support by joining the trust. An additional fan response involved a request to show visible support for the cause by wearing green and gold scarves to matches. This act displayed evidence of supporter disharmony to the 211 territories across the world where the EPL is broadcast. The Red Knights delayed their plans to make a formal offer to buy the club from the Glazers in June 2010, as they believed that the price likely to be asked would be too high (BBC News, 2010). The Green and Gold movement was initially well received by the militant Manchester United supporters who had formed the "fight from within" in 2005. For instance, the February 2010 edition of the *Red Issue* fanzine referred to it as "admirable in its intent and its base simplicity," but warned that it "alone will not have any tangible impact on the Glazers". The views of FC United supporters were split. Although the club made an official statement that offered "its support to the Green and Gold Campaign aimed at unifying supporters", not all fans shared this view. On the *FCUM-unofficial* online message board, a thread entitled "G&G [Green and Gold] is the Fashion, not the

Passion" was started, prompting 225 responses (24 February–12 March, 2010) by FC United fans:

> Well it is, isn't it?! More and more people keep going on about seeing fans wearing g&g scarves yet buying from the kiosks. Well here's the latest when you try to educate them. Posted on Facebook by some guy:
>
> > Quote:
> >   came out of old trafford, saw a bloke wearing GnG with a megawhore [referring to the club "megastore"] bag, let him know what i thought and tried to educate a little, turned around BANG straight into a lampost what a twat i am!! at least i tried!! (24 March 2010)

Subsequent threads reframed the debate to question further the authenticity of those choosing to wear green and gold scarves.[7] Another FC United fan tried to downplay the mobilization, arguing that he had witnessed "delectable student ensembles on Oxford Road over the last couple of days, incorporating the rich colors of the green and gold scarf" (24 March 2010). In both instances, these acts contravened the imagined cultural-geographical boundaries that ground claims of being a "real" fan.

Despite questions among some elements of the supporter base, the Green and Gold campaign did generate a level of success, even in the face of the club's rising debt levels. It was announced in March 2010 that ticket prices would remain at the same level for the following season, and Drasdo declared this to be "an incredible victory". The club's Chief Executive showed that the fan mobilization was agitating at least some in the club when he described the campaign as "a bit tiring" (quoted in Wallace, 2010, p. 76). These events highlight that the development of resistance identities communicated through Internet-based technologies had at least moderate levels of success—despite failing to end the Glazer family's ownership of the club.

LEGITIMIZING IDENTITIES

It is impossible to measure the number of people who identify themselves as supporting Manchester United. In May 2012, the club's official website announced the results of a survey undertaken by market research agency *Kantar*—it had 659 million followers across the world (Manchester United, 2012). Therefore, no matter how impressive the number of people taking part in various fan-led protests, it is almost certain that the majority of supporters display legitimizing identities. According to Castells (2004, p. 8), a legitimizing identity is "introduced by the dominant institutions of society to extend and rationalize their domination *vis à vis* social actors". As such, it is the formation of a personal or a collective identity that shows either apathy or active support regarding the prevailing conditions. In the context of Manchester United, these conditions include the Glazer family's purchase of the club, and the "hyper-commodification" of soccer in general (Walsh & Giulianotti, 2006). These attitudes are not often collectively organized, and so are not negotiated through online fan networks and forums, but they can be articulated in these digital spaces. One such example was provided by *View from Tier 3* blog-writer, Blanchette, who stated:

> Personally . . . I still do not care who owns the club. Having been born into the Martin Edwards era of club ownership, I had seen that they first and foremost cared about money and secondly about the fans. This is the commercial and corporate world that football sits in today . . . The Glazers should prepare to sell the club now. One thing that people do not recognize [is] that at the end of the day Manchester United is an asset in the global business of the Glazer family. And the truth is that it is them that pay the bills . . . not the fans. Yes we contribute with our shirt sales, season tickets, etc etc but they control the purse . . . for example I am wearing a Nike shirt—does it mean I should have a say in their financing? It's of no interest to them to make a loss at the football club . . . It will always be beyond me why supporters take so much interest on what goes on behind the scenes in the politics of a football club. Fans wish to be part of some sort of "family" and therefore think they have some emotional connection to absolutely everything. (Blanchette, 2010a)

Blanchette appears to express a consumer-oriented relationship with Manchester United—likening them to the sports brand Nike—that is at odds with more "traditional" forms of consumption (King, 2002). He does "not care who owns the club". However, after the Green and Gold protest began, his line of argument altered to one reflecting a resistance identity: "I will no longer wear my Red jersey to games anymore. I will now adopt the Green and Gold until this mess is sorted out . . . It's time to get active" (Blanchette, 2010b). This identifiable change of attitude was prompted by, first, leaked details of the refinancing of the club's debt by Glazer, which would increase the annual loan repayments. These details were communicated through the news media and online social media. Second, the aesthetic power of tens of thousands of scarves on display at the match had an impact. Most obviously, this change of position emphasizes the extent to which identifications can change from legitimizing to resistance identities in a short space of time. This positional malleability reflects the volatile environment of professional soccer, and the ways in which changes are announced and discussed in legacy and social media forms.

CONCLUSION: THE LIMITATIONS OF TECHNOLOGIES OF MASS SELF-COMMUNICATION

The power of identity is strong in the network society, and the sites of communication power are people's minds, which can regularly change (Castells, 2009). Blanchette personifies this pattern, as do the members of IMUSA who moved from resistance to project identities following the establishment of FC United. These shifts are also not mono-directional. Throughout the short lifespan of FC United, there have been reports of fans leaving their principal support of the club behind to attend once again matches at Manchester United. Identities, on a collective basis, are potentially powerful, but they are also immensely changeable and certainly far from fixed in time, space and culture. Castells identifies a clear link between power and identity, which may be advantageous to "ephemeral rulers" such as those involved in small-scale project identities because:

> identities anchor power in some areas of the social structure, and build from there their resistance or their offensives in the informational struggle about the cultural codes constructing behavior and, thus, new institutions. (Castells, 2004, pp. 424–25)

As such, supporter movements can alter some of the conditions in which soccer is played. Social networking technologies are able to assist in the formation of these groups, and yet, online communication technologies—in the context of Manchester United, soccer, business, sport or any area of society—can only be the sum of the ways in which they are used. Andy Mitten, the editor of *United We Stand* fanzine, captures the complicated and conflictual reality of this situation:

> The perception of United's whole support is being distorted by empty vessels who make the most noise. Websites, social media and radio phone-ins are full of people who call themselves United fans and yet have never seen the team live. They're an embarrassment, spoilt by too [much] information. They know everything, yet they know nothing. They can quote stats and pass ratios, yet wouldn't be able to recognise United's hardcore from city's [Manchester City] in the street because Sky don't do a slow mo of that and there isn't a link to it on Twitter. (February 2012, p. 3)

Rather than challenging the structures and practices of hyper-commodified soccer, technologies of mass self-communication (Castells, 2009) are routinely used by fans to announce blandly elements of their cultural identity. These acts can amount to little more than goading the supporters of opposing teams. Online forums and other digital network platforms offer the potential to facilitate the development of various identities, but they are not collective actions in and of themselves in the social world.

NOTES

1. Ticket prices had "gone up by an average of 48 per cent . . . and by as much as 69 per cent" in some areas of the club's Old Trafford stadium by the start of 2009–2010 season (Taylor, 2010, p. 1).
2. Rather, resistance identity communities may become an interest group and bargain for a position in the globalized network society (Castells, 2004, p. 357).
3. Rob Blanchette has established the popular blogs *View from Tier 3* (http://viewfromtier3.blogspot.com/) and *The Faithful* (http://thefaithfulmufc.com/).
4. Later renamed MUST or the Manchester United Supporters Trust.
5. For a background on online soccer fan forums, see Millward (2008), Ruddock (2005), Sanderson (2010) and W Wilson (2007).
6. Fans have been given numbers rather than their "real" online names to protect their privacy.
7. Castells (2009) argues that social movements hold greater cultural resonance when they receive celebrity endorsements and, in March 2010 at the end of a Champions League match at Old Trafford between Manchester United and AC Milan, David Beckham wore a green and gold scarf.

REFERENCES

BBC News (2010) Red Knights "to drop £1bn Man Utd bid". 30 May. Online. Available from: http://www.bbc.co.uk/news/10194568 (Accessed 30 May 2010).

Blanchette R (2010a) Why the Glazers should sell United NOW. *View From Tier 3*, 12 January. Online. Available from: http://viewfromtier3.blogspot.co.uk/2010/01/why-glazers-should-sell-united-now.html (Accessed 1 April 2012).

Blanchette R (2010b) MUFC Green & Gold army! United against the Glazers. *View From Tier 3*, 19 January. Online. Available from: http://viewfromtier3.blogspot.co.uk/2010/01/mufc-green-gold-army-united-against.html (Accessed 1 April 2012).

Blanchette R (2012a) Nice to tweet you: social media and its threat to football. *Red News*, January edition.

Blanchette R (2012b) The stinking pot of social media. *The Faithful*, 26 March. Online. Available from: http://thefaithfulmufc.com/2012/03/26/the-stinking-pot-of-social-media-red-issue-muamba/ (Accessed 26 March 2012).

Brady R (2006) *An Undividable Glow*. Manchester: Rubberybubberyboy Parchment.

Bridgewater S (2010) *Football Brands*. Basingstoke: MacMillan Palgrave.

Brown A (2007) "Not for sale"? The destruction and reformation of football communities in the Glazer takeover of Manchester United. *Soccer and Society* 8(4): 614–35.

Brown A (2008) Our club our rules: fan communities at F.C. United of Manchester. *Soccer & Society* 9(3): 346–58.

Brown A & Walsh A (1999) *Not For Sale: Manchester United, Murdoch and the Defeat of BSkyB*. London: Mainstream.

Castells M (1998) *End of the Millennium*. Oxford: Blackwell.

Castells M (2000) *The Rise of the Network Society*. Oxford: Blackwell.

Castells M (2004) *The Power of Identity*. Oxford: Blackwell.

Castells M (2009) *Communication Power*. Oxford: Oxford University Press.

Conn D (2010) Revealed: Truth about Glazer's business empire beyond Manchester United. *The Guardian*, 7 June. Online. Available from: http://www.guardian.co.uk/football/2010/jun/07/glazers-manchester-united-fortunes-wane (Accessed 7 June 2010)

Crossley N (1999) Working utopias and social movements: an investigation using case study material from the radical mental health movement in Britain. *Sociology* 33(4): 809–30.

Crowther P (2006) *Our Club Our Rules: F.C. United of Manchester*. Manchester: Lulu Books.

Freeman J (1973) The origins of the women's liberation movement. *American Journal of Sociology* 78(4): 792–811.

Friedman M (1999) *Consumer Boycotts: Effecting Change Through The Marketplace and the Media*. London: Routledge.

Habermas J (1986) *The Theory of Communicative Action (Vol. I): Reason and Rationalization of Society*. Cambridge: Polity.

Habermas J (1989) *The Theory of Communicative action (Vol. II): Critique of Functionalist Reason*. Cambridge: Polity.

Harris N (2010) Premier League nets £1.4bn TV rights bonanza. *The Independent*, 23 March. Online. Available from: http://www.independent.co.uk/sport/football/premier-league/premier-league-nets-16314bn-tv-rights-bonanza-1925462.html (Accessed 23 June 2010).

King A (1997) The lads: masculinity and the new consumption of football. *Sociology* 31(2): 329–46.

King A (2002) *The End of the Terraces: The Transformation of English Football in the 1990's*. London: Leicester University Press.

Lievrouw L (2011) *Alternative and Activist New Media*. Cambridge: Polity Press.

Manchester United (2012) World's most popular FC. 29 May. Online. Available from: http://www.manutd.com/en/News-And-Features/Club-News/2012/May/manchester-united-global-following-confirmed-as-659million.aspx?pageNo=1 (Accessed 1 June 2012).

Millward P (2008) The rebirth of the football fanzine: using e-zines as data source. *Journal of Sport and Social Issues* 32 (3): 299–310.

Millward P (2011) *The Global Football League: Transnational Networks, Social Movements and Sport in the New Media Age*. Basingstoke: Palgrave.

Mitten A (2012) Editorial. *United We Stand*, February edition.

Robson G (2000) *"No One Likes Us, We Don't Care": The Myth and Reality of Millwall Fandom*. Oxford: Berg.

Ruddock A (2005) Let's kick racism out of football—and the lefties too! *Journal of Sport & Social Issues* 29(4): 369–85.

Sanderson J (2010) Weighing in on the coaching decision: discussing sports and race online. *Journal of Language and Social Psychology* 29(3): 301–20.

Taylor I (1971a) Soccer consciousness and soccer hooliganism. In: Cohen S (ed.) *Images of Deviance*. Middlesex: Harmondsworth, 134–64.

Taylor I (1971b) "Football mad": a speculative sociology of football hooliganism. In: Dunning E (ed.) *The Sociology of Sport*. London: Frank Cass. 352–77.

Taylor I (1984) Professional sport and the recession: the case of British soccer. *International Review for the Sociology of Sport* 19: 7–30.

Wallace S (2010) Gill hits back at Green and Gold. *The Independent*, 28 May. Online. Available from: http://www.independent.co.uk/sport/football/news-and-comment/gill-hits-back-at-green-and-gold-1984930.html (Accessed 28 May 2010).

Walsh AJ & Giulianotti R (2006) *Ethics, Money and Sport.* Abingdon: Routledge.

Wilson J (2007) Premier League is world's favourite league. *The Telegraph*, 6 November. Online. Available from: http://www.telegraph.co.uk/sport/football/2325057/Premier-League-is-worlds-favourite-league.html (Accessed 6 June 2007).

Wilson W (2007) All together now, click: MLS soccer fans in cyberspace. *Soccer & Society* 8(2–3): 381–98.

Wood S (2008) *Trips on Glue: F.C. United of Manchester in the NPL Div 1 North 2007/8.* Manchester: Bookprinting.

11 "Born on Swan Street, Next to the Yarra"
Online Opinion Leaders and Inventing Commitment

Andy Ruddock

Born on Swan Street, Next to the Yarra,
Home or Away, It doesn't matter,
We'll follow you Melbourne to the top of the table,
Fight for your city! Fight for your people!

INTRODUCTION: RHYTHMS OF CULTURAL LIFE IN MEDIATIZED WORLDS

These are the lyrics to a chant by the "Yarraside", the main supporter group for the Melbourne Heart soccer club (henceforth, the Heart). The Heart was founded as the eleventh club in Australia's professional A-League competition, and started playing in the 2010–2011 season. Almost immediately, the Yarraside appeared as a visible body of highly committed supporters. In the words of one of its members:

> Yarraside is the "active" portion of the south end of the stadium. We stand for the length of games coordinating singing, chanting, displays, flags, banners etc. We believe that our support adds to the atmosphere at games and we aid the club on and off the pitch with a strong vocal and visual presence. (Braveheart, 2012)

The song begs the question of how a team that did not exist five years ago could stand for a city and a people that already boasted a championship-winning soccer side *and* nine existing professional Australian Rules clubs that play in the Australian Football League (AFL). To cynics, the irony was especially delicious since an author of the Yarraside anthem was an English migrant whose lasting allegiance was to another team.

Such anomalies are arguably characteristic of contemporary media sport. Indeed, the story of how the Yarraside assumed leadership of the Heart's support base exemplifies key concepts that audience researchers have used to explain how media organize social life. The Heart and its supporters have fabricated a tradition, using a suite of skilled "media practices"—daily habits through which people come to live many aspects of their lives in relation to media (Couldry, 2004). At key points, media practices have been marshaled by "opinion leaders" (Katz & Lazarsfeld, 1955) or people who employ media resources to win peer recognition and exert authority over other fans. These opinion leaders have been a resource for a young club that has struggled to find supporters in a highly competitive Melbourne sports market. The Heart and the Yarraside group of supporters constitutes a case study in the functioning of "media centres" (Couldry, 2003); that is, places that blend cultural rituals—daily practices that buttress deep-seated convictions about the way that life should be—and quotidian media habits. These centers make the presence of media and cultural industries indispensable to social life, and form the foundation of media power. The Yarraside is an intriguing microcosm of this process in action, using mediated opinion to rationalize a complex bargain. The "deal" struck by these fans is with a highly mediated and commercialized soccer club whose success depends on the conspicuous invention of tradition. The Yarraside, a collection of little more than one hundred people in a crowd that rarely tops 7,000 during live games, depicts how audiences help commercial media operations organize everyday life.

In advancing these arguments, this chapter explains how opinion leading complements contemporary approaches to audiences and media power, where the latter focuses on how fans actively participate in the interpretation, circulation and creation of media content. It examines the role that studies of soccer fans have played in theorizing "performance" and "media practice" as key analytical terms in audience research (Abercrombie & Longhurst, 1998; Couldry, 2011). In addition, the chapter presents a method for analyzing the online activities of soccer fans, paying special attention to ways of justifying the validity of small sample qualitative studies. In so doing, it looks at the media practices of Heart supporters and, especially, the digital opinion leading employed by the Yarraside. This examination involves analyzing the content of an Internet message board where potential Heart fans discuss the appeal of the new team. This forum was a crucial resource in two senses. First, it demonstrates how fans framed the appeal of the new club within the discourses of the knowledgeable, committed soccer fan. Second, it demonstrates the synthesis between media-related opinion leading and embodied fandom, as the Yarraside sought to promote itself as an effective and authoritative presence online and at the ground on game day. Ultimately, the Yarraside cleverly negotiates a sophisticated deal between the commercial realities of the media sports cultural complex (Rowe, 2004) and the pleasures of embodied fandom and, in the process, enact an almost seamless integration of media and social life. In this way, the Yarraside is shown to have captured the rhythm of cultural life in mediatized social worlds.

OPINION LEADERS, SOCCER FANS AND PERFORMANCE

Developed in the late 1940s, opinion leading is an important sensitizing concept that changed the direction of early media audience research. When most researchers were studying how advertising, political campaigning and the like could persuade audiences to change the way that they thought and behaved, Elihu Katz and Paul F. Lazarsfeld used this concept to offer a radically different perception of media power. Opinion leading suggested power "flowed" in often surprising directions because it was *mediated* by people. Katz and Lazarsfeld's evidence came from surveys and interviews conducted among 800 women from Decatur, Illinois. The women were asked how media influenced consumption choices, movie preferences, voting decisions and opinions on public affairs. On reading their responses, Katz and Lazarsfeld (1955) concluded that media power was "horizontal" in some respects. When shopping, voting or making their minds up about current events, women were most influenced by the opinions of people whom they knew, trusted and met through their interpersonal networks; not what they read in newspapers or heard on radio. However, these trusted figures—opinion leaders—*did* tend to pay attention to advertising, news and the like, because this content promised peer esteem. A factory worker, for example, may have enjoyed little power in traditional social and workplace hierarchies, but could claim prestige among her peers as a vernacular critic; that is, someone who gave good advice on "must-see" movies.

The apparent partnership between media and opinion leaders masked a deeper form of media dependency, where access to social status rested on access to media resources. Opinion leaders signified an emerging interest in the role that the media played in organizing social communication and identification within peer groups. Katz and Lazarsfeld described this role as a "convergence" between mass and interpersonal communication. Their choice to invoke a term synonymous with the digital age invites media scholars to consider continuities between recent studies of social media and identity, and ways of conceiving media influence that have been around for almost a century. The Yarraside's work in mustering support for the Heart helps demonstrate how these traditions fit together.[1] To understand this process, it is necessary to explore how cultural studies researchers have explained "media dependence" when describing what people do with media, and why soccer supporters have been important in tracking how media have colonized everyday life.

SOCCER FANS AS MEDIA AUDIENCES

Soccer fans make their first significant appearance at the "turning points" of critical audience research in Nicholas Abercrombie and Brian Longhurst's *Audiences: A Sociological Theory of Performance and Imagination*

(1998). This book argued that the global media industries depend on spectacular events whose allure relied significantly on public participation. Audiences become performers during such events and, according to Abercrombie and Longhurst, the transformation of soccer into a media sport encapsulated this shift. Audiences like watching audiences—for example, the appeal of soccer's World Cup is partly due to the spectacle of the packed stadium. The importance of this spectacle as part of the media event affords soccer fans the opportunity to perform national identities for global television audiences (Abercrombie & Longhurst, 1998). By the 1990s, soccer's ubiquity as a media event made it an ordinary resource for displaying identity and commitment almost all of the time—not simply in games that happened once a week or in tournaments played every four years. The spectacularization of professional soccer also depends on the "ordinary" power of the media to organize social life and identity among diffused audiences. Thanks to the media, soccer comes to matter in fairly intense ways to people who never go to live games. "Audience" here remains a pivotal concept for research on changing patterns of media production and public engagements with communications technologies and content, with soccer audiences standing as vivid emblems of these changes (Abercrombie & Longhurst, 2008).

Abercrombie and Longhurst's work was published just before the creation of two phenomena that moved media sport closer to the lives of so many people. First, the "digital plenitude" of networked and online media (Hutchins & Rowe, 2009), and, secondly, the rise of social networking media, which makes it easier for audiences to participate regularly in media sport cultures. Abercrombie and Longhurst's prescient identification of the "spectacle/performance paradigm" established a research agenda on a radical new form of media dependence, where access to media resources was the bedrock of social life, right down to the matter of individual identity. Like Katz and Lazarsfeld they are interested in the "convergence" between everyday and media communication.

When Nick Couldry revisited the purpose of audience studies in 2011, he did so to address the same intersection. His work on media practice focused on what people did with media in the course of doing other things and in thinking of themselves in other ways. Media practice identified the ultimate convergence between social rituals and media habits in a world where it is now rare to have one without the other. The simple act of watching a soccer game on television summarized the sort of "audiencing" power that Couldry wished to describe:

> The fact that people perform a huge range of practices (from fandom to family interaction to group solidarity in a pub to just waiting for something else to do) via the act of watching televised football is itself an example of the time-space coordination of practices through media schedules. (2011, p. 219)

Watching a televised soccer game is a social action that exists in *relation* to media, is a response to the fact of media saturation, and largely accepts the terms on which that saturation is offered. Even if the meaning of that match varies according to the desires of the user, every sort of viewer "act[s] out in formalized ways category differences that reproduce in condensed form the idea . . . that media are our access to society's centre" (Couldry, 2003, p. 52). Media organize social life since life has always depended on ritual, "action that is associated with transcendent values" (Couldry, 2004, p. 22), and rituals are routinely exercised through media habits. Media practices are, therefore, "a special type of ritual action, distinguished by a particular type of relation to . . . media processes" (2004, p. 23). Couldry describes a situation where the convergence between mass and interpersonal communication that had fascinated Katz and Lazarsfeld was happening through the ritual pleasures of mediated soccer.[2]

As a concept, media practice combines notions of performance and creativity to make the point that the power of media industries is a lived experience because it offers substantial social rewards. Phrased this way, media practice clears the path that Katz and Lazarsfeld could only hint at in their work on opinion leaders. Seen from this perspective, the Yarraside and the Heart are interesting as an audience with a stake in using social media to help a new sports media franchise achieve its goals. They do this by leading opinion toward the view that a new, privately owned club is not an opportunistic commercial gambit, but a worthy attempt to command genuine loyalty in keeping with the traditions of soccer fandom.

MELBOURNE HEART AND THE INTERNET

The research presented here uses a simple method that is applied to a "sliver" of the actions of Melbourne Heart supporters. On 14 November 2009, a thread started on the Australian fan website bigfooty.com asked who intended to support the Heart and why, as the club prepared for its launch (Billyboutsis, 2009). The thread was ongoing, running into January 2012, at which point it had attracted 691 posts. This analysis studied 521 of them, covering the period up until September 2011, when attention turned to the team's second season. The thread represented an almost two-year discussion of the club, its foundation, the expectations of the fans, the extent to which those expectations were being met, and the ways in which fans reacted to the packaging of the club as a meaningful experience.[3]

The thread was coded using Nvivo 9 software. Categories of response, which were developed through sensitizing themes derived from the existing literature on media audiences and soccer fans, were classified according to the factors that determined whether or not fans lent their support to the new team. Broadly speaking, classification involved looking for posts that discussed commercial appeals, the role of the media in building the club and aspects of the Heart that were grounded in more traditional sporting concerns, such as the playing and coaching staff, how the new club would fit into the history of Melbourne soccer (particularly in its appeal to different ethnic groups) and feelings about the new stadium. As a media audiences project, coding also looked for posts that expressed opinions on the mediatization of sport, and that exercised forms of "digital opinion leading" through the sharing of media content and active attempts to persuade others that the Heart deserved support. The goal of this exercise was to establish a general, descriptive pattern of the cultural matters and supporting experience that shaped the Heart's first season, and to contextualize how the Yarraside built itself as an integral part of the experience. This approach was then augmented with a more qualitative approach, with posts from Yarraside members used to outline how the group used the thread to promote itself and establish a position of cultural authority.

The method here codes posts into categories of response, sensitized by themes in sports media and audience studies on the phenomena that synthesize media and social life (see Table 11.1). It produces quantitative data that identify patterns of response and general reasons why soccer followers thought that the Heart deserved support (or not). The evidence is then examined qualitatively to look for the cultural and media processes that particular people engaged in to make their decisions. Having delineated the "shape" of the Heart's supporting culture, the study then examines how supporters used online media to sustain that "shape". The purpose of this section is to examine how people construct online identities that win respect for their ability to navigate the cultural and economic realities that constitute contemporary sport.

Table 11.1 Reasons for supporting the Melbourne Heart.

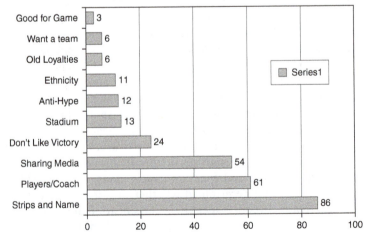

The most conspicuous finding here is that the thread's reflections on marketing were largely positive. Posters were more interested in the prospective name of the club and the design and color of the playing strip than in anything else. This interest signifies how this group of fans was more concerned with the presentation of this new soccer experience than how the Heart might represent existing community or sporting traditions. As much as posters differed in their opinions about the suggested names and strips, no one questioned the validity of using such criteria to decide whether they should follow the team. Moreover, approximately twenty percent of the coded posts involved sharing links to other media content—stories about potential names and signings, images of possible strips and the like. By and large, then, posters saw the spectacle constructed before their eyes, and were happy to accept it into the Australian sporting landscape. Discussions about marketing were slightly more frequent than debates over potential signings, but far outstripped others on how the club could profit from a history of soccer fan rivalry that predated not only the Heart but also the A-League itself.

Against the impression of a "boil kettle and pour" instant club, some suggested that the core of success lay in the Heart's appeal to the city's Croatian community, who had been historically apathetic about the Melbourne Victory, the city's existing club that had won the A-League twice since 2006. This idea attracted only eleven posts, several of which were dismissive of the suggestion. In contrast, twenty-four posters stated that the Heart appealed to them because they had never emotionally connected with the Victory. Most of the people who posted to the thread were more interested in the "now" than the past and were happy to enjoy the novelty of seeing a team created, partly by sharing media content with other fans via social networks. These activities, it seems, were a crucial tactic in preparing for the pleasures of the live soccer event. The Heart appealed to people who wanted to spend time preparing for live games and the presence of social media helped them to share this anticipation with anonymous others online. Heart supporters wanted a satisfying soccer experience, Melbourne's sporting culture had yet to provide them with one, and so they were happy to embrace the "joy of the new" as long as it had the right name, strip, players and ground. These preferences explain the fact that posters were more interested in marketing debates than in discussing the role of the club in the city's sporting history. This fascination also rejected the notion that anyone "seduced" by the commercialized appeals of a brand new club was just a *dilettante*.

The thread supports the claim made by Garry Crawford (2004) that the phatic pleasures of fan gossip are increasingly occupied with discussions of the commercial aspects of sport, with the business of sport having become a source of cultural capital rather than of irritation. This argument is further supported by the lack of criticism about the role of online and news media in creating the club. The Heart attracted attention by enlisting the Melbourne's

Herald Sun newspaper to run a poll where readers could vote for the new name. This tactic, and other commercial aspects of the operation (such as disdain for the way that A-League clubs selected gaudy, attention grabbing names, and the issue of corporate sponsorship of stadiums), attracted just twelve comments ("Anti-Hype").

RECONCILING WITH TRADITION: ENTER THE YARRASIDE

Opinion leading became a relevant factor in this research when considering accommodations between commercial practices and supporting traditions. The online actions of the Yarraside were crucial in this respect, especially in the actions of one key poster, who put considerable effort into creating what we might call the Heart's foundational "myth". On 28 May 2010, "Liverpool Red" announced the formation of the Yarraside in the most substantial post on the thread at almost one thousand words long. The post was more akin to a press release announcing the name, location, dress code, social rituals, joining procedures and, importantly, the website for the group that would promote the Heart's identity as a club worth supporting. In his own words:

> After months of deliberation and toil, Melbourne's newest football club finally has a strong, knowledgeable and clandestine terrace group to match its on field success with off field enthusiasm, passion and active support. (Liverpool Red, 2010)

The use of "clandestine" was a little misleading. Scott Munn, the Heart's CEO, had commented publicly on the good relationship that he enjoyed with the Yarraside. Munn thought this a relationship worth cultivating, as the Yarraside was crucial to the appeal of live games (Ormond, 2011). Indeed, those spectators observe that the group enjoys a cordial relationship with ground stewards. This harmony reflects the fact that, according to the accounts of Liverpool Red at least, the group generally engages with the commercial aspects of the club on positive terms. Yarraside's online presence is, importantly, a significant foundation for game day *bonhomie*, and Liverpool Red a key figure in showing how online identities help the Yarraside maintain its leading position in the Heart's supporter base.

The Yarraside justified its existence on the notion that any "real club" needed an identifiable group of noisy, distinct and visible supporters at home games. This presence depended on a gentle antagonism between this group and the game's authorities. But this was a friendly conflict that accepted the need to build soccer as a spectacle and use media resources where necessary, while also understanding the need for systematic business planning. This logic can be traced from the "publicity release", Liverpool Red's regular posts and the Web activities embraced by the Yarraside. In terms of the embodied, rebellious fan, it was noted:

> The Yarraside will be an active supporter terrace. This means that we show our support for the club we love all the time. As a result, from the kick off to the final whistle, we will stand, chant, sing and support for the full 90 minutes. It is imperative that we show our club and the rest of the footballing public that we are a legitimate, passionate and traditional body of support . . . just because the FFA (Football Federation Australia) wants us to sit in the seat they tell us, it doesn't mean we will give up the feeling of a real football terrace, will we lads! (Liverpool Red, 2010)

At the same time, Liverpool Red constructed himself in other places as a citizen of world soccer who was pragmatically engaged with the global game. Another poster criticized A-League fans that attended games wearing EPL shirts. At this point, Liverpool Red was compelled to make his priorities clear:

> I am a part of the Heart Terrace, but my support for Liverpool has been there all of my life . . . I am a Liverpool fan before I am Heart . . . In saying that, I won't be wearing my Liverpool top at the game, because I don't believe in this whole commercialised football shit, but any fan who does, I won't have a problem with. (Liverpool Red, cited in Billyboutsis)

So, if Liverpool Red did not *believe* in "commercialised football shit", he was certainly willing to engage with it and with those who do. Far from home, Liverpool Red resurrected a clearly cherished supporter identity, helped by a global soccer business where the notion of the franchise is not *anathema* to sporting pleasure. Included here was sensitivity to the importance of online actions. Liverpool Red claimed his authority not only by leading chants in the stadium, but also through online discussions and by competing with commercial news media in "breaking" news about player signings. For instance, he hinted heavily at the signing of John Aloisi, one of Australia's most successful players, before professional journalists got hold of the story.

Liverpool Red's intervention in the *BigFooty* thread indicated how Yarraside's online presence was an important tool for negotiating relations with other fans, marking a distinctive departure from the hostility to "armchair supporters" found in other studies. In my research on *Knees Up Mother Brown* (2005), a forum run for supporters of West Ham United, fans who attended live games used online media to taunt those who did not, or who attended only on rare occasions. No effort was made to explain the attitudes and behavior that onlookers found offensive. In contrast, the

Yarraside expended considerable online effort explaining who they were and why their presence mattered to anyone who was interested in the new club, especially as the group had to form online before it could be appreciated as a core aspect of the live game. For example, online opinion leading was important in legitimating the group's decision to ignore certain rules of behavior, such as its refusal to sit in seats during matches. Online opinion leading made it clear that flouting this law was not meant as an affront to security staff and helped smooth relations with club officials. In this sense, the live experience was situated within a framework of meaning that had been built online.

The patterns described here tell us about how Heart fans understood themselves in relation to established soccer supporter traditions. On one level, literature on soccer supporters suggests that any notion that people can be won over with new teams, shiny strips and consumer-friendly stadiums is an affront to supporting traditions that have long claimed to be about loyalty to local histories. At another level, this same literature presents these traditions as mythic constructions and the Heart provides unique insight into how these myths are made. Longstanding soccer supporters often think about their loyalties in relation to geography. They and their team share common cultural identities by virtue of where they are in the world, and their bond is rationalized as a matter of duty, not of choice (Brown, Crabbe & Mellor, 2008; Millward, 2011). This type of soccer supporter believes that they embody an organic identity that cannot be manufactured by corporate culture. However, it should be remembered that this belief is based on a contestable *argument*. The "traditional soccer supporter" is a myth, insofar as it is a political rationalization that draws on a contestable reading of cultural history (Barthes, 1957).

Reviewing the history of soccer fandom in the UK, Adam Brown, Tim Crabbe and Gavin Mellor (2008) contend that the dogmatism of "traditionalists" both reflects and ignores a deep crisis in the very notion of community. In the UK, professional soccer clubs have largely stayed in the same physical place while the demographic make-up of their community has changed. For all the gloss of global branding exercises, these same clubs have been unwittingly caught up in a debate about what constitutes community in a world of mobility and cultural flux (Brown et al., 2008). Provocatively, Brown et al. argue that this has always been the case. English clubs that command the most intense traditional support were founded in large industrial towns in the nineteenth century where new urban populations initially had little in common, and they succeeded because these clubs were places where people could generate new social bonds. These same clubs began to appeal to supporters from beyond their immediate *environs* from the 1930s onwards. For all their appeal to place, soccer clubs are fundamentally *ideas* that "embody many of the collective symbols, identifications and *processes of connectivity* which have long been associated with the notion of community" (p. 303, emphasis added). The figure of the traditional supporter as the bearer of organic cultural traditions is mythic, insofar as it is first and foremost a principle that is made and defended in daily fan practices.

As Millward (2011, and also in this book) points out, these practices have become increasingly media dependent. He explains how fanzines and then Internet message boards became valuable resources for supporters seeking to achieve peer recognition and respect by *presenting* themselves to others as the true bearers of tradition. Such actions have become especially important when fans of clubs (such as Liverpool FC and Manchester United) attempt to mobilize worldwide support to stop global corporate raiders from buying their teams and stripping their associated assets. Two ideas relate these analyses to studies of media audiences in general and to the case of Melbourne Heart in particular. Soccer support has always been about telling stories of genuine connection made by people in a chaotic world. These stories become myths through organized acts of opinion leading, which has become more widely practiced as it has moved from the relatively limited fanzine culture to the accessible spaces of the Web. The construction of fan myths on the Internet is an example of the sort of media-dependent social identity to which Katz and Lazarsfeld gestured with the figure of the opinion leader—the person whose social status depends on the ability to win respect by mustering media resources. Seen in this way, the rapid invention of the Heart and the Yarraside is a condensation of the cultural processes that have always given soccer meaning. The speed with which this myth was constructed and structured as a media spectacle reflects the intensification of myth making in the digital age (Mosco, 2004). If soccer support is best thought of as a "process of connectivity", a figure such as Liverpool Red shows how digital networks connect media and interpersonal communication. He is noteworthy as a sport media opinion leader; that is, as someone who uses online communities and other media resources to achieve an image of authority by sharing news, analysis and general guidance.

CONCLUSION: LESSONS FOR CRITICAL AUDIENCE STUDIES

The Heart and the Yarraside took shape before any whistle blew or goal was scored. Many prospective fans were happy to confess that the right strip, name and ground could attract them to a team with no history. As an opinion leader, Liverpool Red *gave* them this history by using online forums to frame arguments, share media links, provide journalistic style commentary and information, and generally offer a "benediction", assuring Heart fans that theirs is a rightful place at the soccer fan table. In the world of the global soccer supporter, it is not surprising that an Englishman can sing "Born on Swan Street, Next to the Yarra" with gusto. His decision to follow the Melbourne Heart was a strategic choice designed to extend his "career" as a soccer fan. He and the Yarraside demonstrate how access to media resources, and to other people through them, has become integral to the public life of the soccer supporter. The point made by studies of online soccer fans is that performances on online message boards are as much a part of "being seen" as gathering in the pub before the game or in the stands at kick-off. The Melbourne Heart case study is especially valuable for the field of audience studies. It shows how message boards are part of the materiality of the soccer supporter, allowing the democratized "fabrication" of a tradition to be an authentic and rationalized means of finding pleasure and community in a heavily commodified world.

The case study presented here also speaks to the core of critical audience studies. This field is driven by two questions: how do the public make media power real by completing circuits of cultural production (Lewis, 1992), and to what extent does media pleasure depend on a willingness to accept the rules of the media business that put profit first (Carey, 1989; Couldry, 2004; Gerbner, 1998; Turner, 2011)? Studying how Heart fans interpreted appeals for their support, and how they used social media to recruit others, provides intriguing answers to both questions when viewed through the concepts of performance, media practice and opinion leading. In combination, these ideas show why mediated sports and their audiences are locked into a cycle of unequal codependence. The Yarraside could only claim its rightful place in the hierarchy of authentic soccer fandom by engaging with *media* sport. The story of the Heart and the Yarraside outlines the conditions that have made it impossible to have cultural experiences that feel authentic without entering into bargains with commercial and other media operations.

NOTES

1. Other writers have pointed out that *Personal Influence* was a complex study whose significance is still being unraveled. Lang and Lang (2007) note that many of the exceptions taken to the study were really more about how the work had been adopted by other scholars, rather than what Katz and Lazarsfeld had actually written. Indeed, the delay in publishing the study suggested that even the researchers were at odds over what they had found.
2. See Ruddock (2012) for more on Couldry, online soccer communities and ritual.
3. The thread features an interesting gap from 10 October 2010 to 21 May 2011. That is, it features no discussion of games during the inaugural season. In this sense, the thread is notable as a place where soccer fans seemed to "preview" and review the overall Heart experience, as distinct from the everyday chatter about performances in the league and on the field.

REFERENCES

Abercrombie N & Longhurst B (1998) *Audiences: A Sociological Theory or Performance and Imagination.* London: Sage.
Barthes R (1957) *Mythologies.* New York: Hill and Wang.

Billyboutsis (2009) *Who Intends Being a Melbourne Heart Fan?* Online. Available from: http://www.bigfooty.com/forum/showthread.php?s=bf49b917df288d6e4c-2c12c0aba19189&t=652137 (Accessed 15 January 2012).

Braveheart (2012) The different supporter groups. Online. Available from: http://mhfcsupporters.com/topic/149-the-different-supporter-groups/ (Accessed 28 January 2012).

Brown A, Crabbe T & Mellor G (2008) Introduction: football and community-practical and theoretical considerations. *Soccer and Society* 9 (3): 303–12.

Carey J (1989) *Communication as Culture*. Boston: Unwin Hyman.

Couldry N (2003) *Media Rituals: A Critical Approach*. London: Routledge.

Couldry N (2004) Theorising media as practice. *Social Semiotics* 12 (2): 115–32.

Couldry N (2011) The necessary future of the audience . . . and how to research it. In: Nightingale V (ed.) (2011) *The Handbook of Media Audiences*. London: Routledge, 213–29.

Crawford G (2004) *Consuming Sport: Fans, Sport and Culture*. London: Routledge.

Gerbner G (1998) Cultivation analysis: an overview. *Mass Communication and Society* 1(3–4): 175–95.

Hutchins B & Rowe D (2009) From broadcasting rationing to digital plenitude: the changing dynamics of the media sport content economy. *Television & New Media*. 10(4): 354–70.

Katz E & Lazarsfeld P (1955) *Personal Influence: The Part Played by People in the Flow of Mass Communication*. Glencoe, ILL: Free Press.

Lang K & Lang GE (2006) Personal influence and the new paradigm: some inadvertent consequences. *The Annals of the American Academy of Political and Social Science* 608 (1): 233–50.

Lewis J (1992) *The Ideological Octopus*. London: Routledge.

Liverpool Red (2010) *The Wait Is Over!* Online. Available from: http://www.bigfooty.com/forum/showthread.php?t=652137&page=24 (Accessed 15 January 2012).

Millward P (2011) *The Global Football League: Transnational Networks, Social Movements and Sport in the New Media Age*. London: Palgrave.

Mosco V (2004) *The Digital Sublime: Myth, Power, and Cyberspace*. Cambridge, MA: The MIT Press.

Ormond A (2011). *Marrone's Italian Heartbreak*. Online. Available from: http://au.fourfourtwo.com/print.aspx?CIID=270933 (Accessed 15 January 2012).

Rowe D (2004) *Sport, Culture, and the Media*. 2nd ed. Maidenhead, Berkshire: Open University Press.

Ruddock A (2005) Let's kick racism out of football: and the lefties too! Responses to Lee Bowyer on a West Ham web site. *Journal of Sport and Social Issues* 29(4): 369–85.

Ruddock A (2012) Cultivation analysis and cultural studies. In: Shanahan J, Morgan M & Signorelli N (eds.) *Cultivation Analysis: New Theoretical and Methodological Dimensions*. New York: Peter Lang, 367–85.

Turner G (2010) Approaching celebrity studies. *Celebrity Studies* 1(1): 11–20.

Part III

Content Ecologies, Social Software and Games

12 New Media Technologies in Lifestyle Sport

Paul Gilchrist and Belinda Wheaton

INTRODUCTION: SUBCULTURAL LIFE AND SOCIAL NETWORKING

Detailed attention to the role of "specialist" or subcultural media in the creation and evolution of sporting subcultures, and the construction and performance of identities in different sporting contexts, is surprisingly limited (Wheaton & Beal, 2003). As sociologist Brian Wilson argues, "given the increasingly global character of sport subcultures" and the "long-standing relationship between these groups and both mass and niche media", it is extremely surprising that "so little research in the sociology of sport literature has examined the role of the internet in subcultural life" (Wilson, 2008, p. 149). Our focus here is to explore the location and use of media in the lives of lifestyle sport participants. Discussing the use of social networking sites and platforms in parkour, we locate the adoption of media technologies historically, turning to the more established lifestyle sports of climbing and surfing in order to contextualize the role of the media in subcultural life. Theoretically, our research is located in previous work on sporting subcultural formations (Atkinson & Young, 2008b; Wheaton, 2007) emerging from the post-Centre for Contemporary Cultural Studies (CCCS) conceptualization of youth subcultures (Bennett & Kahn-Harris, 2004; Muggleton & Weinzierl, 2003), and their relationship to mainstream and niche media (Wheaton & Beal, 2003). It is also informed by audience research in media and cultural studies, particularly the "new paradigm" (Abercrombie & Longhurst, 1998) sometimes termed that of "spectacle/performance" (see Chapter 11). This approach recognizes the active role that consumers perform as both performers and audiences in their everyday, media-saturated lives.

Lifestyle sport refers to a range of mostly individualized activities, from established and residual sports like climbing, surfing and skateboarding, to newer activities like parkour, wake boarding, B.A.S.E. jumping, and kite surfing (Wheaton, 2004, p. 140; Wheaton, forthcoming). Numerous commentaries have been produced that identify the key characteristics of lifestyle sports' histories, ideologies and contributions to new forms of social identity. These sports are marked by their negation of, and challenge to, Western "achievement" sport cultures, often taking place in spaces lacking regulation and control and taking on forms that diverge from traditional rule-bound, competitive and institutionalized sport. Importantly for our purposes here, while they are activities that have historically been outside "mainstream" sport media provision,[1] lifestyle sport subcultures such as surfing and skateboarding have also been pioneering in their adoption of media technologies and evolving forms of "do-it-yourself" (DIY) media production and distribution. Indeed, although lifestyle sports have failed to make much of an impact on the mainstream media's sporting schedules, their impact on the broader mediascape is pervasive. For example, ESPN's X Games—the spiritual home of the extreme sport phenomenon—sits at the center of the global diffusion and expansion of lifestyle sport, and has been extremely successful in attracting youth audiences (Rinehart, 2008; Thorpe & Wheaton, 2011). Blurring the boundaries between music festival and sporting event, the X Games offers spectators, viewers and athletes a unique physical, visual and virtual experience that differs from traditional sporting events (Rinehart, 2008). An array of interactive digital media technologies is used actively to engage fans. For instance, during the 2009 Winter X Games, viewers and spectators were given the chance to vote via text message to determine the winners of events such as the Ski and Snowboard Big Air competition. The success of the X Games in attracting younger audiences has been noted by the Olympic movement, which has borrowed many of its strategies in a bid to "modernize" its events (Thorpe & Wheaton, 2011).

This chapter documents the ways in which social networking sites and digital media technologies have had a profound impact on how we view subcultural life, particularly the ways in which it enables interaction and exchange between subcultural groups and participants at a global level. However, we are mindful of tendencies to "overstate the impact of the internet on social life" (Wilson, 2008, p. 141), recognizing that there are important continuities with pre-Internet forms of communication and niche media. Research has tended to explore various online subcultures without adequately acknowledging the multiple ways in which Internet-based experiences (e.g., chat rooms, blogs, emails, social media websites) are also related to off-line activities (see Wilson, 2008; Wilson & Atkinson, 2005). Thus, in assessing the impacts of various new media technologies on lifestyle sport subcultures, a historical perspective is adopted, reminding us that the use of niche DIY media is a longstanding feature of these cultures.

LIFESTYLE SPORT AND THE DEVELOPMENT OF NICHE MEDIA: A GENEALOGY

The application of new technologies has been crucial to the transformation of the mountain as a distant object of Romantic reverence to one of sporting consumption. Advances in optics in the nineteenth century, particularly through the production of telescopes, turned mountaineering into a public spectacle as voyeuristic tourists flocked to the Alps to view climbing bodies. Mountains became theatrical spaces and sites of high drama and intrigue (Colley, 2010). By the latter half of the nineteenth century, the use of cameras by mountaineers brought new and additional meanings to the sport. As Douglas A. Brown argues, photographs were not merely reproductions, they were extensions of what the climber desired to feel. The use of photography allowed climbers to reconfigure their aesthetic expectations, and to gradually dismantle Romantic notions of the picturesque and the sublime that had framed the experience of the mountains for more than a century. The camera lens enabled new relationships between the mountaineer, nature and landscape to form, in the process redefining what was beautiful, spectacular and worth the physical effort (Brown, 2007). By the mid-1920s, the summit photo was a habitual part of the climbing experience, becoming a conventional way of marking personal and group achievement.

Documentary film was embraced by mountaineering expeditions, famously employed in the 1922 and 1924 Mount Everest expeditions to document sporting achievements. Film was also used as a promotional tool and saleable product to defray costs and to garner support for further expeditions. In the post-war era, interest in climbing stimulated by television—which was now able to provide up-close and live images using lightweight portable cameras—enabled a new generation of working-class climbers to forge careers out of the activity, turning them into household names (Gilchrist, 2007; Osborne, 2010). These examples reveal that we need to proceed with a degree of analytical precision and historical awareness when identifying the impact of media technologies on lifestyle sport. This history informs the types of claim that we can make about the role of media technologies in attracting participants and audiences, bringing action into the domestic sphere, creating new celebrities, and altering the social rituals of lived experience.

Nevertheless, changes have occurred. With regard to climbing, it has now become an increasingly accepted practice to use social networking sites to relay progress. The first ascent of the northwest face of the Great Trango Tower in Pakistan in 1999 involved a film crew and daily Web updates via an elaborate satellite link-up to base camp. This arrangement led to fears that, if the practice was widely adopted, the publicity would marginalize achievements on harder routes and lead experienced climbers to chase commercial avenues, rather than to take on new challenges at the boundaries of the sport (Chabaline, Gadd & House, 2000). Despite these misgivings, "from-the-route" uses of social networking sites are now common amongst individual climbers seeking adventure beyond the well-funded large expedition. Climbers in Yosemite in the US, for instance, have provided real-time commentary through the use of solar-charged Apple iPhones to update Facebook pages for thousands of followers. This practice has led the climbing "establishment" to express concern over potentially altered attitudes to risk, or what is known as "Kodak courage"—the tendency to go beyond one's physical limits when photographed or filmed (Gasperini, 1999)—and the diminishment of the concentration needed to execute careful movements. Put simply, how can one climb properly and safely if "glued" to the iPhone? (Lowther, 2011).

The relationship between the culture of surfing and evolving media technologies is also well documented. Here, as with climbing, still and moving images popularized the activity amongst participants and wider constituencies. As Douglas Booth (2001) outlines, the Hollywood beach movies (produced in the 1950s) and surfing niche media, initially films (1950s) and subsequently magazines (from the 1960s) and videos, played a central role in growing the global popularity of surfing. While commercial films about surfing, such as the AIP Hollywood beach movies, were apparently shunned by the surfing "community", specialist surf films "produced by surfers for surfing audiences" quickly became important products, often consumed in communal settings and "explaining surfing and surfers to themselves" (Booth, 2001, p. 94). By the 1980s, mass-produced surf films were replaced by a proliferation of videos and then DVDs, predominantly produced by the surf industry[2] (mainly equipment and clothing manufacturers) as a cost-effective way to promote their products via sponsored riders. These sponsored media texts represented, Booth argues, a "distinctively new post-Fordist form of production" that helped to define the niche market (Booth, 1996).

By the 1990s, magazines were produced and distributed across national boundaries, targeting an increasingly broad and fragmented surfing audience. The magazines served important functions, for instance, deepening the sense of belonging to a unique community of participants. As Wheaton (2003) has argued, they should be seen as both "information bearers" and "membership documents" regarding how they inform readers about the sports value system and lifestyle and, particularly, about forms of insider knowledge concerning equipment, skills and techniques. However, the space of surfing magazines—like the subculture itself—was a (contested) male world in which female performers were tolerated, but only if their presence did not challenge the male hegemony of elite sport (Booth, 1996; Booth, 2008; Henderson, 2001; Wheaton, 2003). While the most popular surfing magazines like *Tracks* centered on young, White and male short-board riders, publications also emerged for female surfers (e.g. *Surfer Girl* and *Wahine*), for "soul" surfers (*The Surfer's Path* and *The Surfer's Journal*), and for paddle surfing specific publications (*SUP*)(see also Booth, 2008, p. 22).

These magazines share conventions with surf films. Action photographs dominate the magazine content, and large telephoto lenses and fast shutter speeds freeze and dramatize the action (Wheaton, 2003). As Ford and Brown (2005, p. 33) argue, surfing is primarily a visual culture, and photography drives the sale of surfing magazines. As in mountaineering culture, the natural environment is pronounced in the visual presentation of this sport, with waves and the ocean taking center stage. Photographic images focus on rhythm and power, using techniques such as under-water photography, boats, jet skis and poles to provide an "authentic representation" of the ocean. These techniques reproduce the surfer's point of view, particularly the experience of being inside waves or "tubes" (Ormrod, 2007).

Despite the centrality of films and magazines to the evolution of surfing subcultures, the last decade has seen a wide range of digital media emerge in the shape of online forums, interactive webpages, Web magazines and films. Commercially produced print magazines have developed online versions (which, in some cases, require a paid subscription) and these texts now sit alongside a range of on-line self-published products. As is documented in relation to climbing and in the case of parkour below, technological advances in video equipment have revolutionized participant-driven audiovisual production and the Internet provides the means for content distribution. Social networking sites are used to relay progress on "surfaris", and DIY movies and images are posted on sites like YouTube and the surf weather forecast site, Magic Seaweed. Yet, these digital media tools have supplemented rather than replaced established media forms, and many of the same stylistic conventions are replicated. As Wilson highlights, the distinctions between the virtual and real are often more relevant for scholars than the subculturalists who use them, as their "cultural lives include relatively seamless and frequent transitions across the appropriate online-offline divide" (Wilson, 2008, p. 135).

NEW MEDIA AND LIFESTYLE SPORT: THE CASE OF PARKOUR

The remainder of this chapter presents a case study developed from research into the emergence and institutionalization of parkour in the UK (see Gilchrist & Wheaton, 2011). Parkour is a form of human movement that focuses on "efficient motion" over, under, around or through "human-made" or naturally occurring obstacles by jumping, vaulting and climbing. The activity originated in the Paris suburbs in the 1980s, although pioneers trace its history back to Georges Hébert's natural method (*méthode naturelle*), originally a military training method for the French army (Ortuzar, 2009, p. 61). Parkour has been described as both sport *and* art, exhibiting forms and styles that intersect with dance, martial arts and gymnastics. Academic research on parkour has tended to describe how parkour provides a novel way of interacting with the (urban) environment that challenges the use and meaning of urban space, metropolitan life and embodiment (see Atkinson, 2009; Bavinton, 2007; Ortuzar, 2009).

Our study had a broad remit, which is to understand the social benefits that accrue from participation in parkour[3], both for participants and authorities that are investing in infrastructure and in the development of the sport. The study took us around the UK. We interviewed young *traceurs* (30 parkour practitioners) in their own communities at nine different sites, and discussed their biographies, aspirations and involvement in efforts to develop the sport. However, it soon became apparent that digital media were an important means of communication, connecting participants translocally and transnationally (for some). We recorded instances where the use of digital media was central to participation and involvement in the subculture. Furthermore, we created a repository of websites and media used by the participants to help us understand the importance of communication technologies within the subculture, as well as the institutionalization and globalization of the sport. What follows is a brief discussion of our findings relating to the centrality of digital media to parkour culture.

Our discussion here focuses on three interrelated themes. First, we highlight the way in which blogs and video-sharing websites (e.g., YouTube) are widely credited as enhancing the transnational popularity of the sport. Second, we explore how, in contrast to the longer-standing lifestyle sport cultures of surfing and climbing, parkour participants predominantly use interactive "social software" tools (Bruns, 2008), rather than the mix of traditional niche media forms observed in most lifestyle sporting subcultures. Third, we explore *how* these digital media tools are used in parkour for communication, learning about the activity and its culture as a creative form of performance and self-expression, and as a potential route to entrepreneurial activity.

THE EMERGENCE OF PARKOUR AND THE MEDIA: CONNECTING THE TRIBE

For much of its existence parkour was an underground activity with low participation rates, and conducted in the back streets and plazas of cities. Many city dwellers were, and still are, unaware of its existence. However, via exposure in the media, parkour has become an increasingly conspicuous cultural commodity. Although digital media and online communications are widely credited as being central to the growing transnational popularity of the sport (Angel, 2011), it is through traditional media that the original founders and leading protagonists of parkour found a wider audience. Luc Besson, the French filmmaker, initially offered (founding participant) David Belle and his colleagues work in his film *Taxi 2*, and later produced a film based on the group titled, *Yamakasi, les samourai's des temps modernes*. This is a big budget action film that follows seven *traceurs* through the *banlieue* (poor, migrant-dense suburbs) of Paris.[4] Parkour has been picked up by a range of advertisers (e.g., Nike, Swatch, KSwiss, Canon, Scion cars and Go-Cat), while pop stars have been keen to use the urban and athletic spectacle that has characterized its media appropriation. Both Madonna and David Guetta have featured parkour in music videos for hit singles, while Sebastien Foucan, a founder of parkour, featured in the opening chase sequence in *Casino Royale* (2006) in the James Bond movie franchise.

The visibility and presence of parkour in the UK changed overnight after the broadcast of a documentary, Mike Christie's *Jump London* (2003) on Channel 4. The film showcased freerunning through the landmarks of the capital and is widely credited with inspiring a new generation of *traceurs*. However, media exposure has been a double-edged sword for leading parkour practitioners. It has helped to raise the profile of the sport and opened up commercial opportunities. Yet, as Wilson (2008, p. 147) reminds us, the media have long played a central role in the "incorporation, mis-representation, and stigmatization" of subcultural groups. Parkour is no exception—the spectacular media production of the action genre, reproducing and replaying cultural connotations and encoded meanings in mainstream media products, can cause understanding of the sport to atrophy, thereby popularizing unsafe practices that contravene care for the body, self and environment (Archer, 2010; Atkinson, 2009).[5] This distortion is a particular concern for coaches who are keen to instill a sense of discipline and risk-management required to perform safely, particularly in a context in which there is no formal regulation or organization of the sport (see Gilchrist & Wheaton, 2011). Online videos of parkour and freerunning have reputedly led to copycat performances, contributing to news reports of deaths as novices attempt moves without adequate caution or regard for personal wellbeing. In Toronto, for example, reports (2004–2006) of this type contributed to moral panics about irresponsible youth in the local media, in which participants were seen as "disruptive" and displaying "aggressive tendencies" (Atkinson & Young, 2008a, p. 68). Commercial news media depictions of parkour as a dangerous activity have also contributed to widespread misinformation about the activity and the degree of risk involved. As one interviewee told us:

> A lot of people just see what's in the media and they assume that's what they are going to be doing, and it's just not the case. (Participant/ Promoter)

Those involved with parkour as educators are acutely aware of these problems. As one sport development officer explained, "You know you get the same old analogies, 'you are teaching the cat burglars of the future'" (Personal interview). Yet our research has shown that media concerns over risk factors are often exaggerated, and that, in some urban spaces, local authorities, the police, businesses, youth workers and parents have worked together to find spaces and programs that can harness the enthusiasm of local *traceurs*. These groups are mindful of parkour's potential for "positive youth development" and wider social benefits (Gilchrist & Wheaton, 2011).

Despite the individualistic nature of parkour, *traceurs* have a strong sense of being part of a local and increasingly transnational collectivity, often being represented as "the community". Research has highlighted how parkour has grown and developed through the use of social software and via a participatory online culture (Bavinton, 2007; Saville, 2008). In so-called "lifestyle sport cultures" like surfing, commercially produced films, DVDs and magazines remain important "organs of communication" that are largely sustained by advertising revenue from companies *within* the surf industry (e.g., clothing, equipment and travel). However, parkour does not—as yet—have material commodities or equipment to be sold (other than bodies themselves). Unusually, and perhaps uniquely in sport subcultures, there is currently no role and a limited market for commercially sustained niche media devoted to parkour. In the absence of more traditional media forms, web-based sources have proliferated. Websites developed by professional parkourists and freerunners (e.g., www.urbanfreeflow.com) provide a space for practitioners to share videos and photographs of their performances, offer guides on locations and routes, host articles on techniques and tips for maintaining a healthy body, supply news of coaching opportunities and events, and house international directories of parkour enthusiasts and groups.

The use of social software is felt in the lived practice of the parkour subculture. *Traceurs* use blogs, message boards, websites and Facebook to organize meet-ups, commonly referred to as "jams" (Atkinson, 2009), which are primarily about meeting new people, sharing styles and techniques, and learning about how to move through new spaces. These activities align with Michel Maffesoli's notion of the "tribe", a group:

> ... without the rigidity of the forms of organization with which we are familiar, it refers more to a certain ambience, a state of mind, and is preferable to be expressed through lifestyles that favour appearance and "form". (1996, p. 98)

The tribe denotes temporal and site-specific gatherings where people with common dispositions and outlooks come together to share interests through informal interactions. We found that it was common for *traceurs* to move around the UK and further afield. These movements were for jams and longer "pilgrimages", such as to the Paris suburb of Lisses where parkour originated. Living arrangements were often "sleepovers" in the homes of acquaintances contacted via social networking platforms.

NICHE MEDIA: PRODUCERS AND CONSUMERS

As detailed above, participants often have ambivalent and contradictory relationships with the media. For some, involvement in paid stunt or media work is seen as a "sell-out" and as antithetical to the values of responsible, ethical and safe practice inherent to the participative ideology of parkour (Gilchrist & Wheaton, 2011). However, we should remain cautious in assessing claims that the parkour "community" has been duped into commodifying the sport into media products for global markets. Reflecting the development of many youth subcultural formations, debates about the degree of incorporation and resistance increasingly consume parkour (Angel, 2011). As Sarah Thornton's work illustrates, despite the "resilient belief" that a "grassroots" or "authentic" subculture resists and struggles with a "colonizing mass-mediated corporate world" (1995, p. 116), youth subcultures are formed within and through the media. Likewise, lifestyle sport subcultures such as snowboarders, skaters and windsurfers are illustrative of the way in which the media have become central to the authentication of popular cultural practices, and the complex and shifting relationships to the seemingly co-opting force of global consumer culture (Wheaton, 2007). In these sporting spaces, participants as producers *and* consumers have a reflexive and dynamic relationship with the subcultural media serving as a crucial network in the "definition and distribution of cultural knowledge" and identity (Thornton, 1995, p. 14).

Many *traceurs* take an active role in producing media content. Armed with the latest mobile video cameras, they have been keen to record their own performances. The availability of cheap and lightweight cameras (GoPros and iPhones) and video editing software has opened up a territory previously controlled by professional photographers and magazine editors. It would be incorrect, however, to suggest that *traceurs* are developing a visual and performative aesthetic independent of other cultural influences, as other media products and narratives are consumed by them and inform their own products and representations. The *Yamakasi* group (of parkour founders), for instance, were avid consumers of Japanese *anime, manga,* Western comics and graphic novels, using this symbolic content to fashion newly constructed senses of self. The incredible action and bravery that they observed in the comics fed into reconstituted understandings of identity, self and body, bringing a heightened sense of being able to push physical limits. As Julie Angel (2011, p. 30) observes: "The friends' culture of self-improvement traversed the realms of fantasy and realism, incorporating an active imagination to create new situations and encounters". Kinesthetic tropes within martial arts, comic books, video games and film can be found in the spectacular presentation of parkour and animate the participative ideologies of some of its participants. Mundane or repetitive movements crucial to the mastery of obstacles are often edited out to enhance the visual spectacle (Angel, 2011, pp. 93–94). Many short films created by *traceurs*, therefore, reproduce tropes key to the film action genre, in particular chase sequences and spectacular moves such as jumping off rooftops. Heroic masculine fantasies are played out, almost always "scripted through with heroic narratives of accomplishment; of highly skilled, mature bodies overcoming the constraints of the environment" (Saville, 2008, p. 892). Films are uploaded onto video-sharing websites to showcase movements in urban settings, with *traceurs* often performing character types of the "bandit" or "outlaw", thereby encoding and legitimating a version of "outsider" masculinity among often privileged White males (Atencio & Beal, 2011). Thus, in parkour—and reflecting youth subcultural formations more broadly—despite participants' belief in an "authentic" unique identity, intertextual media-driven relationships inform the practice, production and consumption of the sport.

NEW MEDIA AND LIFESTYLE SPORT ENTREPRENEURIALISM

Within the evolving cultures of parkour, we argue that YouTube—the world's most popular video-sharing platform—is having the greatest impact in cultivating the social interactions mentioned above. The action footage posted on this site highlights the physical conditioning required, journeys from apprentice to master, and the endurance, willpower and techniques needed to be proficient in the sport (Stapleton & Terrio, 2012, p. 5). Yet, YouTube is more than a distribution channel. Video-sharing, comments and communal evaluation features make the democratization of sport coaching possible. This platform also has the potential to allow a broader range of voices and expressions of subcultural identity to surface. Here we will briefly discuss each of these aspects.

Sport coaching has been an important feature in a previous generation of lifestyle sport media, either as moving image DVDs or as photo sequences with written commentary by the "star" performer. For example, "how to do it" features—ranging from beginner techniques to action photo sequences of maneuvers—are a central part of surf magazines (Booth, 2008; Wheaton, 2003). However, on YouTube participants provide video evidence that can be commented upon by anyone as a form of peer support and pedagogic intervention. The two-way interactive elements of YouTube allow for dialogue and criticism, revealing philosophies and debates about how parkour should be practiced and evaluative commentary on the movements of the participant/performer (see Angel, 2011, pp. 201–02). Participants view this as a positive aspect according to one practitioner:

> I'll watch people and pick up their techniques and then put my own onto it. Not be the same but because they've done it right, if I watch

their technique and pick it up, I'll just change it a little bit, just to make it my own way but still be the same.

Another interviewee, a *traceur* who had been involved in the sport for eighteen months, told us:

In freerunning and parkour, it's your style, how you want to look, how you feel comfortable. That's what draws the community together. It's everybody's individual style. Nobody can be the same as everybody else.

By making their performances, style and movements available on YouTube and personal websites, *traceurs* are able to reach an audience directly, market themselves and build a following or fan base. This capacity is in marked contrast to the ways in which media power operates in off-line niche market media, where various gatekeepers (photographers, sponsors, journalists and magazine editors) decide who is included and excluded from the magazine content.

The online videos confirm the importance of style and distinction to lifestyle sport subcultures, separating individuals from each other and from variants of the sport. Videos convey subcultural status and authenticity (Wheaton & Beal, 2003) and signal forms of value and symbolic power crucial to the professionalization of the sport. However, like the status hierarchies in more traditional sporting fields, power in the parkour field is contested. James, a parkour coach and director of a leading training organization based in London, told us that there is a particular concern with parkour-related Internet forums:

Forums are run by people who think they know all about the history of the art and the philosophy of the art, but actually when it comes down to it they really don't live it, they just write about it a lot . . . same in all disciplines, anyone that spends all their time on Internet forums clearly does not understand what he is doing.

Here (apart from the implicit gendered nature of the forums) James reveals the politics of authenticity underpinning the parkour field; that is, like most other lifestyle sports, authentic identity is *doing* and the inauthentic is *consuming* (Rinehart, 2000; Thorpe, 2011). Evidently, and as other self-defined "real" *traceurs* also claimed, those who spend their time on forums are not "real" *traceurs*.

Traceurs with high levels of physical capital have become elevated in the parkour subculture. They have proved themselves by mastering different levels of ability, cultivating an individual style or through displays of skilled bodily performance. An internal hierarchy and charismatic culture operates structurally to elevate certain individuals, some through their pedagogical reputation—an ability to preach, teach and educate others about their own style and philosophy—and others by claiming a social status through attracting commercial opportunities. In some cases it is a combination of both means, thereby highlighting that power can accrue from work in the cultural industries and from the wider sporting economy. Our interviewees spoke of the seductive cosmopolitan lifestyles available to the proficient and media savvy *traceur*:

> Where I see myself going is teaching and performing full-time. So, going around not only the UK but the world, around the world delivering sessions and performing everywhere. That's where I see it going. If we keep up the hard work we could be doing that kind of thing.

The connection is clear: hard work will translate into global opportunities. Many freerunners whom we interviewed spoke of being inspired by Tim "Livewire" Shieff, a freerunner from Derbyshire, England, who won the 2009 Barclaycard World Freerun Championships. His profile on the Storm Freerun site (http://www.stormfreerun.com/) lists his "vital statistics" and signature parkour moves, and under "work" a brief biography gives details of worldwide travel, corporate engagements and performances in the presence of royalty and celebrities. A video reel plays on the site to emphasize his media appearances and connections, showing his ease in front of the camera as a performer for chat shows, news items, events, films and music videos.

It is also noticeable that many websites of the leading *traceurs* in the world marginalize class and nationality as markers of identity, social difference and affiliation. It is more common to view outsider identities that utilize the semiotics of heroic rebels or urban warriors (Stapleton & Terrio, 2012, p. 7), suggesting alternative transnational (urban) commonalities. The websites give important clues to the mobile lives of the "borderless athlete" and the social identities of the *traceur* as a transnational citizen and entrepreneur. These are men (and very rarely women) who lead highly mobile lives, leaving traces of their business activities and performances in informational space, and who shift to new opportunities as the market demands. For example, *3-Run*, a group of freerunners based in the south of England, markets its services with a distinct cosmopolitan flavor. It practices a more performance-oriented version of parkour that combines acrobatics, gymnastics and "tricking". Its slick website highlights an aim to be the world's leading parkour and freerunning team. In this quest it has worked on *Casino Royale*, developed award-winning commercials for Microsoft Xbox, and set a number of Guinness World Records in front of television cameras. A page on its site (www.3run.co.uk) gives "the story" and includes a montage of photos that includes a sign for Cape Town, a wallet opened revealing several travel tickets and a passport with the words, "Life is an adventure—explore the world", positioned around it. Other photos show bare-chested members posing in exotic locations, their bodies framed by seascapes and mountain backdrops.

It is this sense of freedom, accomplishment and becoming that proved so seductive to the young men whom we interviewed throughout the UK. For instance, the website of a parkour group from the English Midlands (www.leicesterparkour.co.uk) contains a short one-minute video clip of performances and training "that gives a small insight into how hard we've worked to get to where we are today". A brief chronology of activity is situated underneath, emphasizing their humble beginnings from a "group of young lads practicing a past time they love" to local performances, development of the brand, training and coaching others, to the acquiring of professional qualifications, construction of a purpose-built park and the formation of a social enterprise. They were keen to impress upon us that parkour had no limits, having started with nothing and achieved a material product (their own purpose-built park) and regional reputation. Whilst some of the group spoke of potential local investments to be made from their endeavors—for example, owning and running a gym—others were keen to express a desire to "globetrot" and inspire others with their moves.

CONCLUSION: QUESTIONING POWER IN DIGITAL MEDIA SETTINGS

Digital media play a central role in lifestyle sport subcultures. They offer new, low cost and high-speed opportunities for subcultural groups to communicate and to create and sustain online, real time participant networks from the local to the transnational level. We may celebrate the uptake of YouTube by lifestyle sports participants as an example of "mass self-communication" (Castells, 2009), whereby the participant has the potential to reach large audiences whilst retaining control of production through the self-generation of content. Our parkour case study illustrates that new technologies are enabling lifestyle sports participants to convert seemingly peripheral cultural activities into wider cultural value. Physical capital, then, becomes cultural and economic capital within and outside the parkour field. YouTube channels and personal websites distribute the athletic and media proficiency of the participant/performer, and act as pathways to entrepreneurialism and social mobility by signaling an intention to undertake commercial work. As Gerry Bloustien (2007) notes, young people's use of convergent media forms can bring to the fore new agencies, rendering distinctions between public and private self, production and consumption, work and leisure, increasingly blurred (see also Ravenscroft & Gilchrist, 2009). Young people are able to draw upon their social networking and collaboration skills to develop an empowered "sense of self" and to fashion self-fulfilling careers and opportunities (Bloustien, 2007, pp. 451–52).

Despite these observations, it remains an open question as to how far the adoption of digital media technologies is truly transforming lifestyle sport subcultures. It is evident that many of the power inequalities chronicled in the traditional sports media are also reproduced in digital media settings. As we have illustrated, climbing, surfing and parkour media continue to reinforce the hegemonic position of the heroic Western White male adventurer subjectivity (Farley, 2005). Women and non-White men are pushed to the peripheries as playful White masculinities are recurrently represented in mediated spaces (Frohlick, 2005). There is a need to be cautious about the degree to which online media spaces subvert or disrupt subcultural representations and identities. For instance, despite claims that surfing has become a "girl friendly space" (Comer, 2010), DVDs, magazines and films are still male dominated, and still reproduce the gendered and racialized stereotypes "associated with privileged forms of whiteness" (Comer, 2010, p. 21). Krista Comer's revealing discussion of the global surf industry's "penchant for blondes . . . reveals a 'politics of blondness' where the preferred female figure is the 'global California girl' ". Those who do not fit this image have tended to remain on the periphery. Within parkour, similar questions can be raised about the presence of women in its user-generated films and documentaries, which tend to depict *traceurs* as anti-heroes and outlaws. These cultural archetypes do not necessarily aid more inclusive forms of representation of physical achievement.

Online media platforms certainly provide opportunities for the subaltern voice and experience, and the possibility for scripts that challenge the dominant discourses of gender, race, sexuality and dis/ability. Natalie Porter (2003), for example, explores the emergence of a wide range of Internet forums for female skaters, skatezines and all-girl competitions that challenge dominant discourses of skateboarding and masculinity. In parkour, too, participants expressed a genuine desire to be inclusive, and to provide "real" and mediated spaces for female participants (Wheaton, forthcoming). One group of teenage male *traceurs* made provision for female participants on their website, despite the reality that there were no local female participants. In surfing, too, a cursory trawl through surfing-related Web materials illustrates the broad range of surfing experiences that are promoted (e.g. groups for female surfers, surfing "mums", "silver" surfers, indigenous surfers, gay surfers, surfers with disabilities, political surfing movements and a broad range of environmental protest groups). Furthermore, independent and some commercially produced documentary films are challenging the dominant histories and myths about surfing culture, including representations of race and gender.[6] Within these media spaces, multiple and competing discourses of femininity and masculinity are produced, discourses that are also reflective of the complex shifting identities evident in contemporary short-board surf culture (see Waitt, 2008).

While networked digital media has transformed some of the practices and cultures of lifestyle sport, we retain a sociological skepticism and sobering sense of historical perspective concerning how far this is a profound and empowering development. We should not uncritically laud web-based media as instruments for self-expression, creativity and enhanced democratic communication. More research needs to be conducted on actor-network relations produced by or transformed through new media within various lifestyle sport subcultures. It is time to probe deeper into the winners and losers, and structures and constraints that come into being as technologies are adopted and opportunities are distributed.

NOTES

1. With the exception of the Winter Olympics and surfing, particularly in Australia (see Thorpe & Wheaton, 2011).
2. It should, though, be noted that many who work in the surf industry are surfers themselves. Furthermore, this insider status is a way for brands to assert their authenticity (see Wheaton & Beal, 2003).
3. In this chapter we use parkour to refer both to the activities of parkour and freerunning. We are aware that there are important philosophical differences between these two activities, and the cultures that underpin them (see, for example, discussion in Atkinson (2009) and Wheaton [forthcoming]). These differences, however, do not impact on our discussion of social media.
4. A full history of the development of parkour is beyond the scope of this chapter. For more detail on this subject, see Atkinson (2009), Atkinson & Young (2008a), and Edwardes (2007).
5. An attempt to rectify this issue is offered by Julie Angel's participative "shared cinema" ethnography of parkour (Angel, 2011).
6. See, for example, Nike's *12 Miles North* (Yelland, 2012) and also *White Wash* (Trespass Productions, 2011), a film that explores "the complexity of race in America through the struggle and triumph of the history of black surfers".

REFERENCES

Abercrombie N & Longhurst B (1998) *Audiences: A Sociological Theory of Performance and Imagination*. London: Sage.
Angel J (2011) *Ciné Parkour*. Self-published book.
Archer N (2010) Virtual Poaching and altered space: reading parkour in French visual culture. *Modern and Contemporary France* 18(1): 93–107.
Atencio N & Beal B (2011) Beautiful losers: the symbolic exhibition and legitimization of outsider masculinity. *Sport in Society* 14(1): 1–16.
Atkinson M (2009) Parkour, anarcho-environmentalism and poiesis. *Journal of Sport and Social Issues* 33(2): 169–94.
Atkinson N & Young K (2008a) *Deviance and Social Control in Sport*. Champaign, IL: Human Kinetics.
Atkinson N & Young K (2008b) (eds.) *Tribal Play: Subcultural Journeys Through Sport*. Bingley: Jai.

Bavinton N (2007) From obstacle to opportunity: parkour, leisure, and the reinterpretation of constraints. *Annals of Leisure Research* 10(3–4): 391–412.

Bennett A & Kahn-Harris K (2004) *After Subculture: Critical Studies in Contemporary Youth Culture*. Basingstoke: Palgrave Macmillan.

Bloustien G (2007) "Wigging people out": youth music practice and mediated communities. *Journal of Community & Applied Social Psychology* 17(6): 446–62.

Booth D (1996) Surfing films and video: adolescent fun, alternative lifestyle, adventure industry. *Journal of Sport History* 22(3): 313–27.

Booth D (2001) *Australian Beach Cultures: The History of Sun, Sand and Surf.* London: Frank Cass.

Booth D (2008) (Re)reading the surfers' bible: the affects of *tracks. Continuum: Journal of Media and Cultural Studies* 22: 17–35.

Brown DA (2007) The modern romance of mountaineering: photography, aesthetics and embodiment. *International Journal of the History of Sport* 24(1): 1–34.

Bruns A (2008) *Blogs, Wikipedia, Second Life and Beyond: From Production to Produsage*. New York: Peter Lang.

Castells M (2009) *Communication Power*. New York: Oxford University Press.

Chabaline P, Gadd W & House S (2000) Commercialization and modern climbing: three views. *The American Alpine Journal* 42(74): 151–59.

Colley AC (2010) *Victorians in the Mountains: Sinking the Sublime*. Farnham: Ashgate.

Comer K (2010) *Surfer Girls in the New World Order*. Durham and London: Duke University Press.

Edwardes D (2007) Parkour. In: Booth D & Thorpe H (eds.) *Berkshire Encyclopedia of Extreme Sports*. Great Barrington: Berkshire Reference Works, 233–36.

Farley R (2005) By endurance we conquer: Ernest Shackleton and the performances off white male hegemony. *International Journal of Cultural Studies* 8(2): 231–54.

Ford N & Brown D (2005) *Surfing and Social Theory: Experience, Embodiment and Narrative of the Dream Glide*. London: Routledge.

Frohlick S (2005) "That playfulness of white masculinity": mediating masculinities and adventure in mountain film festivals. *Tourist Studies* 5(2): 175–93.

Gasperini K (1999) Kodak courage. *Mountain Sport and Living*, January–February, 43.

Gilchrist P (2007) Reality TV on the rock face—climbing the Old Man of Hoy. *Sport in History* 27(1): 44–63.

Gilchrist P & Wheaton B (2011) Lifestyle sport, public policy and youth engagement: examining the emergence of parkour. *International Journal of Sport Policy and Politics* 3(1): 109–31.

Henderson M (2001) A shifting line up: men, women and *tracks* surfing magazine. *Continuum: Journal of Media and Cultural Studies* 15(3): 319–32.

Lowther A (2011) On ledge and online: solitary sport turns social. *New York Times*, 11 December, D6.

Maffesoli M (1996) *The Time of the Tribes: The Decline of Individualism in Mass Society*. London: Sage.

Muggleton D & Weinzierl R (2003) What is "post-subcultural studies" anyway? In: Muggleton D & Weinzierl R (eds.) *The Post-Subcultures Reader*. Oxford: Berg, 3–23.

Ormrod J (2007) Surf rhetoric in American and British surfing magazines between 1965 and 1976. *Sport in History* 27(1): 88–109.

Ortuzar J (2009) Parkour or l'art de deplacement. *The Drama Review* 53: 54–66.

Osborne C (2010) An extraordinary Joe: the working class climber as hero. In: Wagg S & Russell D (eds.) *Sporting Heroes of the North*. Newcastle: University of Northumbria Press, 48–70.

Porter NL (2003) *Female Skateboarders and Their Negotiation of Space and Identity*. PhD thesis, Concordia University, Canada.

Ravenscroft N & Gilchrist P (2009) The emergent working society of leisure. *Journal of Leisure Research* 41(1): 21–38.

Rinehart R (2000) Emerging arriving sport: alternatives to formal sport. In: Coakley J & Dunning E (eds.) *Handbook of Sport Studies*. London: Sage, 504–19.

Rinehart R (2008) ESPN's X Games: contests of opposition, resistance, co-option and negotiation. In Atkinson M & Young K (eds.) *Tribal Play: Subcultural Journeys Through Sport*. Bingley: Jai. 175–96.

Saville SJ (2008) Playing with fear: parkour and the mobility of emotion. *Social & Cultural Geography* 9(8): 891–914.

Stapleton S & Terrio S (2012) Le parkour: urban street culture and the commoditization of male youth expression. *International Migration* 50(6): 18–27.

Thornton S (1995) *Club Cultures: Music, Media and Subcultural Capital*. Cambridge: Polity Press.

Thorpe H (2011) *Snowboarding Bodies in Theory and Practice*. Basingstoke: Palgrave Macmillan.

Thorpe H & Wheaton B (2011) The Olympic movement, action sports, and the search for generation Y. In: Sugden J & Tomlinson A (eds.) *Watching the Olympics: Politics, Power and Representation*. London: Routledge, 182–200.

Trespass Productions (2011) *White Wash*. Santa Monica, CA.

Waitt G (2008) "Killing waves": surfing, space and gender. *Social & Cultural Geography* 9(1): 75–94.

Wheaton B (2003) Lifestyle sports magazines and the discourses of sporting masculinity. In: Benwell B (ed.) *Masculinity and Men's Lifestyle Magazines*. Keele: Sociological Review/Blackwell, 193–221.

Wheaton B (2004) Introduction: mapping the lifestyle sport-scape. In: Wheaton B (ed.) *Understanding Lifestyle Sports: Consumption, Identity and Difference*. London: Routledge, 1–28.

Wheaton B (2007) After sport culture: rethinking sport and post-subcultural theory. *Journal of Sport and Social Issues* 31(3): 283–307.

Wheaton B (forthcoming) *The Cultural Politics of Lifestyle Sport*. London: Routledge.

Wheaton B & Beal B (2003) "Keeping it real": subcultural media and the discourses of authenticity in alternative sport. *International Review for the Sociology of Sport* 38(2): 155–76.

Wilson B (2008) Believe the hype? The impact of the internet on sport-related subcultures. In: Atkinson M & Young K (eds.) *Tribal Play: Subcultural Journeys Through Sport*. Bingley: Jai, 135–52.

Wilson B & Atkinson M (2005) Rave and straightedge, the virtual and the real—exploring online and offline experiences in Canadian youth subcultures. *Youth and Society* 36(3): 276–311.

Yelland R (2012) Director's cut: inside 112 miles North. *The Inertia: Distributor of Ideas*. Online. Available from: http://www.theinertia.com/business-media/12-miles-north-black-surf-documentary/ (Accessed 23 March 2012).

13 Blogging the Beijing Olympics
The Neoliberal Logic of Chinese Web 2.0

Haiqing Yu

INTRODUCTION: THE MEDIA ECOLOGY OF THE BEIJING 2008 GAMES

The 2008 Beijing Olympic Games made history in many ways, including thirty-eight new world records and eighty new Olympic records. Yet, Olympic history is not only written by athletes "going for gold" but by global constituencies competing for resources, power, influence and money, including those with television and/or multimedia broadcasting coverage rights. Beijing organized widespread media coverage of the longest—and least harmonious—torch relay and presented Olympic telecasting with the most sophisticated technologies. China hosted the largest world media festival to date, with 56,000 registered journalists, and 1.12 billion people watching the Games on China Central Television (CCTV) alone (Sohu.com, 2008). Despite the dramatic events in the lead up to the Beijing Olympiad, which included unrest in Tibet and the tragic Sichuan earthquake, the Games provided few major surprises. It was a "coming-out" party and "coming-of-age" celebration for the People's Republic of China as an emerging great power (Close, Askew & Xin, 2007). This mega-event was also a reward for China's reintegration into the world community:

> . . . coming outside and coming onside as a capitalist social formation
> . . . having embraced mainstays of the Western cultural account and
> above all, of Western-style capitalism (albeit with Chinese characteristics) (Close, 2011, p. 11).

The Games were a technical and logistical marketing success and media spectacle, reporting an extraordinary budget ($2.8 billion), revenue ($3 billion) and television audience (4.7 billion or seventy percent of the world's population). They are also an exemplary case of the elective affinity between modern Olympism and the logic of market capitalism (Close et al., 2007).

Interest in the legacy of the 2008 Beijing Games has concentrated on three dimensions: the global, the regional and the domestic. The Games reinforced Western neoliberal rules in marketization of sports and the unequal distribution of resources and participation of countries (Short, 2003). They also worked to rebalance power in East Asia (particularly *vis-à-vis* with Japan) (Close, 2011) and potentially impacted China's economic, social, legal and cultural (though not necessarily political) conditions (Brownell, 2008; Ong, 2004). Many commentators have discussed the Beijing Olympics in the context of the social, cultural and historical development of modern sport in China, the intersections of geopolitics and elite-level sport, and the sizable communication divide between China and Western democracies over the former's human rights record, the independence of Tibet, press freedom and environmental issues (Brownell, 2008; Caffrey, 2008; Jarvie, Hwang & Brennan, 2008; Price & Dayan, 2008; Xu, 2008). The Beijing Games were, therefore, a "polyphonic, multivoiced, many themed" sign and platform (Price & Dayan, 2008, p. 2) seized by both international and Chinese domestic media, as well as by marginal and established groups to advance a range of agendas, values and ideologies.

There is, however, a conspicuous lack of discussion about the role of the Internet and networked digital media in staging mega-events and media sport spectacles in the Chinese context. While broadcast media dominated the sports programming of all networks, Beijing was the first ever Olympiad available live on the Internet and on mobile phones. "Multimedia"—ranging from TV (including terrestrial, cable, satellite, transit, outdoor and mobile television), radio, newspapers, magazines, the Internet, mobile phones and their various combinations—was a key word during the 2008 Olympics. This media ecology introduced multimodal experiences of the Olympics. Watching events in stadia was combined with television viewing, radio listening and newspaper reading, and the Games could also be experienced on the Internet and via mobile phones in textual and audio-visual forms. High definition, IPTV, video-streaming and 3G mobile technologies allowed blogging and microblogging[1] to be part of this massive media event.

Networked digital media are introducing new ways to deliver and consume sports content (Boyle & Haynes, 2003). Neologisms—such as "produser," "prosumer" and "viewser"—seek to describe the changing role of new media users in the *habitus* of "anywhere, anytime" connectivity. Among all the forms of new media, the Internet has been hailed as the "Trojan horse" of grassroots participation and activism, particularly in the era of Web 2.0 (Couldry & Curran, 2003). It opens up opportunities for cultural expression, exchange and resistance, as exemplified by the anti-Olympic movement and Olympic watchdog groups' use of the Internet and of independent media centers (Lenskyj, 2006). At the same time, the contestation of media power is limited in scope, quality and diversity, as was witnessed during the Games. Nationalist sentiments, rather than any alternative or dissenting views, were fortified by the state's monopoly over media and communication, and its strategic alliances with commercial content providers, ISPs, blog operators, and WAP operators. The rise of transnational corporations in the Chinese media and telecommunications market further undermines the democratic potential of "Chinese Web 2.0". While consumers are empowered by the freedom to participate in content generation via their desktop, laptop or handheld devices, their roles as co-creators and prosumers of content are also harnessed and entrapped in a neoliberal market logic. In other words, participation does not necessarily lead to emancipation.

This chapter examines the incorporation of digital media, particularly through blogging, in the presentation of the Olympic variety show by Chinese mainstream media, telecommunications operators, commercial content providers, local tabloids and individuals. It illustrates the extension of the commodification of sport, the party-state's desire to control and profit from the sports media industries and individual aspirations for cultural participation. Through blogging the Olympics, Chinese elite athletes, journalists and urbanites—the kinds of newly empowered and entrepreneurial consumer subjects targeted by business—are pivotal in the formation of the media festival enabled by the Olympic Games. During August 2008, Chinese netizens acted out their desires for creativity, freedom and belonging through blogging and problogging via their mobile phones and computer interfaces. They presented a diversified, amateur version of the Olympic spectacle. At the same time, they were also willing participants in new forms of productive cooperation designed by the "money-power-knowledge iron triangle" to harness their immaterial labor for political and corporate gain.[2]

The aim of my analysis is to illuminate the dynamics of blogging the Beijing Olympics and the neoliberal logic of the Internet in the context of the Chinese media sports cultural complex. I do not focus on the fraught politics of the Beijing Games, which is discussed elsewhere,[3] but rather on the intricate relations between key players who blogged the Games and how digital media practices such as blogging are colonized at the level of production. Before detailing the dynamics of blogging the Beijing Olympics, I first contextualize the Chinese case within the history of the Olympics and digital media.

BLOGGING THE OLYMPICS

Winning the rights to stage the XXIX Olympic Games in July 2001 led to a surge of specialized sports websites in China, initiated by the private sector and joined by state-owned media and communication entities such as China Telecom (sports.21cn.com), CCTV (www.cctv.com/sports), *People's Daily* (sports.people.com.cn) and Xinhua (www.xinhuanet.com/sports). Staging the Olympics can transform a host city into "the nexus of a massive media information network and flow of capital", whether it is in Sydney or Beijing (Schaffer & Smith, 2000, p. 217). While global news media presented a struggle over meanings in their polysemous interpretations of the Beijing bid and the Olympiad (Polumbaum, 2002), a semiotically over-determined meta-narrative characterized Chinese media discourses that "read the sports events as both metaphors and metonyms of China's greatness in an international context" (Sun, 2002, p. 123). The contestations and debates over representations of China, or the search for the "real China", were also staged in the new media (Latham, 2009). Networked digital media were essential to China's aim to present a "High-Tech Olympics", one of the three themes proposed by Beijing, which also included the "Green Olympics" and the "People's Olympics".

China sees a universal narrative of technological innovation as key to showcasing the country's advancement. This narrative is about transforming the widely held perception of "made in China" to a framework centered on "created in China" (Humphreys & Finlay, 2008). This techno-narrative of "created in China" is a state-led, top-down drive to boost its information technology and telecommunications sectors. As such, broadband, wireless, high-definition, the Internet and 3G mobile were among the buzzwords that bombarded people from street billboards and on television, mobile phones and computers. Blog services became a standard feature of business models for ISPs, content providers and blog operators. Telecommunications providers and mobile phone carriers also joined the wave of blogging the Beijing Olympiad through newly released 3G platforms. These developments drove an exponential growth of the Chinese blogging market, which saw a 245 percent expansion from 2007 to 2008 (Figure 13.1). By the end of December 2008, 162 million, or 54.3 percent of an estimated 298 million Chinese netizens, had blogged (CNNIC, 2009a).

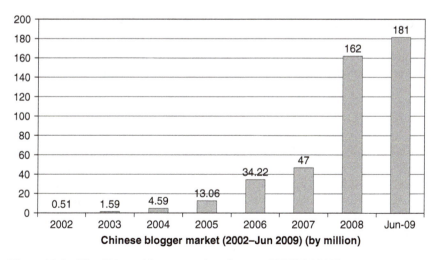

Figure 13.1 The Chinese blogger market. Source: CNNIC 2009b.

The Beijing Olympics official website (www.beijing2008.cn) featured all the important information about the 2008 Olympics and Paralympics, including a rich repertoire of photos and videos. But, like many official government sites, it lacked interactive features and had no user-generated content. This gap was filled by numerous websites offering live video streaming, photo-sharing, and most of all blogging and problogging services. Again, we see major blog operators/content providers, mainstream media, telecommunications companies and transnational corporations playing a key role in the promotion of blogging activities across multimedia platforms. In the lead-up to the Games and during their seventeen days in August 2008, Chinese people were mobilized to blog the Beijing Olympics—some did it at the invitation of (and were paid by) mega-corporations, and others willingly donated their time to blog. Together, they presented an alternative media spectacle that supplemented the CCTV version.

In mid-2008, China had more than 253 million netizens, eighty-six percent of whom accessed Olympic-related content, with twenty-five percent surfing the Internet each day during the Games in August (Nielsen, 2008). The number of netizens increased to 298 million by the end of 2008. This figure included 270 million broadband users and 117.6 million mobile Internet users (CNNIC, 2009a). With the largest numbers of Internet and mobile phone users in the world, China was at the forefront of invigorating the media sports cultural complex (Rowe, 2004), fueled by Beijing Olympics "fever". Enabled by 3G wireless and broadband platforms and high definition video streaming and photo-sharing technologies, blogging and problogging were an everyday reality for anybody with a smart phone or personal digital assistant (PDA). The addition of social networking platforms further promoted the growth of blogging. Apart from foreign social networking services like Facebook, Twitter and Cyworld, Chinese domestic social networking services such as 51.com, Xiaonei.com, Kaixin.com, Chinaren.com and Qzone.qq.com were part of a massive effort to mediate the Olympics. Sport journalists, commentators and editors, previous and current Olympians, academics, freelance writers, sports fans and celebrities were all solicited and recruited by media operators and The Olympic Partner (TOP) program sponsors to offer a "grassroots" version of the spectacle that was compatible with the official version conveyed by CCTV and its business partners.

CCTV is China's only national television network and has a monopoly over broadcasting rights for major international sporting events. Its monopoly extends to networked digital media platforms, with its official website CCTV.com having embedded blogging services since 2005. Journalists are encouraged (or ordered) to blog their programs, hyperlink to CCTV channels and other mainstream news media in their blogs, and to cultivate a cult of personality as "star" bloggers and celebrities. A cursory examination of blog.cctv.com finds many famous names, among whom are sports journalists and commentators who blogged the Olympics throughout August 2008.

Their fame is considerably enhanced by their blogging *personae*. Veteran sports commentators like Zhang Bin, Han Qiaosheng, Sun Zhengping, and Liu Jianhong are among the CCTV blogger team forming a derivative, if not parasitic relationship, with CCTV. In the lead-up to the Games and throughout the Games, CCTV j-bloggers (journalists who blog) enjoyed privileged access to exclusive events and interviews and blogged "insider" stories that supplemented the "normal" programs that they hosted, directed or organized at CCTV.

This kind of j-blogging usually "normalizes" a new format to fit traditional journalistic norms and continues to perform a "gatekeeping" function in a more participatory and communicative environment (Yu, 2011a). The personal touch, conversational style, hyperlinks and interactive components of these blogs do not, however, conceal commercial motives, including self-marketing and cross-promoting individuals, programs and CCTV itself. Olympic j-bloggers employed by CCTV continued the agenda-setting function of traditional journalism, thereby reinforcing rather than challenging the dominant framework of news production and consumption.

While CCTV's Olympic blogs centered on its team of star journalists and programs,[4] its Olympic campaign partner, Lenovo (also the first Chinese TOP sponsor of the Beijing Olympics), enlisted international athletes to blog their Olympic experiences in August 2008. Lenovo is both an emerging global brand in computer manufacturing and an important representative of the Chinese government (the largest shareholder of the company). It was the major supplier of information technology equipment for the 2006 Winter Olympics in Turin and the 2008 Beijing Olympics. Collaborating with CCTV, Visa, Coca Cola and major content providers, Lenovo launched its US$150 million Olympic campaign, which included strategies to market the Olympic torch relay, social welfare projects, product innovation initiatives, blogging and integrated communications.[5]

For the first time athletes were also allowed to blog their Olympic experiences as long as they obeyed the strict rules of the International Olympic Committee (IOC), particularly regarding the production of audio and video content in Olympic venues.[6] Lenovo invited one hundred Olympians from twenty-five countries and twenty-nine sports to blog their way to and through the Beijing Olympics in a campaign called "Voices of the Summer Games Lenovo Blogger Program". Athletes participating in the program were provided with Lenovo Ideapad laptops and video cameras to capture their experiences. These Lenovo-sponsored athlete bloggers all placed a badge on their blogs indicating that they were part of the program and agreed to allow their blog posts to be pulled into Lenovo's "Voices of the Summer Games" website. In this branded blog platform the athlete bloggers could write about their experiences on their road to Beijing in any way that they liked. It aimed "to bring a real insider's perspective on what is happening during the Games to fans at home around the world". Lenovo's blogging and social media marketing project, which was partnered with

Ogilvy 360 Digital Influence and Google, produced more than 1,500 posts and received more than 8,000 comments from sports fans in various countries. At the same time, Lenovo undertook a grassroots blogging initiative to involve the "masses" through the "Lenovo Olympic Blogger Contest". This contest was launched at the same time as the "Voices of the Summer Games" program in May 2008, attracting 393 contestants and considerable traffic on its websites.

While China Mobile, CCTV and Lenovo had global markets at the center of their Olympic campaigns, Chinese content providers and blog operators focused their efforts on domestic media users, particularly with regard to the online video market. According to a survey by the China Internet Network Information Center (CNNIC) on netizen-consumer behavior during the Beijing Olympic Games, video streaming and still images topped all other online content as the most utilized categories (Figure 13.2), followed by commentaries, which may include those pulled from individual blogs and bulletin board systems. This survey shows that the right to broadcast or publish timely audiovisual content and the ability to attract top commentators are crucial to the success of new media portals.

Sohu.com took the lead by signing up with CCTV.com in June 2008. This site became the first strategic new media partner to telecast the opening and closing ceremonies and all events of the Beijing Olympic Games through its network video content. The partnership between Sohu.com (the Olympic content service provider) and CCTV.com (the Olympic official Internet/mobile phone broadcaster) heralded unprecedented live Olympic coverage. Other portals quickly provided various forms of coverage. Sina.com, Netease.com, QQ.com, UUSee.co, PPLive.com, PPS.tv and Ku6.com

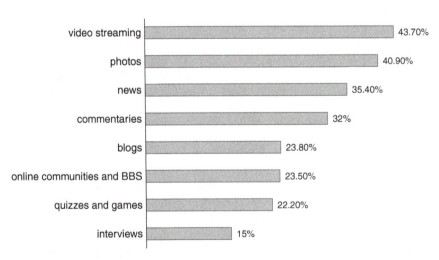

Figure 13.2 Olympic content utilized by Chinese netizens. Source: Figures sourced from CNNIC 2008.

paid RMB50–60 million (US$8–9.5 million) to CCTV.com for the rights to live video streaming and/or video upon demand.

As the sole new media sponsor of the Games, Sohu.com was given the first opportunity to interview Olympic champions and their teams, and to invite the Olympians to participate in a live online talk show, "Face to Face with Champions". Its Olympic blog channel recruited more than forty-four of the best athletes in China, including former Olympians, such as Yang Yang (short-track speed skating Olympian and current IOC member) and Liu Xiang (the 2004 Athens Olympian hurdler). Liu's blog had more than ten million hits for only a handful of very short posts within four months after his blog at Sohu.com was opened in July 2007 (liuxiang.blog.sohu. com). On 18 August 2008, Liu withdrew from the Olympic 110 meter hurdles due to an Achilles tendon injury, leaving his fans at the stadium in silence, confusion and tears. The following day on 19 August, Liu made a public apology to the Chinese media and posted it on his blog entitled, "Please believe in me; I'll be back". This 275-character post was read more than 1.5 million times and elicited 28,391 comments in the next few days.[7] Securing star athletes like Liu on its blog site, and priority access to Olympians for interviews and online chat, saw Sohu.com enjoy unprecedented traffic and commercial returns during the Games.

Besides athlete bloggers, commercial operators also mobilized journalists, academics/experts, celebrities, sports fans and general observers to blog the Beijing Olympics. As Sohu's biggest competitor, Sina.com centered its Olympic blog campaign on "stars" such as China's most popular athletes (e.g., the springboard diver diva Guo Jingjing) and journalists (e.g., Li Chengpeng from *Soccer* newspaper, Dong Lu from Beijing TV and ex-CCTV commentator, Huang Xianxiang). Rather than utilizing the "star" effect, QQ.com took a "grassroots" approach that targeted the youth market. Its Qzone, enabled by mobile and wireless technologies, was preferred by students and young athletes alike to blog and live blog their Olympic experiences. Chinese Olympian gymnast, Cheng Fei, is one of the Chinese athletes who moblogged at Qzone. One-and-a-half hours after she led China's women's gymnastics Olympic team to achieve a first ever gold medal, Cheng uploaded the following message via her mobile phone:

> I'm [still] very excited. All my hard work has finally paid off today. Thank you my coach and thank all my family, relatives and friends who care about me. I have succeeded! . . . I didn't do very well in vault and I am used to be[ing] the last to perform. I was surprised at the order of our performances, so I was a bit nervous. But the nervousness didn't lead to failure. I did my best despite pressure and in the end we won! I've got the gold medal! Mom and Dad, be happy for me!

Within the next few hours, this post attracted more than 50,000 replies, all responding to its timely content and personal touch. This example shows how mobile Internet has started to register within China's telecommunications market. Like Tencent's highly successful instant messaging tool QQ (Koch, Koch, Huang & Chen, 2009), Qzone enables user access through computer, mobile phone or any other wireless device. The seamless and real-time interaction between computer and mobile networks made QQ and Qzone a big hit in the Chinese market, particularly among the young and the "information have-less" (Qiu, 2009). A range of blogging practices and formats during the Beijing Olympic Games saw athletes and spectators transformed into "prosumers", enhancing the media sports cultural complex through networked digital co-production networks.

THE NEOLIBERAL LOGIC OF CHINESE OLYMPIC WEB 2.0

The mediatization of the Beijing Olympics is governed by the dual logics of neoliberalism and centrism. Neoliberalism is understood as a type of economic policy, a cultural structure, a set of particular attitudes towards individual responsibility, entrepreneurship and self-improvement within an institutional framework that emphasizes market imperatives. In China, neoliberalism becomes manifestly hybridized and incoherent in the context of the country's socialist legacy and pursuit of capitalism. The outcome is the construction in China of "a particular kind of market economy that increasingly incorporates neoliberal elements interdigitated with authoritarian centralized control" (Harvey, 2005, p. 120). As mentioned earlier, the Olympics were a celebration of China's coming of age as a member of the global market economy. As a key part of the Games' infrastructure, China's media and communication industries are equally guided by such principles. By the time that the Beijing Olympic Games were held, commercial media and communication networks were focused on sports coverage. While a "turf war" was still part of the new media and communication market, cross-media promotion and the cross-flow of resources were actively sought between old and new media, media and telecommunications networks, and state and private/transnational companies.[8]

Sport is a staple of merged systems in this setting. Social networking, video sharing, blogging and microblogging increasingly create "digital plenitude" in the restructuring of the media sport content economy (Hutchins & Rowe, 2009). Such restructuring, however, has its limitations and constraints. I have written elsewhere about the disingenuous neoliberal nature of Chinese media and communications (Yu, 2011b). I argue that China is an economic system in which the marketplace is shaped by a cozy relationship among government, industry and capital. The disingenuousness of Chinese neoliberalism lies in the passion for intervention described as "selective non-intervention", all in the name of harmony and "one dream." The market is far from free, dancing with the magic wands of both market capitalism and the Chinese authoritarian state. Thus, neoliberal logic walks hand-in-hand with the logic of centrism.

The logic of centrism emphasizes the role of the state in boosting and restructuring the Chinese media and telecommunications industries. Beijing's ambition was not only to chase gold medals (Fan, 2008), but to strengthen the media and communication industries through the Games. This mission started in the mid-1990s with the push toward conglomeration by the central government. Thought to be "messy, protracted, confusing, and confused, littered with odd, even counterintuitive institutions, structure, and practices", the process of media conglomeration (Zhao, 2000, p. 3) has turned out to be effective in ensuring the party-state's continued control of media resources at the cost of social equity (Yu, 2009, pp. 7–8). All major players in the media and telecommunications sector are either directly or indirectly part of the state-controlled "hybrid Chinese socialism-cum-neoliberalism" (Sigley, 2004, p. 566). During the Beijing Olympic Games, Chinese bloggers were subject to double centralism by the IOC and the Chinese government. To prevent ambush marketing and broadcast media rights infringement, the IOC issued "Blogging Guidelines" with conditions and tight limits on what could be blogged by athletes and members of national teams. Such guidelines were not without contradictions, and athletes and national team managers were required to be vigilant about how and to what extent athletes expressed themselves online during the Games (Hutchins & Mikosza, 2010). At the same time, the Chinese government had not loosened its control over media operations and management. Rather, it actually tightened media control and censorship, while selectively promoting competition among state-owned enterprises in the media and communication industries.

Established sport and media organizations in China have extended their brands into blogging and social media platforms in a similar fashion to their European and American counterparts (Mahan & McDaniel, 2006). Research in these Western contexts finds that digital media technologies are used to control the flow of information and maximize capital flow (Real, 2006; Dart, 2009). This logic of neoliberalism is also prevalent in China, a post-socialist state governed by a disingenuous form of neoliberalism. Yet, here we see a unique and unwieldy combination of neoliberalism and crony capitalism in the so-called "socialist market economy with Chinese characteristics".[9] Operators in the Chinese Olympic media sports cultural complex are either directly or indirectly part of the state-dominated "socialist market economy" and so subject to the dual logics of neoliberalism and centrism.

Under this peculiar neoliberal centrism, blogging the Beijing Games was not just about networked digital media sport, but the reconfiguration of power relations in the media sports cultural complex. Political aims and economic gains dominate media and communication policies, operational models and management. For businesses, blogging is a communications tool, a listening device, a marketing technique and a public relations platform used to build a positive image for the company and to interact directly with consumers. Scholars in marketing, corporate communication and business management have contributed to discussions about the creative use of new social software such as blogs and social networking services to revolutionize sales by turning consumers into prosumers (Wright, 2006). Prosumers are part of the chain of "value co-creation" (Prahalad & Ramaswamy, 2000). The co-creationist concept is applied to blogging the Olympic Games when communication carriers, broadcasters and new media portals harness, as at Beijing 2008, consumer creativity and productivity in content production to generate value-added revenue for commercial companies.

For minor players without accreditation or access to the Olympic venues, the co-creationist concept was utilized to generate traffic and revenue. In most cases they adopted a strategy of "piggyjacking" (a combination of piggybacking and hijacking) (Miah, Garcia & Tian, 2008, p. 339) by forming a second-tier alliance with CCTV and its official partners. This strategy allowed them to capitalize on the work of others and, at the same time, infiltrate "legal" spaces with additional and competing publicity. China's popular video sharing website Youku.com is an example of piggyjacking marketing. As an unaccredited new media portal, Youku.com was not allowed to have any video streaming content sourced from CCTV or its nine new media partners. But the site still managed to capitalize on the Olympics by mobilizing vbloggers to upload videos about fans and events outside the Olympic stadia. This alternative site attracted more than 2,000 video uploads per day during the Beijing Games, with some receiving more than one million hits. Youku.com's loyal users appeared to be competing to upload the fastest and best pieces about the Olympics. Less than five minutes after Liu's withdrawal from the race on 18 August 2008, a video stream of people's reactions outside the stadium was uploaded to its website, which was immediately followed by numerous others. Local tabloid newspapers, such as the *Jinan Times* in Shandong Province, also employed this piggyjacking strategy. In the lead-up to the Games, the *Jinan Times* enlisted thirty people to form a team called "amateur Olympic Journalists". All were volunteers or service and maintenance staff at various venues, or simply avid Olympic fans who bought tickets to view multiple sporting events. A QQ group was created by the *Jinan Times* to facilitate instant communication and file transfers between the "amateur journalists" and editors based in Jinan. As such, this newspaper was able to cover the Olympic events without sending a single journalist to Beijing.

The analysis presented here suggests that blogging can be viewed as a new form of cooperative production of Olympic media. On the one hand, consumers are empowered to act out their desires for creativity, control, freedom and belonging in an affective community supported and fostered by service providers. On the other hand, behind the veneer of consumer empowerment is the logic of "creationist capitalism" (Boellstorff, 2008): the sense of empowerment is translated into added value when the prosumers "donate" their products (blog writings, postings, images, audio and video files) to corporate projects. As Olympic organizations, broadcasters and sponsors considered how best to build their brand names, exploit advertising opportunities, and maximize profits, they were joined and facilitated by a Chinese government eager to profit from the business of Olympic media. The "masses" were just as self-motivated to contribute to the success of the Beijing Olympic Games. The result in 2008 was "production without alienation" or a mutually beneficial relationship between consumers and companies.

This co-creationist capitalism is increasingly employed by networked media sport businesses worldwide to capture large repositories of technical, social and cultural competence at minimal cost. These practices underline the neoliberal logic of Chinese Web 2.0: the drive to make huge profits goes hand-in-hand with the demand to be politically responsible (to the state and its main agendas). In co-creating the Olympic spectacle, the drive and the demand were neutralized through:

> . . .experimenting with new possibilities for value creation that are based on the expropriation of free cultural, technological, social, and affective labor of the consumer masses. (Zwick, Bonsu & Darmody, 2008, p. 166)

The consumer masses were willing participants in the expropriation of their desire for empowerment and expression. Through blogging the Beijing Olympics, they offered an alternative form of Olympic media that supplemented, rather than competed with, the official coverage of the Games.

ALTERNATIVE VIEWPOINTS?

The widespread availability of blogs offered the potential to offer powerful counternarratives about the Beijing Olympic saga. Yet, there was no record of contending stories on the Chinese Internet before or during the Games. This eventuality went against suggestions made prior to the Games:

> While the High-Tech theme of the Olympics may connote Chinese technological progressivism and innovation, the increased adoption and prevalence of advanced information technology, including mobile technology, may provide opportunities for such a narrative to be hijacked and for counternarratives to emerge. Camera and video mobile phones provide a means of sousveillance [monitoring authority from below] through which everyday citizens can monitor, record, and disseminate official acts and behaviors of abuse or negligence. (Humphreys & Finlay, 2008, p. 302)

In the lead-up to the Games, most Chinese netizens rallied behind the Chinese mainstream media, particularly in relation to the Tibetan riots, a disrupted Olympic torch relay and the Sichuan earthquake. Any independent voices and alternative views that could challenge this orthodoxy were possibly deleted quickly by moderators or drowned in the digital sea of articles and posts that were part of Beijing's "charm offensive". The overwhelming sense drawn from the available evidence is of nationwide celebration and self-congratulation. Just as James Leibold (2008) anticipated, if there were any protests outside the stadia, the Chinese media completely ignored them, while international media cautiously covered them. There was also no evidence of protests on video sharing sites. This situation captures an important dimension of the neoliberal logic of Chinese Web 2.0: the drive to make huge profits and the demand to be politically responsible accompanies the prosumer desire for empowerment, expression and change. Yet, this "empowerment, expression and change" is contingent upon the dynamics of online activism at any given time (Yang, 2009). In the case of blogging the Beijing Olympic Games, the prosumers mostly consisted of urbanites that supported the national effort to initiate China's formal entry into the realm of great world powers.

The seemingly diverse views on Liu's withdrawal from the 110 meter hurdles, for example, tell us less about prosumer empowerment or an "alternative" perspective on the Olympics than about the marketing strategies of China's "big four" Internet services (Sina, Sohu, QQ and Netease) and their business partners. Posts by two of China's best-known sports journalists/commentators were selected as "recommended blog posts" to attract traffic and more posts. Michael Real (2006, p. 182) reminds us of the consequence of convergence and consolidation of media ownership in this context:

> . . . the likelihood of a Spiral of Silence emerges, one in which fringe minority voices get less hearing and are gradually brought into conformity. Similarly as dominance of the web reverts, as seems to be happening, towards the media monopolies, the hegemony of the privileged over Web content and values will marginalize less powerful groups as it has in other media.

Furthermore, the star j-bloggers (Dong and Huang) represent the "champion" consumers of the nation. Chinese bloggers were usually the urban middle class who could afford the trip to the "Bird's Nest", watch different kinds of sporting events and share their excitement through blogs, Qzone or QQ groups. They were willing participants in co-creationist capitalism, and happy consumers of a spectacle afforded by "super-investment" in telecommunications and the "super-capacity" of broadband and 3G mobile networks. China's telecommunications infrastructure, like the society itself, is fractured and characterized by "one country, four worlds": the first world of the ultra-modern and high-income metropolitan cities; the second world composed of large, middle-sized and small cities in the coastal areas and prosperous high-income rural areas; the third world of middle- and low-income rural areas; and the fourth world composed of minority and border areas and extremely poor and low-income rural areas (Hu et al., 2001, p. 167, cited in Zhao, 2007a, p. 102). Additionally, the "champion" prosumers of the Olympic media tend to ignore the "real politics" behind the "harmonious" blogosphere, such as Falun Gong's "resistance politics", workers' "proletariat politics" and farmers' "right defense politics" (Zhao, 2007a). As Yuezhi Zhao and others have pointed out, the Chinese telecommunications industry is governed by state-led, "market-oriented, high-end customer-centered and profit-driven development strategies" (Zhao, 2007b, p. 109). It is also marked by inequitable access, and short-term and top-down paternalism combined with mercantilist approaches to the digital divide. This situation has seen the rural and urban poor—including laid-off workers, retirees and rural migrants—and the vast hinterland and less developed areas left out of the telecommunications boom.

CONCLUSION: CHINA'S OLYMPIC MEDIA AND CO-CREATIONIST CAPITALISM

This chapter has critiqued the neoliberal logic of Chinese Olympic media in the context of blogging the Beijing Olympics. I have argued that digital media and communication technologies are increasing the chances for cross-promotion and concentration of the media sports cultural complex. When "old" media migrate to "new" media and multimedia platforms, they are in a stronger position to create spirals of silence and consensus. The seemingly diversified views afforded by blogging practices, and the huge number of blog posts and videos posted during the Beijing Games, only serve as a facade to mask the uneven development and unfair access to telecommunications and media markets in China.

The scale and resources of CCTV, Lenovo, China Mobile, Sohu.com and other new media portals allow them to cross-promote one another, and their domination of Chinese television, mobile communications and digital media markets enables them to maximize profit, as well as to shape and guide public opinion. CCTV and its business partners—most are state-owned enterprises, while others hold state-issued licenses for audio-video content—are able to consolidate their cross-media business models by adopting user-generated content through blogging and problogging. They are able to moderate what is posted in blogs and to set media agendas and shape public opinion by selectively promoting certain posts while deleting others. Under co-creationist capitalism, consumers are transformed into co-producers that donate their labor to corporations. While transforming prosumers' creativity and productivity into added value, big businesses can also harness such creativity and productivity in line with the Chinese state's expectations of its citizens and with how the IOC wants athletes to behave online. Part of the neoliberal logic of Chinese Web 2.0 lies in deliberate cooperation among the corporate sector, the government and dominant Chinese netizens to marginalize less powerful groups and minority voices.

NOTES

1. Microblogging ("weibo" in Chinese) did not take off in China until after 2009 when Sina.com launched its popular weibo platform. The role of microblogging in representing the Olympics is not a focus of this chapter, as blogging rather than microblogging dominated networked media sport in China in 2008.
2. The term "money-power-knowledge iron triangle" refers to the interlocking relationships and alliances among expert knowledge (of elite economists), economic capital and bureaucratic power to implement neoliberal hegemony in Chinese economics, which excludes subordinate social classes (such as workers) without money and discursive power (Zhao, 2008).
3. In addition to the studies cited in the introduction section, see the special issue, "Preparing for Glory: Beijing 2008—Chinese Challenge in the 'Chinese Century' ", of *The International Journal of the History of Sport* 25(7), 2008.
4. CCTV also tried to mobilize grassroots bloggers in its Olympic blogger project. It enlisted bloggers worldwide to provide comments on Olympic events at blog.cctv.com, and invited fourteen selected netizens to participate in live online commentaries with professional commentators.
5. Lenovo signed a five-year agreement with Visa as Olympic strategic collaborators on 22 December 2004. In 2006, Lenovo signed a similar agreement with Coca Cola to expand its involvement in the Olympic campaign. Some of the high-profile campaign strategies by Lenovo include, internationally, its online philanthropic auction of limited-edition notebook computers inspired by the Lenovo-designed 2008 Olympic Torch and an online search for "New Thinkers" to participate in the Olympic torch relay (with the help of Google); and domestically, a one-year "roadshow" in 1,000 second- and third-tier cities and rural areas, and a five-month torch bearer selection campaign called "You are the torch bearer" (both telecast on CCTV). See Ye and Lei (2009) for a discussion on Lenovo's Olympic marketing strategies.
6. For IOC blogging guidelines, see: http://blogs.journalism.co.uk/editors/wp-content/uploads/2008/03/iocblogguidlines.pdf (Accessed 10 October 2009).
7. Almost all of the comments expressed similar messages, such as, "We love you and support you no matter what" and "You are our pride; get better soon!" These sentiments resonate with the message conveyed by the mainstream media.
8. Famous partnerships in the digital media sport business during the Beijing Olympiad include China Mobile & SMG, China Mobile & CCTV, China Unicom & CRI, Nike & Sina.com, Nike & QQ, 361° & QQ, and NBA & SiTV.
9. Aihwa Ong (2006) completed a groundbreaking ethnographic study of manifestations of neoliberalism in East and Southeast Asian states, in which she argues that the Chinese "socialist market economy" is underlined by the twin modalities of neoliberal governmentality: "neoliberalism as exception" and "exceptions to neoliberalism". While the former refers to state engineered practices to embrace the market dynamism in order to compete in

the global market, the latter illuminates the struggles between the governing and the governed, power and knowledge. It is not within the scope of this chapter to provide a comprehensive coverage of debates about neoliberalism in China.

REFERENCES

Boellstorff T (2008) *Coming of Age in Second Life: An Anthropologist Explores the Virtually Human*. Princeton: Princeton University Press.

Boyle R & Haynes R (2003) New media sport. In: Bernstein A & Blain N (eds.) *Sport, Media, Culture: Global and Local Dimensions*. London and Portland: Frank Cass, 95–114.

Brownell S (2008) *Beijing's Games: What the Olympics Mean to China*. Lanham: Rowman & Littlefield.

Caffrey K (2008) Olympian politics in Beijing: games but not just games. *International Journal of the History of Sport* 25(7): 807–25.

Close P (2011) The Beijing Olympiad's achievement and legacy in global perspective. *Play the Game*, 24 January. Online. Available from: www.playthegame.org/knowledge-bank/articles/the-beijing-olympiads-achievement-and-legacy-in-global-perspective-5091.html (Accessed 1 Feb 2012).

Close P, Askew D & Xin X (2007) *The Beijing Olympiad: The Political Economy of a Sporting Mega-Event*. London: Routledge.

CNNIC (2008) Research report of Chinese netizens' Olympic media consuming behaviours in 2008 [2008 nian zhongguo wangmin aoyun meiti xiaofei xingwei yanjiu baogao]. Online. Available from: http://www.cnnic.cn/hlwfzyj/hlwxzbg/mtbg/201206/P020120612508644430906.pdf (Accessed 11 March 2010).

CNNIC (2009a) Statistical survey report on the internet development in China. Online. Available from: research.cnnic.cn/img/h000/h10/attach200906160930580.rar (Accessed 10 February 2010).

CNNIC (2009b) Research on Chinese blogger market and behaviors 2008–2009 [Zhongguo boke shichang ji boke xingwei yanjiu baogao]. Online. Available from: http://www.cnnic.cn/hlwfzyj/hlwxzbg/sqbg/201206/P020120612509155387996.pdf (Accessed 10 October 2009).

Couldry N & Curran J (eds.) (2003) *Contesting Media Power: Alternative Media in a Networked World*. Lanham: Rowman & Littlefield.

Dart J (2009) Blogging the 2006 FIFA World Cup finals. *Sociology of Sport Journal* 26(1): 107–26.

Fan H (2008) *China Gold: China's Quest for Global Power and Olympic Glory*. Great Barrington, MA: Berkshire Publishing Group.

Harvey D (2005) *A Brief History of Neoliberalism*. Oxford: Oxford University Press.

Humphreys L & Finlay CJ (2008) New technologies, new narratives. In: Price ME & Dayan D (eds.) *Owning the Olympics: Narratives of the New China*. Ann Arbor: The University of Michigan Press, 284–306.

Hutchins B & Mikosza J (2010) The Web 2.0 Olympics: athlete blogging, social networking and policy contradictions at the 2008 Beijing Games. *Convergence* 16(3): 279–97.

Hutchins B & Rowe D (2009) From broadcast rationing to digital plenitude: the changing dynamics of the media sport content economy. *Television and New Media* 10(4): 354–70.

Jarvie G, Hwang DJ & Brennan M (2008) *Sport, Revolution and the Beijing Olympics*. Oxford and New York: Berg.

Koch PT, Koch BJ, Huang K & Chen W (2009) Beauty is in the eye of the QQ user: instant messaging in China. In: Goggin G & McLelland M (eds.) *Internationalizing*

Internet Studies: Beyond Anglophone Paradigms. London and New York: Routledge, 265–84.

Latham K (2009) Media, the Olympics and search for the "real China". *The China Quarterly* 197 (March): 25–43.

Leibold J (2008) Duelling dreams at the 2008 Beijing Olympics. *China Beat*, 18 July. Online Available from: thechinabeat.blogspot.com/2008/07/duelling-dreams-at-2008-beijing.html (Accessed 2 August 2008).

Lenskyj HJ (2006) Alternative media versus the Olympic industry. In: Raney A & Bryant J (eds.) *Handbook of Sports and Media.* Mahwah, New Jersey: Lawrence Erlbaum Associates, 205–16.

Mahan J & McDaniel S (2006) The new online arena: sport, marketing, and the media converge in cyberspace. In: Raney A & Bryant J (eds.) *Handbook of Sports and Media.* Mahwah, New Jersey: Lawrence Erlbaum Associates, 409–31.

Miah A, Garcia B & Tian Z (2008) "We are the media": nonacrredited media and citizen journalists at the Olympic Games. In: Price M E & Dayan D (eds.) *Owning the Olympics: Narratives of the New China.* Ann Arbor: The University of Michigan Press, 320–45.

Nielsen (2008) Who were the real winners of the Beijing Olympics? Online. Available from: cn.en.nielsen.com/site/documents/Olympic_en.pdf (Accessed 20 February 2010).

Ong R (2004) New Beijing, great Olympics: Beijing and its unfolding Olympic legacy. *Stanford Journal of East Asian Affairs* 14(2): 35–49.

Ong A (2006) *Neoliberalism as Exception: Mutations in Citizenship and Sovereignty.* Durham and London: Duke University Press.

Polumbaum J (2003) Capturing the flame: aspirations and representations of Beijing's 2008 Olympics. In: Lee CC (ed.) *Chinese Media, Global Contexts.* London and New York: RoutledgeCurzon, 57–75.

Prahalad C & Ramaswamy V (2000) Co-opting customer competence. *Harvard Business Review* 78 (January–February): 79–87.

Price ME & Dayan D (eds.) (2008) *Owning the Olympics: Narratives of the New China.* Ann Arbor: The University of Michigan Press.

Qiu J (2009) *Working-Class Network Society: Communication Technology and the Information Have-Less in Urban China.* Cambridge, MA: The MIT Press.

Real M (2006) Sports online: the newest players in media sport. In Raney A & Bryant J (eds.) *Handbook of Sports and Media.* Mahwah, New Jersey: Lawrence Erlbaum Associates, 171–84.

Rowe D (2004) *Sport, Culture, and the Media.* 2nd ed. Maidenhead, Berkshire: Open University Press.

Schaffer K & Smith S (2000) The Olympics of the everyday. In: Shaffer K & Smith S (eds.) *The Olympics at the Millennium: Performance, Politics and the Games.* New Brunswick, NJ: Rutgers University Press, 213–23.

Short J (2003) Going for gold: globalizing the Olympics, localizing the games. *Globalization and World Cities Research Bulletin* 10. Online. Available from: http://www.lboro.ac.uk/gawc/rb/rb100.html (Accessed 2 Feb 2012).

Sigley G (2004) Liberal despotism: population planning, subjectivity, and government in contemporary China. *Alternatives* 29(5): 557–75.

Sohu.com (2008) CCTV attracted 1.12 billion pairs of eyes and 2 billion yuan during the Olympics [Yangshi aoyun qijian xiyin 11.2 yi shuang yanjing, zhuan 20 yi yuan]. 27 August. Online. Available from: news.sohu.com/20080827/n259232218.shtml (Accessed 13 February 2010).

Sun W (2002) Semiotic over-determination or "indoctritainment": television, citizenship, and the Olympic Games. In Donald SH Keane M & Yin H (eds.) *Media in China: Consumption, Content and Crisis.* London and New York: RoutledgeCurzon, 116–27.

Wright J (2006) *Blog Marketing: The Revolutionary New Way to Increase Sales, Build your Brand, and Get Exceptional Results.* New York: The McGraw-Hill Companies.

Xu G (2008) *Olympic Dreams: China and Sports 1895–2008.* Cambridge, MA: Harvard University Press.

Yang G (2009) *The Power of the Internet in China: Citizen Activism Online.* New York: Columbia University Press.

Ye N & Lei X (2009) On the motives and strategies of Lenovo Group's marketing in Beijing Olympic Games [Lianxiang jituan Beijing aoyun yingxiao dongji ji celuo]. *Journal of Capital Institute of Physical Education* 21(5): 554–56.

Yu H (2009) *Media and Cultural Transformation in China.* London and New York: Routledge.

Yu H (2011a) Beyond gatekeeping: J-blogging in China. *Journalism: Theory, Practice and Criticism* 12(5): 1–15.

Yu H (2011b) Dwelling narrowness: Chinese media and its disingenuous neoliberal logic. *Continuum: Journal of Media & Cultural Studies* 12(1): 33–46.

Zhao Y (2000) From commercialization to conglomeration: The transformation of the Chinese press within the orbit of the party state. *Journal of Communication* 50(2): 3–26.

Zhao Y (2007a) After mobile phones, what? Re-embedding the social in China's "digital revolution". *International Journal of Communication* 1(1): 92–120.

Zhao Y (2007b) "Universal service" and China's telecommunications miracle: discourses, practices and post-WTO challenges. *Info* 9(2/3): 108–21.

Zhao Y (2008) *Communication in China: Political Economy, Power, and Conflict.* Lanham, Maryland: Rowman & Littlefield.

Zwick D, Bonsu S & Darmody A (2008) Putting consumers to work: "co-creation" and new marketing govern-mentality. *Journal of Consumer Culture* 8(2): 163–96.

14 Sports Journalism and Social Media

A New Conversation?

Raymond Boyle and Richard Haynes

> The lesson for journalists is don't just think of social media as a place to show off and chat to your friends. It's also a place where an individual act of journalism can become a networked campaign.
>
> *Charlie Beckett, Polis Blog, 25 January 2012*

> The process has become the product.
>
> *Jeff Jarvis, What Would Google Do?* (2009, p. 92)

INTRODUCTION: ARE SOCIAL MEDIA TRANSFORMING SPORTS JOURNALISM?

Sports journalism has always adapted to its media environment, responding to transformations in technology, institutions, professional practices and sporting cultures. As with most social and cultural changes, this response has often been incremental, involved hegemonic struggles for authority and affected practice in differential ways over time and space. Social media networks, globally dominated in contemporary public culture by Facebook and Twitter, present one of the latest challenges and opportunities for sports journalism as a profession. There are struggles for continuity in sports journalism—for the survival of established codes and conventions of work, for authority and exclusivity—as well as innovative departures from the quotidian "sports beat" of print journalists established over a century of sports reporting. For the journalist this task has involved mastering the utility and language of digital technologies, as well as incorporating new forms of communication into the production and consumption of sports news. Indeed, precisely what is meant by "sports news" is unstable and under constant revision in the digitally networked media environment.

This chapter examines the extent to which social media are transforming sports journalism, focusing on the ways in which media-source relations between journalism and the "world of sport" and its stars are changing. It is also about how the relationship between sports journalists and their audience is transformed by "a new conversation" taking place inside social networking media. Issues covered include how sports information is circulated in the context of social media and how such information is sourced and made into news stories. We also discuss whether new storytelling techniques have emerged in sports journalism as a response to social media. A small range of high-profile professional sports are discussed in order to ascertain how the culture and practices of social media and sports journalism have changed the nature and form of sports news, focusing on the commonalities and differences across different sports. This approach does not only recognize the specificities of news cultures within different sports, but also how social media practices may vary across them. For instance, are there any discernible differences between the social media practices in team as opposed to individual sports? Or are common trends emerging across different sports that signify new ways of reporting from sport and new methods of producing or consuming sports news? If so, how do we identify and analyze them?

The chapter begins with an overview of recent critical thinking on journalism and social media with a view to conceptualizing the place of sports journalism in a convergent digital news culture. We focus on the sports of soccer and golf to unpack some of the specific issues faced by sports journalism in these fields. Case studies are based on responses from sports journalists about the use of Twitter, as well as textual and narrative analysis of sports news stories generated in social media. Debates about the regulation of news-source relations in the "Twittersphere" are also examined. We identify the range of strategic measures used by athletes and their advisors (agents, publicists, clubs, associations and governing bodies) as they seek to manage the complex relations created by social media, and in particular by micro-blogging sites such as Twitter. Our observations are then summarized and some initial responses provided on how critically to understand what is happening in contemporary sports journalism and its social media practice.

SPORTS JOURNALISM AND SOCIAL MEDIA

The relationship between journalism and social networking sites (boyd & Ellison, 2007) has been framed largely in two ways. The first is by reference to the processes of convergence that accelerated in the 1990s with the rise of the Internet and digital production processes that made multimedia news practices the norm. The second relates to how we identify what journalism actually is, and indeed, what it is not. Like their colleagues in other forms of print journalism, sports journalists are expected to be adaptable to a changing media environment. They must be adept enough to work across different media, producing copy for print and online versions of the publications that they work for, as well as creating blogs, tweets and pod-casts, or appearing on radio and television when required. Historically, the pan-media sports journalist is nothing new. In Scotland, for instance, sports audiences have long been familiar with journalists providing commentary or analysis on television one moment, presenting or conducting interviews on radio the next and publishing a column in a national newspaper for publication on the following day (Haynes & Boyle, 2008). However, with the rise of citizen or participatory journalism, the voice of the professional sports journalist has a new challenger as the "gatekeeper" of sports news and information. This challenge comes from fans, bloggers, tweeters and, increasingly, those from within sport itself—the sports star who may be one or all of the former. The sports star as producer of "user-generated content" represents a particular form of disintermediation; that is, cutting out the journalist as an intermediary. This development has destabilized the news-source relationships in sport that for many years were characterized by the "beat" reporting of old (Boyle, 2006) and has recently been replaced by professionally managed media relations (Boyle & Haynes, 2011). Although sport stars have long contributed guest columns, often ghost written, or offered opinion as television panelists, they have rarely ventured into what might be termed independent or alternative media forms, such as fanzines. Sport stars creating blogs, Facebook pages or Twitter feeds present a dif-ferent order of mass self-communication, lying outside mainstream media organizations and circumventing the need to connect with their audience via journalists.

As Wolfgang Donsbach (2011, p. 43) has suggested, the threat to the identity of journalists is a problem of "a disappearing social function" of journalism, where access to information no longer resides with the occu-pation of journalists. As is well documented in the endemic global decline of newspaper circulations, knowledge, information, comment, analysis, gossip and news proliferate on the Internet. These are a mere Google search away on every networked device, with search engines and their algorithms increasingly providing our hierarchy of news rather than jour-nalists (Halavais, 2008). In the context of sport, this shift has profound consequences for audience engagement with sports cultures. How sports gain attention from their audiences is now differentially distributed and aggregated by computers, not editors. People increasingly get their daily dose of sports information through a Google search (or more precisely via an aggregated source such as Google News) instead of the back page. Social media have personalized this distribution and aggregation of sports news even further, as users order, read, compile and connect to informa-tion gathered by those individuals and organizations that they "follow" and confirm as "friends".

The heightened competition for attention in a global, multimedia, net-worked world of communication is, therefore, intense and has led Hutchins and Rowe (2012) to characterize sports journalism as a "leaking craft". Most sports have accommodated and managed this challenge through strategic commercial partnerships with media corporations, exclusive television rights deals, targeted marketing communications and niche television and web channels. Much of this activity is reliant on professionalized and commercially driven promotional industries: advertising, marketing, sponsorship and public relations. This development, in turn, has had some profound consequences for sports journalism. For example, critiques of the influence of public relations activity on the practice of journalism, in its extreme form labeled "churnalism" by Nick Davies (2009), equally apply to the coverage of sport. Sport now sits squarely at the center of the entertainment industries and is heavily influenced by both the economics of the media (television especially) and the cult of celebrity that drives the fascination and populist interest in sport stars. Access to sport stars is now routinized and sanitized in "flash interviews" immediately after an event, and usually in front of a backdrop of strategically placed sponsors' logos. More considered star profiles are commonly based on opinion and sensationalism rather than reflective analysis, and long-form interviews are placed and managed by agents and publicists as part of a wider marketing function. In this rather glib, gloomy version of contemporary sports journalism, investigative approaches to sport are increasingly rare. There are exceptions, such as investigations of match-fixing, performance-enhancing drugs, corruption in the governance of sport and financial irregularities. The subject competence of sports journalists in some of these areas, including sports finance, is often found wanting, as they step into areas of expertise beyond their comfort zone. So the "bread and butter" of sports journalism remains soft news stories based on quotes from press conferences or press releases, with additional gossip thrown in from a network of sources.

A number of questions arise from this state of affairs. How have the dual processes of convergence and professional dissolution impacted the mainstream field of sports journalism? When combined with "convergence culture" (Jenkins, 2006), has the capacity to turn consumers into the producers of celebrity sports media undermined the gatekeeping role of journalists to inform and interpret the world of sport for its fans? Do fans any longer need the sports journalist to provide their "daily fix" of sports information and gossip? The continued existence of professional sports journalists suggests that sports fans do. But the kinds of information available in social networks also suggest that there are other modes of writing and understanding that require no form of journalism training, practice or skills. In the age of social media, the conversation has got much bigger and the position of the sports journalist in informing their audience is no longer as privileged as it used to be. This circumstance begs another important question: what kind of information and knowledge on sport is being produced in social media contexts, and to what extent does any of this represent what is understood as journalism, news or reportage?

In a review of the personalized nature of news in digital networks, Kate Crawford asks another pertinent question: "When is Twitter journalism?" (Crawford, 2010, p. 117). The question raises further issues about who we might actually identify as a sports journalist and how sports information as a news source is identified, managed and controlled by differentiated groups of producers (journalists) and consumers (audiences), who in many cases are one and the same (so-called prosumers). The blurring of the boundaries between those who write and read social media is, of course, one of the key signatures of digital media itself. Governing bodies of sport, and professional sports institutions such as clubs, are concerned that athletes and elite sports stars in the public eye have a potentially free reign to communicate their inner thoughts or the banal trivialities of their everyday lives, which has led to the introduction of guidelines or codes of conduct in an attempt to regulate social media practices (Hutchins & Mikosza, 2010). Sports journalists also have to manage the erosion of the boundaries between their professional (public) and private lives, not least because, in the social media environment, their working lives may appear to be always "switched on". This ceaseless routine is why so many journalists indicate on their Twitter or blog profiles that what is being written in these spaces represents their own opinions and not that of their employer. There is also an implicit informality in social media that, in many ways, runs against the grain of the formal, objective voice of traditional journalism practice.

The practices discussed here are the subjects of an ongoing area of debate and tension between journalists and the news organizations that employ them. In February 2012, Sky News in the UK announced new social media guidelines for all its journalists that limited what they could retweet to followers (it could only be posts from other Sky journalists) and reminded them of the importance of posting breaking news online via the Web before using Twitter. Organizations such as Sky and the BBC are protecting their brands, as well as exercising editorial control over content distributed in their names, even if indirectly through a reporter. Interestingly, such guidelines have emerged as other news agencies, notably Reuters, have broken stories via their Twitter feed. Thus, the rules of engagement are continually evolving as journalists and organizations adapt and make sense of the possibilities and challenges involved in positioning social media as a central element of news culture.

Another dynamic aspect of distinctions between news/non-news and journalism/non-journalism occurs when social media postings are picked up by corporate news media. This phenomenon has been well established since the first blossoming of blogging and "citizen journalism", particularly after the terrorist attacks of 9/11 in 2001. With the increasing use of micro-blogging on Twitter, the potential for sports journalists to pick up on emerging themes and stories—specifically where a topic, individual or organization is "trending" with a high frequency of interest—has also increased. In the next section we examine how this relationship and use of social media by sports journalists has impacted their work, both in terms of how they are influenced by the circulation of information in social media and the ways in which they have increasingly "joined the conversation" in an attempt to influence both the source and use of news from these online spaces. Research on news journalists suggests that many are now freely expressing opinion beyond the objective norms of newsgathering while, at the same time, increasing the accountability and transparency of their work practices (Lasorsa, Lewis & Holton, 2012). Journalists can also use social media and their followers to ask questions and use these responses to inform what they write. Generating sources in this way is a far more open and transparent method of working and requires a "leap of faith" by journalists themselves who, by sharing their everyday thoughts on sport, now open themselves up to public scrutiny and criticism. This practice has become of particular interest when sport stars also use social media to corroborate or dispute the interventions of sports journalists in relation to an emerging news story. As we shall see, there have been a number of high profile disputes between sport stars and journalists in this context.

SHAPING THE NEWS AGENDA

Immediacy has always been an integral part of news culture. The rise over the last two decades of "24/7" rolling news has meant that "breaking stories" have become part of the mainstream lexicon of news culture. Micro-blogging sites such as Twitter now act as news feeds, despite the already-noted restrictions put on them by organizations such as Sky and the BBC. When we saw the dramatic resignation of the England national soccer team manager, Fabio Capello, in 2012—on the same day that the potential future England manager, Harry Redknapp, was found not guilty of tax evasion—it was social media sites that helped shape the news agenda and the reporting of the stories through mainstream news outlets. Sky's Martyn Ziegler broke the Capello story via Twitter even before the FA tweeted the announcement of his resignation (ironically, this would be less likely to happen now under Sky's new social media guidelines). At one point on that day, with Redknapp's acquittal taking place in the morning and Capello resigning in the late afternoon, almost 4,000 tweets a second were being posted. Thus, for those with access to sites such as Twitter the news and story moved at a fast pace, with updates from journalists being posted. Feedback and comments from fans, players and even soccer officials all contributed to the conversation. This group, although large and international in scope, is also, of course, self-selecting. Most people still got news of the dramatic announcements from either radio or television broadcasts. Many people then went online to news webpages for further information. The key point here is that, while only a minority (albeit substantial) was micro-blogging as the story evolved, this group was dramatically shaping the story and the manner in which it would be relayed to the majority of the audience via traditional media outlets.

A new departure in news-source relationships was the scale of Twitter feeds of England soccer squad players reported via the news media. Within minutes of Capello's resignation, the media were reporting the thoughts of current international players such as Wayne Rooney, Glen Johnson and Rio Ferdinand, as well as those of former England stars and media pundits such as Gary Lineker and Stan Collymore. Their thoughts on Capello—many appeared glad he was gone—and their belief that the next manager should be English and preferably Redknapp, may not have come as a shock to those following the story closely, but did shape the tone and tenor of the mainstream news coverage. Thus the attitudes of large sections of the England squad became public knowledge and provided an important news element of the story as it developed on that Wednesday. It was print and broadcast media then that delivered the information to a wider national audience the next day. Newspapers ran headlines such as, "Capello rule had run its course and the players will shed no tears" (Kay, 2012) and printed the tweets from players and celebrities across the pages that it devoted to the resignation.

Not only was Twitter deployed to "break" aspects of the story, but its use as a news and information source by journalists shaped reports to some extent. The tweets of players, officials and supporters helped make sense of events for the majority of the public not using micro-blogging sites, but who access news stories that are now heavily informed by users of such social media. Journalist and broadcaster Jon Snow commented on these changes that journalism is experiencing due to technological and commercial pressures:

> We are in the age of answer back, better still we are in the age in which "we the people" have their greatest opportunity ever to influence the information agenda. (Snow, 2012)

However, this "answer back culture", or the supposed eradication of traditional journalism hierarchies of news values, is at best uneven and at times contradictory.

SOCIAL MEDIA AND THE PUBLIC "PRIVATE" ATHLETE

While social media networking sites disrupt traditional club-player-media-fan interactions, it is also important to note that players often use such platforms for differing reasons. For some players and their sponsors, social media offer another channel through which to raise brand awareness and to connect with fans in a manner that established marketing mechanisms increasingly struggle to do. In the UK, these efforts are often crude. Tweeters such as Manchester United captain, Ferdinand (with other sports stars), have been investigated by the Advertising Standards Authority (ASA) over a series of posts that endorsed the chocolate bar Snickers, having been paid by the company to do so. The ASA investigation focused on whether it was made clear that these "teaser" tweets were, in fact, part of an advertising campaign. The Office of Fair Trading (OFT) had previously been involved in a case in 2010 and had taken action against a public relations agency that had been paying bloggers to write and tweet about its products. As the *Daily Telegraph* noted:

> Heather Clayton, Senior Director of OFT's Consumer Group, said: "The internet plays a key role in how people purchase products and services and the importance of online advertising continues to grow . . . The integrity of information published online is crucial so that people can make informed decisions on how to spend their money. We expect online advertising and marketing campaigns to be transparent so consumers can clearly tell when blogs, posts and microblogs have been published in return for payment or payment in kind. We expect this to include promotions for products and services as well as editorial content." (Barnett, 2012)

However, in the US this aspect of marketing is such that social media clauses are now increasingly common in sports sponsorship contracts. Incentive payments are made to sports stars to endorse products and services and who are able to demonstrate a growth in followers month-on-month. A balance is then required between alienating fans through a hard sell and a less transparent approach to endorsement. The downside for sponsors can be when players or athletes go "off-message", and there have been cases in the US of sponsors cancelling endorsements because of tweets they deemed to be inconsistent with the brand values of the sponsor.

These arrangements serve to highlight the extent to which a new medium for communication can quickly become commercialized. These platforms are viewed by some corporate organizations and sports stars as another way in which to monetize the relationship that fans often have with sports culture. Thus, for some analysts such as David M. Carter (2011), the rise of social media is simply part of a wider process of convergence between the sporting and entertainment industries. Carter views social media not as a means to enhance cultural exchange or deepen our understanding of sports culture but as part of marketing and business culture. Organizations can, then, enhance their integration with sports culture and profit from the forms of convergence that he identifies as taking place in the home, away from the home and in the sporting venue. This narrow, commercially driven and top-down (and ultimately limited) view of the role and potential of social media suggests an extension of existing relationships in the sport-media nexus, rather than an emergent and more democratic model of sports culture.

Even those players who reject this commercial and promotional model of social media face challenges, as new media platforms co-exist with already established channels of communication. For some high-profile players such as Joey Barton (an avid tweeter), the platform allows the projection of an enlarged view of a player who has suffered from an image problem (he has twice been convicted of common assault and affray and served time in prison as a result of his first conviction in 2008). In a comment piece written for *The Times* newspaper, Barton claimed that he had become a Twitter convert when he realized:

> After years of interviews, it became clear that no journalist was willing to tell my tale. Anything I said, anything I did, was given an angle to fit in with the bad-boy image . . . I was [an] enigma . . . They projected someone who was not the real me: it was the me that the press wanted to project . . . No longer would I let journalistic interpretation to [sic] run wild without any accountability. I didn't have many choices. I decided to tweet! (Barton, 2012)

The irony of this piece is that Barton only got his message out to a wide audience by publishing this article in an established British newspaper and its associated online website.

Barton's approach signifies that the chronic breakdown of trust between soccer players and sports journalists identified previously (Boyle, 2006) has not been eradicated by social media platforms. Barton's honesty about his ability to by-pass "media distortions" of his image may be laudable, particularly when placed against a growing commercial and sometimes cynical use of social media as an extension of a player's marketing and sponsorship portfolio. However, his tweets may also have a limited impact on broader public perceptions of Barton, whose violent actions against Manchester City players on the final day of the 2011–2012 Premier League season led to a twelve-match ban and further public indignation that cut through the "smokescreen" he had presented on Twitter.

The case of Barton reveals a disjunction between the player's self-image and what others have read (perhaps honestly) into his character from his actions both on and off the pitch. Indeed, at times players, agents and even managers are all using social media platforms to extend the public relations activity that has been played out traditionally through newspapers and television, often with the objective of shaping opinion or setting news agendas (Boyle, 2012). For instance, the Chief Sports Correspondent of *The Times* newspaper, Matt Dickinson, and Ferdinand of Manchester United, had a public falling out on Twitter. Dickinson suggested that Ferdinand's public utterances via Twitter over his relationship with fellow England international John Terry did not tally with information he had received from other sources about their relationship. Ferdinand reacted angrily on Twitter, indicating that, when the time came to tell the full story about the alleged racial abuse by Terry of Ferdinand's brother Anton (a West Ham United player), then Dickinson "wouldn't be anywhere near the list of people I'd talk to—Poor journalism" (@rioferdy5). Dickinson replied via @Dickinson-Times with, "Won't embarrass you or anyone around you by disclosing what has been said, but u seem full of denials and no explanations re JT". While this exchange offers public insights into some of the private tensions between journalists and players, these types of exchanges gain wider profile when picked up by mainstream media. It should also be remembered that reporting conflict and fallouts in sport has always been a mainstay of sports journalism.

In the longer term, new patterns of trust may emerge as the dialogue between fans, journalists and players is expanded. However, print and broadcast media will remain an important source of news and image shaping for players and their sports. There are also indications that, if a dialogue or conversation is being expanded between all of sport's stakeholders, it is often a "dialogue of the deaf". The anonymity afforded by social media means that it also offers a platform for abuse rather than conversation. A number of high-profile sports stars have closed Twitter accounts due to the level of abuse, often racial in character, to which they have been subjected. For instance, it was reported in 2012 that Manchester City's England international representative, Micah Richards, had closed his account because of racial abuse directed at him (BBC News, 2012). In March 2012, a Welsh student was sentenced to fifty-six days in prison for making a racist comment about the critically ill Bolton Wanderers player, Fabrice Muamba, via a social networking site (Morris, 2012). In Scotland, the police have prosecuted fans for posting sectarian abuse, often aimed at the Celtic manager Neil Lennon on social networks such as Facebook. When David Craig—one of three-high profile cases in later 2011 and early 2012—was found guilty of abuse aimed at Lennon (including calling for the Celtic manager to be shot), his defense was that it was "simply banter" that conventionally goes on between fans of Celtic and Rangers. Such has been the political and public profile of online sectarian abuse that new legislation has gone through the Scottish Parliament to strengthen the power of the police and the courts. The Offensive Behaviour at Football and Threatening Communications (Scotland) Act 2012 allows jail sentences of up to five years for those convicted under the Act. Yet, this initiative can also be viewed as a process that specifically criminalizes soccer fans and fails to recognize that previous laws were actually adequate to deal with the issue of hate speech online.

ON THE ROAD . . . CONVERSATIONS ON TOUR

For some sports stars, the rise of social media has become an important mechanism through which to manage their image and public persona, thereby challenging wider perceptions of their individual character. Where careers are based on individual performance, as in the potentially lucrative professional sports of tennis or golf, social media have been incorporated into the culture and lifestyle of leading players with astonishing rapidity and impact. Leading tennis players and golfers (almost exclusively male) regularly appear in the top earners in sport, but also attract phenomenal numbers of followers on their Facebook and Twitter pages. In February 2012, for example, Rafael Nadal had more than 1.6 million followers, Tiger Woods had more than 1.8 million, and Serena Williams over 2.5 million. While such numbers may actually be meaningless as indicators of any genuine engagement between fans and the stars that they follow, they are significant as crude indicators of popularity. Popularity for a sports star is a form of symbolic capital that can have tangible rewards. It is, therefore, unsurprising to observe forms of canvassing for popularity, both by the stars and their fans. For example, witness the following tweet by Northern Irish golfer, Rory McIlroy (with more than 800,000 followers), who made the following plea on behalf of his tennis star girlfriend, Carol Wozniacki: "Ok tweeps, my beautiful girlfriend @CaroWozniacki is very close to 300,000 followers. Let's see if we can get her to 500,000 ASAP!!" (@rorymcillroy, 27 February 2012). Although McIlroy is clearly supporting his partner, he is also using the power of networks to ratchet up her popularity through social media.

For journalists and sports fans, the extent to which any of this "sports chatter" is news is less clear. The high-profile British golfer, Ian Poulter, provides a useful case study in this respect. Poulter had more than 1.2 million followers of his Twitter page in February 2012. To adopt a marketing synonym, having that many "eyeballs" looking at the daily musings of a leading professional sportsman obviously has immense commercial potential for brands. As Poulter's agent has remarked:

> He's so big on Twitter that his sponsor relationships have been impacted. Now, when we talk to a company, they will ask us if he will tweet about the product or the product's website. Ian doesn't do it to be a pitch man. He does it because he's authentic. He's very comfortable in his own skin, very comfortable sharing his thoughts, his experiences, his life, and I think people who follow him on Twitter sense that with him. (DiMeglio, 2011)

Although a lot of activity surrounding professional golf invariably has some commercial purpose associated with it (leading brand TaylorMade has, for example, introduced a "Twitter hashtag" for its golf brands worn by players), the "authenticity" claimed by Steve DiMeglio on behalf of Poulter is itself a piece of "spin". It would be misleading, though, to suggest that all of Poulter's engagement with social media is simply another form of marketing communication. His use of the medium is diverse and blends his public and private worlds. A significant percentage of his tweets consists of rather mundane and intimately personal content regarding his family; hardly the exciting backstage news from a "jet-set" sports star. But the fact that he is already well known, if not notorious in a golfing context, means that his contribution to the participatory culture of social media gains purchase and meaning for a wider audience. Therefore, an inane comment on the day's events—what we might term a non-news tweet—may actually become an important news source if this piece of information is judged to be significant by journalists, broadcasters or, indeed, by fans.

The timing and flow of such social media communication presents a challenge to print journalism. Both the incessant flow and randomness of when and where tweets emerge mean that the traditional news cycle is destabilized. Castells (2009) has referred to this process as "timeless time", whereby networked digital technologies create a random sequencing of social actions and events. For the likes of professional golfers and tennis players, who may be "on the road" for half of the year, Twitter provides a powerful, peripatetic form of commentary and communication. The ready availability of powerful 3G smartphones, combined with user-friendly social media "apps", account for widespread access to such activities. Indeed, the frequency with which some tennis and golf stars tweet provides an autobiographical narrative of both a public and private life that many sports journalists would once only have dreamed of accessing. A brief sample of Poulter's tweets from his experiences at the Match Play Championships in Tucson in the US in February 2012 yields a surprising range of insights into the life of a leading professional golfer. But these messages also illustrate the complexity of discursive shifts from the private to the public:

> 30 minute power nap. I'm on twitter until my battery runs out again. Twitter smashing thru the battery keeping my little brain entertained. (20 Feb)

> Days like today makes me realize how fortunate I am to be able to afford to fly on Marquisjet a good chunk of the year. Life's been kind. (20 Feb)

> Friends it's been a lot of fun on twitter today. We are descending into Tucson, time for me to sign off, brush my furry mouth & get to work. (20 Feb)

> RT @TweeterAlliss @IanJamesPoulter A most enjoyable twitter feast as ever young IJP. Quite remarkable. >> my pleasure glad you enjoyed it. (20 Feb)

> It's Matchplay time folks love the feeling you get in Matchplay when can look ur opponent straight in the white of his eyes & get that buzz. (22 Feb)

> That was simply rubbish, 5 bogeys I had today, I beat myself. I wouldn't have given many a good game today. It's a shame I love Matchplay. (22 Feb)

Well Bruce Chritchley [sic] talks complete bollox most of the time anyway. Sorry sky sports viewers for having to listen to his crap every week. (22 Feb)

Should be on twitter or even have a business interest, oh no I'm a golfer I should be a boring idiot that reads his yardage books every day. (22 Feb)

I am a bad loser I've never known a good 1. I'm more disappointed with my own performance. Bae done enough to beat me. Congrats to him. (22 Feb)

Back home with my family & they are really happy to see me good play or bad play. Puts things into perspective. (23 Feb) (@Ianjamespoulter, Accessed 25 February 2012)

In these few Tweets we learn of Poulter's use of Twitter as entertainment to relieve boredom; the luxury lifestyle of one elite professional sport star; a direct connection to his followers and fans; the psychological challenge of match play golf; auto-critique of his poor performance; a direct and rude challenge to media pundits; humor to deflect the criticism; a confession about the deep hurt of losing; and the relief and solace of being back home. Access to such emotive and personal information from a leading player is a departure from any form of sports news and journalism that we have witnessed before.

Precisely how many of Poulter's 1.2 million followers were figuratively travelling with him through this online narrative of life on tour can never be known. But, amid the global media spotlight of golf, which is heavily sponsored and fills hours of television around the globe, Twitter and other social media provide a new space for engagement with this world. Poulter makes links to his fans by providing snapshots of his day and constantly updating his autobiographical narrative in real time. This practice often leads to unexpected consequences, such as an increased profile for him and his sponsors, and a self-serving mechanism for communicating his distrust or critique of the golf media. The increasingly diverse media practices of sports stars and journalists who follow them generate criticism. In Poulter's case, journalists have claimed that his social media activity distracts him from the main event—playing golf. Bruce Critchley, a former Walker Cup player who now works for Sky Sports, remarked that Poulter was not focusing on his golf as much as he should. Another golfer turned television pundit, Sir Nick Faldo, also commented that Poulter's "Twitter addiction" was distracting him from proper practice and had harmed his performances on the Tour. Crude metaphors of addiction are increasingly used to describe excessive use of digital media, particularly in relation to gaming and social media. However, they are unhelpful in understanding why leading sports stars use Twitter and what they hope to achieve by doing so. It is far more useful to analyze the ways in which such activity changes the relationships between sport, the media and audiences, and transforms the nature of the messages and narratives produced, distributed and received. Although regulations on the use of social media have not, as yet, emerged within professional golf, there have been instances of self-censorship. In 2010, during the Ryder Cup, both teams abstained from using their mobile phones during the tournament, thereby removing access to social media platforms. It can only be guessed as to whether performances were enhanced by such a move. But what it does reveal is that, in a team event, individual actions—both front and backstage—have an impact across the group of players, including inappropriate messages coming from public communications in social media.

CONCLUSION: THE CO-EXISTENCE OF MEDIA FORMS

Sports journalists engage with social media for a variety of reasons. Twitter is a news feed from official and unofficial sources, including other journalists and players. It also offers a snapshot of fans' opinions on particular issues and represents a conversation of sorts. Finally, Twitter is a platform to promote and raise athlete profiles and news stories. Social media platforms play a role in shaping news stories, yet the manner by which these stories gain widespread attention or traction is more often through traditional media outlets, so suggesting a coexistence of media forms rather than dominance by any one platform. As with other areas of the digital landscape after the initial period of start-up, the nature of a platform changes as growing commercial opportunities are recognized. Micro-blogging and other social media continue to shape and alter practice and even forms of journalistic output. These developments and energy devoted to them make the production of robust, well-funded journalism challenging in the midst of a social media news maelstrom.

REFERENCES

Barnett E (2012) ASA investigates Rio Ferdinand Snickers tweets. *The Daily Telegraph*, 26 January. Online. Available from: http://www.telegraph.co.uk/technology/twitter/9042288/ASA-investigates-Rio-Ferdinand-Snickers-tweets.html (Accessed 26 January 2012).

Barton J (2012) Thanks to Twitter I'm not just a bad boy now. *The Times,* 31 January, 18.

BBC News (2012) Micah Richards closes Twitter page after "racist abuse". 11 February. Online. Available from: http://www.bbc.co.uk/news/uk-16994086 (Accessed 11 February 2012).

Beckett C (2012) Are you fit enough to face a Twitter trial? *Polis*, 25 January. Online. Available from: http://blogs.lse.ac.uk/polis/2012/01/25/are-you-fit-enough-to-face-a-twitter-trial-lafitness/#more-7608 (Accessed 26 January 2012).

boyd D & Ellison N (2007) Social network sites: definition, history, and scholarship. *Journal of Computer-Mediated Communication* 13(1): 210–30.

Boyle R (2006) *Sports Journalism: Context and Issues*. London: Sage.

Boyle R & Haynes R (2011) Sport, the media and strategic communications management. In: Trenberth L & Hassan D (eds.) *Managing Sport Business: An Introduction.* London: Routledge, 318–37

Boyle R (2012) Social media sport? Journalism, public relations and sport. In: Krovel R & Roksvold T (eds.) *We Love to Hate Each Other: Mediated Football Fan Culture.* Gothenburg: Nordicom, 45–62.

Castells M (2009) *Communication Power.* Oxford: Oxford University Press.

Carter DM (2011) *Money Games: Profiting from the Convergence of Sports and Entertainment.* Stanford: Stanford University Press.

Crawford K (2010) News to me: Twitter and the personal networking of news. In: Meikle G & Redden G (eds.) *News Online: Transformations & Continuities.* London: Palgrave, 115–31.

Davies N (2009) *Flat Earth News.* London: Vintage.

DiMeglio S (2011) Poulter thrives in social media, fashion and on the golf course. *USA Today*, 22 February. Online. Available from: http://usatoday30.usatoday.com/sports/golf/pga/2011-02-22-wgc-accenture-match-play-championship_N.htm (Accessed 26 January 2012).

Donsbach W (2011) Journalists and their professional identities. In: Allan S (ed.) *The Routledge Companion to News and Journalism.* London: Routledge, 38–48.

Halavais A (2008) *Search Engine Society.* London: Routledge.

Haynes R & Boyle R (2008) Media sport. In: Blain N & Hutchison D (eds.) *The Media in Scotland.* Edinburgh: Edinburgh University Press, 253–70.

Hutchins B & Mikosza J (2010) The web 2.0 Olympics: athlete blogging, social networking and policy contradictions at the 2008 Beijing Games. *Convergence* 16 (3): 279–97.

Hutchins B & Rowe D (2012) *Sport Beyond Television: The Internet, Digital Media and the Rise of Networked Media Sport.* New York: Routledge.

Jarvis J (2009) *What Would Google Do?* New York: HarperCollins.

Jenkins H (2006) *Convergence Culture: Where Old and New Media Collide.* New York: New York University Press.

Kay O (2012) Capello rule had run its course and players will shed no tears. *The Times*, 9 February. Online. Available from: http://www.thetimes.co.uk/tto/sport/football/international/article3314190.ece (Accessed 10 February 2012).

Lasorsa D, Lewis SC & Holton AE (2012) Normalizing Twitter. *Journalism Studies* 13 (1): 19–36.

Morris S (2012) Student jailed for racist Fabrice Muamba tweets. *The Guardian*, 27 March. Online. Available from: http://www.guardian.co.uk/uk/2012/mar/27/student-jailed-fabrice-muamba-tweets (Accessed 27 March 2012).

Snow J (2012) Poised for journalism's golden age. *The Hugh Cudlipp Lecture*, 23 January, London College of Communication.

15 Carnival Mirrors
Sport and Digital Games

Steven Conway and Mark Finn

INTRODUCTION: MARKETING AUTHENTICITY AND THE LOGIC OF MEDIATED SPORT

The sports digital game is a fictional account of both representation and play. Yet it is often a fiction full of verisimilitude, a fiction that chafes in discomfort at such labeling. Many products within the genre are constructed as non-fiction, as accurate, holistic representations of sports connected to a range of allied industries. As the longstanding motto of the monolithic digital game publisher, EA Sports, proudly announces, "If it's in the game, it's in the game". The product does not claim to provide its own image of the world. It is instead marketed as a reflection of the existing one, which is evident in the promotion of such digital games[1] as not game but "simulation". The aim of this chapter is to illustrate how these digital game products are not simply a reflection of the sport-as-played, but, in fact, are a rigorous, careful construction of the game as an extension of the cultural logic of the "media sports cultural complex" (Rowe, 2004). This is not the logic of sport-as-played but of sport-as-mediated.

The conception of the sport videogame as simply "the real thing" is perpetuated even by those directly involved with sport-as-played, claiming to use the latest sports videogames as a didactic resource. As the general manager of the NBA's Houston Rockets, Daryl Morey, remarked in an interview, "I don't play EA Sports as a game. I use it as a tool" (Good, 2008). This comment was made in response to the incorporation of a feature known as "Dynamic DNA" into the *NBA Live* series (EA Sports, 1995–present). This system uses data gathered from the latest NBA matches, analyzed and categorized by a real-time video-indexing engine created by Synergy Sports Technology. This analysis is then applied to in-game player and team information (player behavior and success rates, favored movements and tactics). What occurs in the physical world of basketball is reflected, at least statistically, in the digital version. This feature is utilized by the developer and wider industry to invoke a scientific discourse that furthers their claim to simulation—a mirror held up to the "real world". This assertion is outlined in Electronic Arts' description of a similar feature in the *FIFA* soccer series (EA Sports, 1993–present), called "My Live Season":

> The new My Live Season . . . will feature weekly updates of player form, transfers, injuries, suspensions, fixtures, results and league standings, creating a mode that mirrors the real world, where gamers play their favourite real-world teams' games in complete authenticity. (Electronic Arts Ltd., 2009)

Thus, the product attempts further to erase evidence of its own overt mediation through such discursive strategies, as Andrew Baerg (forthcoming 2012) states:

> The determinist element of the Dynamic DNA metaphor also suggests the potential transparency or even invisibility of the digital game medium. If Dynamic DNA data represents how real world basketball players have acted in a given game and determines how players will respond in the simulation, the medium ostensibly disappears. To see the real game is to increasingly see the virtual game. To see the virtual game is to increasingly see the real game. Graphical verisimilitude may be important, but the integration of DNA data into the simulation blurs the line between the real and the virtual to a new degree. (p. 18)

We demonstrate in this chapter that the employment of this scientific rhetoric reflects a "system of nonsocial, nonpolitical truths grounded in nature and thus objective, universal, and unchallengeable" (Fiske, 1989, p. 183). This rhetoric is required to mask the fact that these videogames are developed from an inherently biased and partial position in accordance with contemporary paradigms of cultural production. They are creating simulacra (Baudrillard, 2004) that offer a utopian, mediated and often spectacle-laden vision of the sport; a sport euphemism that has never existed and never can exist. As Jean Baudrillard laments in *The Perfect Crime vis-à-vis* the simulacrum's technical supremacy, "the world has become real beyond our wildest expectations" (1996, p. 64). Building upon this argument, we suggest that such digital products are more than remediations (Bolter & Grusin, 1999) of sports production and consumption. We thus introduce the term "reludification" to describe how they incorporate not only certain forms of representation and models of interaction captured by the concept of remediation (Bolter & Grusin, 1999), but also certain rules and mechanics that are not conducive to sport-as-played. Rather, the emphasis here is on spectacle and media presentation, i.e., sport-as-spectacle. Additionally, it is illustrated how remediation and reludification exist in a network of symbiotic relationships, whereby the digital version of the sport now has a tangible impact upon the physical world version, its media representation, formal and informal play, and *vice versa*. To anchor this analysis and allow consistent movement between the abstract and the concrete, this chapter focuses on digital games that market themselves as faithful reproductions of soccer, whilst also commenting upon other sports (notably motor racing) that incorporate "realistic" features.

ELECTRIC PERFORMANCE AND THE MUNDANE CIRCLE

On Wednesday, 18 November 2009, the Republic of Ireland lost to France in a major qualifying match for soccer's 2010 FIFA World Cup finals. This defeat gained instant notoriety, first because French player, Thierry Henry, had obviously cheated in the build-up to the winning goal by handballing the ball twice. Secondly, the sports news media used this event as an anchor for further discussions about sport regulation and culture. This discussion produced an instance of "vortextuality" (Whannel, 2010), quickly turning into a political issue and receiving extensive attention in the news media. Demands were made by media commentators, selected players and the Football Association of Ireland to replay the match in the spirit of sportsmanship. In an interview with French soccer magazine *L'Equipe*, French defender Patrice Evra responded, "The replay, I'll do it when you want on a PlayStation" (Daily Mail, 2009).

Following Arsenal's elimination from the Champion's League by Barcelona on 6 April 2010, Arsene Wenger was quoted in British newspaper, *The Guardian*. He praised Barcelona player Lionel Messi as "like a Playstation", in a detailed article by Keith Stuart where he asks, "Who's better: the real Messi or the virtual one?" (2010, p. 2), playing a variety of digital games to reenact Messi's goals from the match. In 2008, EPL club Everton announced it had officially paid for the rights to use the *Football Manager* series' (Sports Interactive, 2004–present) digital game database as a scouting tool. Everton manager David Moyes could search the records of 380,000 players compiled by 1,500 researchers across the globe, whilst Northern Ireland manager, Lawrie Sanchez, contacted Sports Interactive (developers of the *Football Manager* videogame series) for scouting advice on lower league players eligible for the national team (Macaskill, 2009). Various boundaries between entertainment and politics, fiction and non-fiction, technology and society, the virtual and physical, are seen to be merging, moving and even eroding in these examples. As Jean-François Lyotard (1984) perhaps anticipated, such blurring is an inevitable conclusion of media production and consumption in the late capitalist context.

Soccer has a long history as a form of both entertainment and political expression. But it is no longer a sport understood simply through live spectatorship, or supported by local communities living in close proximity to the team ground. Indeed, unmediated reality is now sold at an escalating premium, with Manchester United season tickets being sold (at the time of writing) for £950 (US$1,533), allowing the buyer attendance at nineteen home matches. In comparison, satellite television provider Sky's sports package costs £200 (US$323) for the entire soccer season, gaining the subscriber access to a minimum of 115 EPL matches (approximately £1.74 [US$2.81] per game). Commodification of the "real" is also evidenced by the current premium paid for high definition television sports channels. Reality in a mediated environment is a mode of production based upon technological differentiation, whereby greater resolution and audio fidelity correlates with more "reality" (Bell, 2009). Media producers hope that the sports fan—existing "in the denial of the real" by constantly utilizing the "simulacrum of the world" and its concurrent "alibi of participation" (Baudrillard, 1998, p. 35)—will purchase such technological upgrades marketed as reality enhancers.

Contrasting season ticket prices with the comparatively low cost involved in watching sport on television, it is clear why the modern game is supra-sentential (Price, 1998); that is to say, broadcast globally live on television, radio and online, appearing on our personal computers and digital game consoles, and discussed in newspapers, magazines and Web forums. It is apparent that the audience's experience of sport is now largely a mediated phenomenon. Consumption is influenced by various formats, sources and personalities, some of which may have little to do with the actual playing of the game itself, but all of which can impact upon the reception and comprehension of the sport in an intertextual manner. To paraphrase Ted Friedman, "Any medium . . . can teach you how to see life in new ways" and may "reorganize perception" (1999, p. 133). Therefore, the digital game medium has significant consequences for how we experience sport culture.

Crawford (2011) and others have argued that Johan Huizinga (1949) was wrong in describing the "magic circle" of games and play as a distinct area cordoned off from the "everyday" world, leading to an assumption that engagement with sport involves momentarily shedding other identities and responsibilities. All kinds of games take up our time, change our mood, communicate ideas and values, influence our behavior and have the capacity to involve objects traditionally (or initially) considered outside the formal boundaries of the circle. Whether that boundary is the chalk line of the pitch, the stadium gates or the television screen, games find ways of "bleeding" into our everyday lives in both purposeful and accidental ways (Conway, 2010a). Games also push against and interlock with various other circles or "frames" (Goffman, 1986). All kinds of media now offer their own commentary upon how we should view and consume sport, while simultaneously cannibalizing and engaging in an incestuous relationship with the technical and stylistic conventions of other media.

As Joe Booth and Michael Muller-Mohring (lead producer and data manager respectively for EA Sports' *FIFA 08*) have commented, the very construction of these digital games rests upon an intertextual approach to the sport, particularly in quantifying and deciding upon the virtual player's statistics:

> Our database researchers watch live football games to evaluate and rate the skills and abilities of each player. They also rely on television, internet, magazines and newspapers for information. (Booth & Mohring, 2008)

Media consumption does not occur in isolation, but is situated within a similarly inter- and pantextual environment. The follower of sport, whether they choose it or not, is figuratively bombarded from all sides by networks of distribution pushing sports-related content to their mobile phones, tablets, television, radio, magazines and, of course, their personal computer and game console. The term "sports media" is becoming redundant in an era where, to many fans, sport *is* media (cf. Hutchins, 2008; Hutchins & Rowe, 2012). The following section uses soccer games to extend our arguments in this regard.

THE STARTING LINEUP

Soccer games are generally divided into three subgenres: the televisual, extreme and management. Each is unique in its representational and ludic characteristics, in how it interpolates the player (Ruggill & McAllister, 2011), and how it presents the culture of soccer. The televisual subgenre is one that claims, above all others, to offer an "authentic" and "real-world" experience that EA Sports perpetuates in its marketing, which, as indicated by the genre's moniker, is, in fact, an attempt to reproduce sport as a mediated exhibition. A simulational veracity of televisual convention is constructed that eclipses the televisual presentation of sport and the digital game genre's remediating effects, so that one informs the other in a cyclical relationship. The stylistic conventions of television enhance the televisual authenticity of the digital game, whilst the smooth, almost frictionless technological interface of the videogame informs the presentation of data during television broadcasts, including formations and tactics, plus virtual reenactments of key moments.

In this environment, photo-realistic graphics are paramount due to their signification of the "real" (Bell, 2009) and their multi-modal marketability in a popular culture that has an insatiable appetite for spectacle:

> The spectacular involves an exaggeration of the pleasure of looking. It exaggerates the visible, magnifies and foregrounds the surface appearance, and refuses meaning or depth. When the object is pure spectacle, it works only on the physical senses, the body of the spectator, not in

the construction of a subject. Spectacle liberates from subjectivity. Its emphasis on excessive materiality foregrounds the body, not as a signifier of something else, but in its *presence*. (Fiske, 1989, p. 84)

Soccer games enact these qualities by allowing popular players certain graphical concessions. Lionel Messi and Cristiano Ronaldo are, for example, painstakingly recreated, often with their own unique animation routines, hairstyles and even friendship bracelets.

The immediacy of the audio-visual patina is reinforced by the mechanical layer, where sophisticated physics systems are employed accurately to render player and ball movement, collisions, wind, humidity and weather patterns, culminating in a vast assortment of interactions for the user. Again, the "star" player is awarded special dispensation, aligning once more with their conventional media representation, as Whannel (1998, p. 23) explains:

> Sport is presented largely in terms of stars and narratives: the media narrativises the events of sport, transforming them into stories with stars and characters; heroes and villains.

Well-known players have exclusive mechanics, meaning that they can perform tricks that others cannot, move faster, hit a harder shot or make the ball curve in a more dramatic fashion. These players are "hyper-ludic"[2] agents within the game space (Conway, 2010b).

The extreme simulation in its modern form, from the EA published *Need For Speed: Underground* (EA Black Box, 2003) franchise onwards, began as photorealism. Further iterations moved towards caricaturism as a way to distinguish itself from the televisual genre, and also to incorporate what film scholar, David Bordwell, terms "expressive amplification" (2000, p. 232). This is a method originating in film production in which impressive choreography, special effects, sound editing, set design and cinematography merge to amplify the action within the scene, invoking a heightened response in the audience:

> These films literally grip us; we can watch ourselves tense and relax, twitch or flinch. By arousing us through highly legible motion and staccato rhythms, and by intensifying their arousal through composition and editing and sound, the films seem to ask our bodies to recall elemental and universal events like striking, swinging, twisting, leaping, rolling. (Bordwell 2000, p. 244)

For instance, the appearance of the game world in the *FIFA Street* (EA Sports, 2005-present) series allows each movement to be exaggerated, each shot to be spectacular through the addition of inflated sounds and impossibly colorful settings in line with its arcade heritage, which, as will be discussed, is similar to many arcade-style motor racing videogames. The grotesque embellishment applied to the character models of well-known players (e.g., AC Milan's Gennaro Gattuso is impossibly barrel-chested, and Tottenham Hotspur's Peter Crouch is preposterously thin and long-limbed) also speaks to the subversive quality of the product and its appeal to a younger demographic. Fiske contextualizes these visual conventions:

> Bakhtin (1968) suggests that the grotesque is linked to a sense of earthy realism; indeed, he talks about "grotesque realism." The realism of the grotesque is opposed to the "aesthetics of the beautiful" (p.29) represented in sport's vision of the perfect body. The grotesque body is "contrary to the classic images of the finished, completed man" (p.25); cleansed of, or liberated from, the social construction and evaluation of the body, it exists only in its materiality. If the body beautiful is the completed, formed social body, then the body grotesque is the incomplete, the unformed. Its appeal to children (whose heroes, such as the Incredible Hulk or Mr. T, often have grotesque bodies) may well lie in the relevance they see between the grotesque body and their own childishly incomplete, unformed ones. The grotesque allies their incompleteness with adult strength . . . The grotesque is properly part of the vernacular of the oppressed. (1989, pp. 88–89)

Finally, the management genre maintains the abstractionism long ago abandoned by the televisual genre, and that was limited through the 1980s by technical capacity. This form of representation can be ingeniously simple or startlingly complex. The management simulation is an abstract representation of the world of soccer management, boasting an extraordinarily informatic visual template that remediates common Web browser interface design. For example, the player uses an email client to communicate with their team and others, the template's architecture is based upon the "upside-down L" Web page design (whereby main menu options exist at the top of the screen, with a content listing on the left side), hyperlinks are used and so on. This format also remediates a British-style presentation of sports media, as the majority of the information that the user receives about fan and player contentedness ratings is via "simulacral" tabloid headlines and anchoring text delivered to the player's inbox.

The user must also negotiate his or her[3] avatar through page upon page of numerical statistics, text-laden communiqués and drop-down menus to find satisfactory solutions to their team's problems. The representational facade is quite unimportant. Rather, what is important to the player is the underlying system of rules, regulations and parameters that is never revealed to the user, but always presents itself as an obstacle and challenge. This system stands in stark contrast to other forms of gaming, from *Chess* to *Pictionary* to *Trivial Pursuit*, where the rules and parameters of play are clearly and necessarily outlined before commencement. In no other form of game is the "interactive trial and error" (Jones, 2008, p. 74) method of progress, championed by digital games, so central to the play experience. This is doubly so for the management genre, where gaining a complete understanding of the rules and parameters of the simulation would undermine the entire ludic experience, which is predicated on the user's incomprehension of the system's purposefully obtuse inner-workings.

The dressing of soccer culture, from the sardonic media tabloid headlines to the team talk and match day procedure, is in many ways a narrativization of the underlying system that makes it attractive to a certain gamer demographic. As Raph Koster (2005, p. 85) points out:

> The stories in most video games serve the same purpose as calling the über-checker a "king." It adds interesting shading to the game but the game at its core is unchanged.

In other words, whether it is soccer, American football or basketball, the system itself stays unaffected and the gamer plays the product in the same manner; only the visage changes to attract interest from a particular group. Again, digital media reveal their impartiality towards content (Flew, 2005) and their modular structure (Manovich, 2002) regarding the program's various components (graphical, audio and mechanical). This quality allows for substantial modification, addition, or deletion to cater for different demographics, or for the fan to take the role of developer. Indeed, a game editor is packaged with each edition of the *Football Manager* series that encourages such user-led activity.

Soccer management games also encourage the player to adopt the mindset of the information economy worker, albeit with a distinctive sporting inflection. Everything is reduced to data, codified and quantifiable—personality, race, national identity and age. Management is translated into a mathematical model designed around the goal of maximizing output, profit and efficiency, and minimizing the costs of (athletic) labor and production. Playing management games is not so much about understanding an opponent as the *system*. Understood critically, middle-class labor practices have infiltrated the realm of popular entertainment in this context:

> [A]esthetics is a disciplinary system, an attempt by the bourgeoisie to exert the equivalent control over the cultural economy that it does over the financial. "What is at value in aesthetic discourse . . . is nothing less than the monopoly of humanity" (Bourdieu, 1984, p. 491). Aesthetics is naked cultural hegemony, and popular discrimination properly rejects it. (Fiske 1989, p. 130)

The aesthetic design of the management genre is positioned in relation to the middle-class knowledge worker, and its mass appeal speaks to the changing tastes of an increasingly affluent society (Galbraith, 1998).

RELUDIFICATION

While soccer games exemplify the increasingly convoluted relationship between the sport-as-played and sport-as-media, the motor racing genre takes this one step further in terms of the *ludic* interaction between sport and videogame. As is the case with soccer, professionals working in motor racing are turning to games to improve their own performance, with some drivers using commercial video games to familiarize themselves with new tracks prior to racing on them (Hutchins & Rowe, 2012, pp. 164–65). For example, as part of his preparations for the first ever Indian Grand Prix, Ferrari driver Felipe Massa stated that:

> I spent a day on the simulator to get a general impression of the track and I've also got the latest version of the 2011 Formula One computer game that features this circuit, which means I at least have a feel for it and know where the corners are. (Massa, 2011)

That Massa was able to use a commercial game serves as an indication of the emphasis that is placed upon a particular conception of realism in the development of these games. But, as noted previously, we are dealing here with a carefully constructed myth of the real that exceeds the limitations of that which it represents. "Realism" is, in fact, the criterion by which racing games are often judged, with most racing games capable of being placed on a spectrum that ranges from "arcade" at one end to "simulation" at the other.

At the extreme end of the range are vehicle combat games such as *Twisted Metal* (SingleTrac, 1995), which feature an exaggerated visual presentation style and physics parameters, allowing players to perform maneuvers that would be impossible in real life. From here, racing games gradually increase in graphical photorealism and adherence to real world physics models. The *Need for Speed* franchise offers photorealistic cars and a physics model that attempts to replicate proper vehicle dynamics, while also allowing players to execute moves that would be impossible in a real car. At the other end of the spectrum are games like the *Gran Turismo* series (Polyphony Digital, 1997–2010) that actively position themselves as accurate representations of the driving experience. Marketed as "the real driving simulator," *Gran Turismo 5* features more than 1,000 officially licensed cars and a physics model that attempts to translate realistic vehicle behavior through the limitations of a handheld control-pad attached to a game console. Games based on the Formula One World Championship are generally slanted towards the simulation end of the genre, featuring complex handling and vehicle models that seek to replicate their season-specific counterparts, including the individual sponsor's decals on the car's bodywork.

Claims to realism in motorsport videogames extend far beyond physics and visual models. The ways in which the sport's rules are implemented help to define whether the game is perceived to be realistic. While it is sometimes assumed that rules work only to limit what a player can do, Jesper Juul (2005) reminds us that in computer games they serve a dual purpose:

> The rules of a game also set up potential actions; actions that are meaningful inside the game but meaningless outside. It is the rules of chess that allow the player to perform a checkmate—without the rules, there is no checkmate, only meaningless moving of pieces across a board. Rules specify limitations and affordances. (Juul, 2005, p. 58)

Fares Kayali and Peter Purgathofer (2008, p. 110) argue that rules in digital sports games follow a multi-layered logic, working both to translate the rules of the original sport *and* to impose additional rules specific to the game simulation.

Formula One game titles present a range of technical and competitive rules dictated by the sport's governing body, the Fédération Internationale De L'Automobile (FIA). Some of these rules, such as pit lane speed limits, are designed to ensure the safety of the drivers and their crews and have little impact on game play. However, the failure to include these rules would potentially offend many players by undermining the "authenticity" of the game experience. Other rules transposed from sport to videogame are designed to promote competition, with a good example being the regulation governing the passing of a lapped competitor. In both the physical sport and many of its simulated representations, drivers being lapped are required to move aside to allow the faster car to pass (commonly referred to as "blue flag conditions") so as not to impede the progress of front-running competitors. Such rules, in particular, represent what Juul (2005) describes as affordances.

Unlike many sports where the rules have remained stable for decades, motorsport continually adjusts its regulations to encourage technical innovation and consistently even competition between race teams. Like most major spectator sports, motor racing derives a significant proportion of its income from the sale of television rights, and the promotion of aggressive racing tactics with frequent overtaking by cars makes for compelling television viewing. There is, nonetheless, a fundamental problem in achieving these race conditions. Modern racecars are able to achieve high levels of performance primarily through the use of aerodynamic down force that can create problems for overtaking. Once a chasing vehicle gets close behind another car, the aerodynamic effect on the following car is greatly reduced (referred to as "dirty air"), meaning that it is difficult for the second car to overtake.

To promote competitive racing, both Formula One and the American Indycar Series have adopted strategies that are similar to the game mechanics found in many digital game arcade racers. One of the key differences between arcade racers and simulations is that the former often feature "assists" to help slower drivers catch up, thereby encouraging closer racing. In some cases these assists are subtle, such as the "rubber-banding" effect in which the program manipulates the speed of computer-controlled vehicles so that slower cars have a chance to catch the leaders. In other games the assists are much more explicit, with drivers having the ability to activate various boost mechanisms to improve the performance of their machine for a short period. This mechanism is particularly evident in successful titles such as Nintendo's *Mario Kart* series (Nintendo, 1992–2011).

In Formula One, two systems have been introduced to overcome the difficulties in passing created by the reliance on aerodynamic down force. The first of these is referred to as the Drag Reduction System (DRS) (Formula1. com, 2012a) and takes the form of a small slot in the racecar's rear wing that can be opened by the driver at specific points around the circuit. The resulting decrease in drag allows a chasing car to increase its top speed temporarily, thereby increasing the likelihood of a passing move. The second mechanism, the Kinetic Energy Recovery System (KERS) (Formula1. com, 2012b), uses batteries inside the car to store some of the energy that is generated during braking, and then rereleases that energy in the form of a power boost initiated by a button on the steering wheel. As with DRS, the effect is to give the car a short burst of additional speed, potentially allowing it to overtake the car in front or to defend if being overtaken.

The technology used in Indycar is even more reminiscent of video game mechanics and is commonly referred to as "push-to-pass." Like KERS, push-to-pass is activated by a button on the steering wheel. But in this case, the boost in power comes from an increase in the number of revolutions that the engine can perform, as well as a change in the fuel mixture that provides an instant boost of up to twenty horsepower. As with the assists in Formula One, the use of push-to-pass is restricted to a limited number of instances per lap (Cavin, 2009) and requires the driver to use the increased power at strategic points throughout the race.

While there is no evidence to suggest that motorsport administrators have based these changes on videogames, the ludic implications of such *hyper-ludic* features (cf. Conway, 2010b) offer insight into possible commercial motivations. Just as games like *Need for Speed* (EA Canada, 1994–present) and *Burnout* (Criterion Games, 2001–2011) use artificial assists to encourage close racing, the measures introduced by professional motorsport organizations are designed to make the competition more agonistic. An article discussing the introduction of push-to-pass to Indycar in *Wired* magazine made the link explicit:

Mario had super mushrooms he could use in the *Mario Kart* games to blast past his opponents and take the lead. Now, drivers in the Indy Racing League have them too. The cool new power up is a "push to pass" or "overtake assist" button on the steering wheel of every Indy Racing League car. Mashing it unleashes a sudden jolt of horsepower,

> giving drivers a strategic edge that's brought back some of the side-by-side racing excitement from the Indycar racing of old. (Lundin, 2009)

Perhaps ironically, the introduction of these assists into professional motorsport has posed problems for video game developers, who have had to revise their code to keep up with the changing regulations. Codemasters, who took over the *Formula One* game franchise in 2008, have been widely criticized in online game forums for their implementation of both KERS and DRS. Some players claim that it provides too much of an advantage, while others are adamant that it provides too little.

Significantly, such complaints are framed in the context of two distinct, though interrelated discourses. The first of these refers to the idea that the assists are detrimental to gameplay, allowing less-skilled players to keep up with more skillful players. Interestingly, a professional Formula One driver recently made the same complaint concerning DRS, arguing that:

> The way the wings work is for me a little ridiculous. Overtaking is not really a great art anymore. You just put the wing down and go past easily. The guy in front can't really do anything. But I agree that at least it makes the show better. (Raikkonen, 2012)

The second discourse takes a different view. It proposes that Codemasters' implementation of the assists is flawed simply because it is *unrealistic*, giving more or less of an advantage than the real system. This criticism stems, at least partially, from the almost obsessive emphasis on "realism" and "authenticity" that developers (and many players) imbue the game with, from the satellite-mapped accuracy of the tracks to the impact of technical rule changes on the handling of the cars. This conundrum is nicely illustrated in an interview with Steven Hood, Codemasters' creative director for *F1 2012*, where he describes the relationship between a new rule change and the handling of the cars in the game:

> There's another rule-change that's had a profound effect on the cars this year, with the banning of blown diffusers creating a more skittish, unpredictable ride. "We weren't specifically replicating blown diffusers because we can replicate the effect of the diffuser," says Hood. "It was making the car stick to the ground more. In 2011 we made the cars a lot more skittish. We didn't have that in 2010 because the cars had too much grip, but when we introduced that in 2011 it made it more problematic for some players to drive. In 2012 we have new physics in the suspension and we're seeing cars sliding around more." (Robinson, 2012)

It is important to remember here that the experience of gamers is not a simulation of the sport-as-played, but a simulation of the sport-as-mediated, in this instance via television. It is the real once removed. When players criticize the game for being unrealistic, they are saying that it does not reflect the spectacle of the sport as broadcast on television. Unlike Raikkonen, the gamers generally have no direct experience of the sport as a participant. The end result is a complex situation in which expectations about the sport, its televisual representation and the representation of that representation in game form collapse into one another. These dynamics create a scenario in which it is not only appropriate for sports to draw inspiration from their digital counterparts, but is arguably necessary in order to maintain the spectator's engagement.

CONCLUSION: VERISIMILITUDE AND THE SPORTS VIDEOGAME

As discussed in the introduction, the marketing that surrounds the genre of sports digital games propagates the notion that these products carry an aura of authenticity and objective truth through the invocation of scientific rhetoric. In cultivating the pretense of impartial reflection, digital sports games claim to be a mirror held up to the sporting world. To extend the metaphor, such products are, in essence, carnival mirrors, distorting the image and exaggerating certain features and their stylistic and thematic conventions, whilst diminishing others to the point of negation. Such products are clearly interpretations of sport-as-mediated rather than sport-as-played, pushing the interpretation to the point of euphemism. Sport-as-played is sterilized and sanitized even before translation, motivated by the need to provide the consumer with excitement and spectacle above all else. This pattern holds not only in terms of representational formulation, but also within *ludic* configuration (i.e., the game mechanics), hence the need for the introduction of the term "reludification".

Each subgenre along the spectrum, from televisual to management, arcade to simulation, presents a different mirror, simultaneously accentuating and lessening the numerous constituents of the sport spectacle. As members of a postmodern culture that expresses "incredulity towards metanarratives" (Lyotard, 1984, p. xxiv) alongside claims to epistemological and ontological stability, it is not that the consumer necessarily believes sports videogames to be *real*. Instead, it may be the case that they see many aspects of their culture as equally fictitious, as equally *unreal*, as Baudrillard summarizes:

> Disneyland is there to conceal the fact that it is the "real" country, all of "real" America, which is Disneyland (just as prisons are there to conceal the fact that it is the society in its entirety, in its banal omnipotence, which is carceral). Disneyland is presented as imaginary in order to make us believe that the rest is real, when in fact all of Los Angeles

and the America surrounding it are no longer real, but of the order of the hyperreal and of simulation. It is no longer a question of a false representation of reality (ideology), but of concealing the fact that the real is no longer real. (Baudrillard, 1983, p. 25)

The verisimilitude of the sports videogame is seen to be as authentic as the live sports event broadcast, the accompanying radio commentary, the website match report, online forum discussion and the ritual of the pre-match interview. In this mediated environment, digital games disregard the notion of presenting themselves as imaginary, as not reflective of reality. Thus, the question needs to be posed: in comparison to what? The sports genre of the digital game, located firmly within the aesthetics of postmodernity, finds truth relevant only in relation to other, more pertinent questions:

No longer will it respond to the question "Is it true?" It will hear only, "What use is it?" "How much is it?" and "Is it saleable?" (Lyotard, 1984, p. 51)

NOTES

1. Whether referred to as digital game, computer game or videogame, this chapter uses such terms as synonyms for games played through the medium of electronic computing regardless of format.
2. Empowering the user (whether that be human or AI) more dramatically to affect the gamespace (e.g. *Super Mario*'s mushrooms or *Pac-Man*'s power-pellets).
3. Until recently, the *Football Manager* series did not allow for gender selection, assuming the user to be male.

REFERENCES

Baerg A (forthcoming 2012) Genetic metaphors, the body and digital basketball: dynamic DNA in NBA Live "09". *Journal of Communication Studies* (forthcoming).
Baudrillard J (1983) *Simulations*. New York: Semiotext(e).
Baudrillard J (1996) *The Perfect Crime*. London: Verso Books.
Baudrillard J (1998) *The Consumer Society*. London: Sage.
Baudrillard J (2004) *Simulacra and Simulation*. Ann Arbor: University of Michigan Press.
Bell P (2009) Realism and subjectivity in first-person shooter video games. *Gnovis*, 3. Online. Available from: http://gnovis.georgetown.edu/articles/pr009_Realism&SubjectivityF.pdf (Accessed 13 February 2012).
Bolter JD & Grusin R (1999) *Remediation: Understanding New Media*. Cambridge, MA: MIT Press.
Booth J & Muller-Mohring M (2008) FIFA Soccer 08 on Next-gen Blog 5. *FIFA. com*. Online. Available from: http://de.fifa.com/mm/document/tournament/competition/fifa08_ng_blog_5_player_ratings_23404.pdf (Accessed 13 February 2012).
Bordwell D (2000) *Planet Hong Kong: Popular Cinema and the Art of Entertainment*. Cambridge: Harvard University Press.

Bourdieu P (1984) *Distinction: A Social Critique of the Judgement of Taste.* London: Routledge.

Cavin C (2009) Indycar Series adopts "Push-To-Pass" button, effective immediately. *Autoweek.* Online. Available from: http://www.autoweek.com/article/20090729/ IRL/907299994 (Accessed 19 March 2010).

Conway S (2010a) A circular wall? Reformulating the fourth wall for videogames. *Journal of Gaming and Virtual Worlds* 2(2): 145–55.

Conway S (2010b) Hyper-ludicity, contra-ludicity and the digital game. *Eludamos: Journal for Computer Game Culture* 4(2): 135–47.

Crawford G (2011) *Video Gamers.* London: Routledge.

Daily Mail (2009) France star Patrice Evra offers Ireland World Cup replay . . . on his PlayStation. *Mail Online,* 21 November. Online. Available from: http://www. dailymail.co.uk/sport/football/article-1229815/France-star-Patrice-Evra-offers-Ireland-World-Cup-replay—PlayStation.html (Accessed 22 March 2012).

Electronic Arts Ltd. (2009) FIFA 10 Live Season 2.0 tutorial video. *Playstation Store.*

Fiske J (1989) *Understanding Popular Culture.* London: Routledge.

Flew T (2005) *New Media: An Introduction.* 2nd ed. Melbourne: Oxford University Press.

Formula1.com (2012a) *Aerodynamics.* Online. Available from: http://www.formula1.com/inside_f1/understanding_the_sport/5281.html (Accessed 5 June 2012).

Formula1.com (2012b) *Kinetic Energy Recovery Systems (KERS).* Online. Available from: http://www.formula1.com/inside_f1/understanding_the_sport/8763.html (Accessed 5 June 2012).

Friedman T (1999) *Civilization* and its discontents: simulation, subjectivity and space. In: Smith G M (ed.) *On a Silver Platter: CD-Roms and the Promises of a New Technology.* New York: New York University Press, 132–50.

Galbraith JK (1998) *The Affluent Society.* 40th anniversary edition. New York: Houghton Mifflin Company.

Good O (2008) *NBA Teams Scout and Evaluate Talent Using Video Game. Kotaku.* Online. Available from: http://kotaku.com/5099975/ (Accessed 23 March 2012).

Goffman E (1986) *Frame Analysis: An Essay on the Organization of Experience.* Boston, MA: Northeastern University Press.

Huizinga J (1949) [1938] *Homo Ludens: A Study of the Play-Element in Culture.* London: Routledge.

Hutchins B (2008) Signs of meta-change in second modernity: the growth of e-sport and the world cyber games. *New Media & Society* 10(6): 851–69.

Hutchins B & Rowe D (2012) *Sport Beyond Television: The Internet, Digital Media and the Rise of Networked Media Sport.* London: Routledge.

Jones SE (2008) *The Meanings of Video Games: Gaming and Textual Strategies.* Abingdon: Routledge.

Juul J (2005) *Half-Real: Video Games between Real Rules and Fictional Worlds.* Cambridge, MA: The MIT Press.

Kayali F & Purgathofer P (2008) Two halves of play: simulation versus abstraction and transformation in sports videogames design. *Eludamos: Journal for Computer Game Culture* 2(1): 105–27.

Koster R (2005) *A Theory of Fun for Game Design.* Scottsdale: Paraglyph Press.

Lundin C (2009) *Mario kart* power-ups come to Indycar racing. *Wired.com,* 21 August. Online. Available from: http://www.wired.com/autopia/2009/08/ push-to-pass/ (Accessed 12 September 2010).

Lyotard JF (1984) *The Postmodern Condition: A Report on Knowledge.* Manchester: Manchester University Press.

Macaskill S (2009) Fantasy championship manager becomes football reality. *The Telegraph,* 8 March. Online. Available from: http://www.telegraph.co.uk/sport/

football/leagues/premierleague/4958515/Fantasy-Championship-manager-becomes-football-reality.html (Accessed 30 March 2012).

Manovich L (2002) *The Language of New Media*. Cambridge, MA: MIT Press.

Massa F (2011) India preview quotes—Ferrari, FIA, Renault, Force India & more. Online. Available from: http://www.formula1.com/news/headlines/2011/10/12681.html (Accessed 20 February 2012).

Price S (1998) *Media Studies*. London: Longman.

Raikkonen K (2012) Raikkonen slams "ridiculous" DRS. *ESPNF1*, 8 February. Online. Available from: http://en.espnf1.com/lotusf1/motorsport/story/69718.html (Accessed 20 April 2012).

Robinson M (2012) F1 2012 preview: staying on track. *Eurogamer*, 19 April. Online. Available from: http://www.eurogamer.net/articles/2012–04–19-f1-2012-preview-staying-on-track (Accessed 20 April 2012).

Rowe D (2004) *Sport, Culture, and the Media*. 2nd ed. Maidenhead, Berkshire: Open University Press.

Ruggill J & McAllister K (2011) *Gaming Matters: Art, Science, Magic and the Computer Game Medium*. Tuscaloosa: The University of Alabama Press.

Stuart K (2010) Who's better: the real Messi or the virtual one? *The Guardian*, 8 April. Online. Available from: http://www.guardian.co.uk/football/2010/apr/07/lionel-messi (Accessed 20 April 2012).

Whannel G (1998) Individual stars and collective identities in media sport. In: Roche M (ed.) *Sport, Popular Culture and Identity*. Aachen: Meyer & Meyer, 23–36.

Whannel G (2010) News, celebrity, and vortextuality: a study of the media coverage of the Michael Jackson verdict. *Cultural Politics* 6(1): 65–84.

Games

Criterion Games (2001–2011) *Burnout* (Electronic Arts)

EA Black Box (2003) *Need For Speed: Underground* (Electronic Arts)

EA Sports (1993–present) *FIFA* series (Electronic Arts)

EA Sports (2005–present) *FIFA Street* series (Electronic Arts)

EA Sports (1995–present) *NBA Live* series (Electronic Arts)

Nintendo (1992–2011) *Mario Kart* series (Nintendo)

Polyphony Digital (1997–2010) *Gran Turismo* series (Sony Computer Entertainment)

SingleTrac (1995) *Twisted Metal* (Sony Computer Entertainment)

Sports Interactive, *Football Manager* series (Sports Interactive 2004–present)

16 Privileged Men and Masculinities

Gender and Fantasy Sports Leagues

Luke Howie and Perri Campbell

INTRODUCTION: MASCULINIZED "FANTASYSCAPES" AND "MANLY" MEN

Playing fantasy sports is a past time for a particular type of person. The game and marketing operator, *World Fantasy Games* (2011), has compiled a range of data on fantasy sports participants. Their account of the typical "consumer profile" of fantasy athletes reads as follows:

37 year-old male, married with kids
Bachelor degree graduate and homeowner
An average household income of US$94,000
Spends 3–4 hours per week online
Large amounts of disposable income that is spent on beer, Internet services, prescription drugs, logo hats, running shoes, liquor, magazines and laptops. Almost half operate in two-screen environments (simultaneous use of televisions and laptops)

Middle-aged white men with lots of money are a much sought after target demographic in the marketplace. Competitors are estimated to spend US$800 million per year on fantasy sports with a total consumer impact estimated at around US$4.48 billion. Around one-fifth of men in Canada and the US had played fantasy sports in the previous year according to one recent study (Ipsos Public Affairs, 2011). The participation rate for women is far less—five percent in the US and eight percent in Canada.

Privilege in fantasy sports is tightly bound to questions of gender. The fantasy sports league discussed in this chapter operates at *Yahoo!® Fantasy NBA*. Fantasy basketball is the fourth most popular fantasy sport in the US. Participation in NBA fantasy games is generally lower when compared to other major US sports such as football and baseball, but the participant numbers are still sizable. An estimated twenty-eight percent of fantasy basketball players attended an NBA game, compared to eight percent in the general population (see *World Fantasy Games* 2011). According to the jargon used in fantasy NBA, the league under investigation is a 9-cat rotisserie with a live draft and a non-keeper format. This means that participants in this league battle over nine statistical categories ("9-cat") that accumulate ("rotisserie") over the course of one NBA season ("non-keeper"). The participants in the league gather once a year for a live fantasy draft day in October where teams are selected and later added to the online game.

The theory and data presented in this chapter comprise the first published account from our research. The study is ongoing and involves interviews with fantasy basketball participants and their partners. Here we focus on some of the visual and textual features used by competitors to manage their teams' identities. In particular, we report on the history of this league, team names and the message board discussions from the 2011–2012 NBA/ Fantasy NBA season. The aim of this approach is to understand the types of masculine practices enacted in an online fantasy sports league, which reveals these settings as masculinized "fantasyscapes" where "manly" men toy with the limits of heteronormative realities. Our analysis also responds to the "underdeveloped" nature of the literature exploring fantasy sport (Dwyer & Drayer, 2010, p. 209). Whilst some attention has been paid to fantasy gambling, communications and participant motivations (Bernhard & Eade, 2005; Farquhar & Meeds, 2007; Lomax, 2006), an understanding of fantasy sports leagues as gendered and cultural experiences is comparatively lacking. The chapter is organized in the following way. First, we survey some of the key literature that relates to fantasy sport, masculinities and privilege. An account of the selected roles played by gender in a fantasy league is then presented. This account is drawn from data collected from the online platform where this league is conducted.

PLAYING FANTASY BASKETBALL

Playing fantasy NBA basketball intensely is a quintessentially masculine experience. It involves watching and witnessing male team sports, quantifying the movements and achievements of disciplined bodies and statistically analyzing the results. It involves the use of smartphones, social networking websites and complex digital networks for round-the-clock updates on scores, trades, injuries, crime reports, scouting reports and team management decisions. In 2011, playing fantasy basketball meant nervously awaiting the resolution of a widely publicized NBA player lockout and then watching real events unfold in discursive codes embodied by "box scores". This is an activity that demands time, attention and dedication, especially for the player who wants to excel. Following the example of Sherry Turkle (1995), we might assume that those competing in fantasy basketball leagues are part of a "nerdy" subculture that wish to be "kings" and "warriors" for a day before returning to their humdrum lives. If we follow the arguments of Hutchins and Rowe (2012), fantasy sports connect to a sporting spectatorship that extends *beyond television* and into "digital plenitude" where sports spectatorship is an active, engaged and online experience. Ruddock, Hutchins and Rowe (2010) also argue that online media have facilitated sports fandom in spaces that extend beyond, and in cohabitation with, television. Exploring the online, interactive world of managing a semi-professional soccer club via a website, they argue that MyFootball-Club blends "simulated" and physical sport, reflecting "perennial desires to resurrect organic social and community bonds with the rhythms of media sports culture" (p. 324). *Yahoo!® Fantasy NBA* certainly incorporates multiple rhythmic realities, coinciding as it does with professional sports teams, their performances, injuries, trials and tribulations. Perri Campbell and Peter Kelly's (2009) research suggests that fantasy basketball players are practicing a digital-self. Engaging with a community of like-minded people is a way of practicing an identity that cannot be easily realized in non-digital spaces. Yet, there is another critical dimension to playing fantasy sports that demands extensive and ongoing investigation. As initially identified by Nickolas Davis and Margaret Carlisle Duncan (2006), playing fantasy NBA is about being a *privileged man*.

The league under investigation was first formed for the 2000–2001 NBA season and stands as one of the longest running online leagues that we have encountered. According to Davis and Duncan (2006, p. 246), contemporary fantasy sports leagues first emerged in the early 1980s in the US. Journalists Glen Waggoner and Daniel Okrent are often credited as the "founding fathers" of fantasy baseball (Hu, 2003), but the history of fantasy football extends even further back in time. Frank Shipman (2001) argues that fantasy sports have been around since 1962, beginning as a laborious exercise in "paper and pencil" bookkeeping and developing into the lucrative computer-mediated industry that it is today. There is even evidence to suggest that fantasy football dates back even further, with a form of fantasy Professional Golfers' Association (PGA) golf developed in the mid-1950s arguably representing the founding moment of fantasy sports and fantasy sports leagues (Esser, 1994). The history of fantasy basketball is not well understood, but it likely emerged during the 1990s when a rapid increase in interest in fantasy sports roughly coincided with an explosion in Internet use after the release and spread of the World Wide Web (UFL.edu, n.d.). Despite the heavy reliance on online spaces and computerized calculations of statistics, it is also worth noting that fantasy competitors also make wide use of various "offline" and traditional media sources to manage their teams with greater efficiency (Drayer et al., 2010, p. 129; Hutchins & Rowe, 2012, pp. 167–72).

The competitors who formed the league examined here were drawn from a dedicated group of NBA aficionados studying at a major southeastern Australian university in the late 1990s and an extended network of friends who attended high school together. At the time of writing, seven have a university degree, of which one has a PhD and two are studying for postgraduate degrees. All ten members hold down professional careers, and the average salary of the group is around AUD$81,000 (US$85,000). All are heterosexual males in long-term relationships. The oldest player is thirty-four years of age and the youngest is thirty-one. Five played college basketball in Australia (which is more of a social activity when compared to the prestigious US system); one played at a semi-professional level; and another former member played professionally in Australia's National Basketball League (NBL). The group also has decisively liberal and progressive political attitudes. For instance, all voted for left-of-center political parties and Green (environmental) candidates in the last federal election. One is employed as a journalist; two are tenured academics; and another member is a Muslim with a heightened awareness of the politics of Islam and Islamophobia.

Despite these characteristics, their fantasy NBA competition often descends into an environment that displays overtly masculine characteristics and even misogynistic attitudes. The various team names that have been created over the years are revealing indicators of this behavioral frame (and are discussed later). These materials—the archived histories of league, team names and message board content saved on the *Yahoo!® Fantasy NBA* platform—form a dense collection that highlights the meanings and consequences of fantasy basketball in the lives of these male competitors.

MEN AND MASCULINITIES

According to Donald Levy (2005a), "The voluntary, personal, nonsexual relationships of men with other men are one way in which men *do* gender" (our emphasis). Levy's (2005a) account follows from the useful tautology of "men as men". *Men as men* are able to experience and enjoy same sex, heterosexual relationships. *Men as men* are capable of experiencing these relationships in ways other than just in contradistinction to men's relationships with women. His chief concern is with hegemonic gendered relations where the "manly" pursuits of "friendship" and "comradeship" are at stake. Levy's analysis also occurs in a particular context—his doctoral thesis explores masculinities in fantasy sports leagues (2005b). Placing masculinity at the heart of fantasy sport, Levy argues that men in these contexts are not assumed to be hypermasculinist. They are thought to have privileged occupations, routine access to the Internet and the supposedly feminizing traits associated with higher educational achievements. Education of this type is thought to rely on so-called "feminist ideology" and collaborative "methods of decision-making". In short, higher education makes men pursue the unmanly directions of compromise, but Levy (2005a) adds that men in online social groups might be "less complicit with hegemonic masculinity than some other groups".

Toby Miller (2001, p. 47) draws attention to the legacies of thought that have emerged around the conceptualization of hegemonic masculinity. Following Raewyn Connell, Miller situates this concept as an outcome of social forces that preserve historically relevant systems of domination ("no longer dominant but still influential") in "emergent" systems that are dominated by particular "ruling" and "upcoming" classes of people. Building critically on Connell's applications of these ideas to gender theory, Miller argues that the idea of hegemonic masculinity is an appropriate way to study gender and sports "where aggression, bodily force, competition, and physical skill are primarily associated with straight maleness" (Miller, 2001, p. 48). The expectation is that men be "straight, strong, domineering" and oppress "the many men excluded from it"; even " 'subscribers' may find its norms unattainable" (Miller, 2001, p. 49). He argues for a reading of men's bodies as sites of contestation and of complicated and diverse meanings. Whereas Connell's and Miller's studies equated gayness and unmanliness as being at odds with hegemonic masculinities, it may be that even hegemonic masculinity shows itself to be a category of instability. Whilst male-on-male sexual desire in male team sports is denied both on and off the field, it also involves a certain appreciation of masculine bodily desire. Or, as one of the league names from the 2006 fantasy NBA season articulates, some might be in a "League of Masculine Love" (see Table 16.1).

The "problem" of hegemonic masculinity and sport was, for instance, conspicuously emphasized during an Australian radio sports program in 2006. Playing a word association game, a well-known Australian Rules footballer, Nick Riewoldt, responded to the word "homosexual" with the word "die" (Australian Coalition for Equality, 2005–2006). A popular sports blog hosted a discussion about this slip-of-the-tongue. For the most part, its contributions were critical and disappointed with the comments, but some were eager to add to the homophobic commentary:

> If homosexuals are allowed to come out of the closet, homophobes should be allowed to do the same. Who are we to discriminate against homophobes. It's not their fault . . . they were born that way.
> He shouldn't have said that. *That's the sort of thing you might say with your mates*, but on Triple M and Fox Footy . . . it's asking for trouble (our emphasis).
> So he doesn't like Homosexuals. Where's the discrimination?
> I think you're confusing hate and discrimination. I hate eating broccoli but I don't discriminate against them.
> Not sure I can see anything wrong with this at all.
> Please everyone stop trying to take the moral high ground just so you can get some kudos from your internet buddies, most of us do discriminate against Homersexuals (sic), that's life. They choose to act like an insecure female so they deserve all they get. No one makes them gay—they choose to be. (Big Footy Forum, 2006)

These contributions were not representative of all the available responses, but around a quarter of message board comments expressed a negative attitude towards homosexuality. In an odd and perverse twist, Riewoldt's relationship to sexuality was again in the public spotlight in early 2011 when private photographs emerged of him standing completely naked, holding his penis in the presence of a near-naked teammate (Robinson, 2011). Hegemonic masculinities, homophobia and straight male homo-eroticism are not, then, rigid categories. "True masculinity" always emerges from the male body (Connell, 2005, p. 45). Masculinity is inscribed on the human body and through male bodily desire; that is, the types of body that men admire. The body "drives and directs action" and can be witnessed through aggressive behavior, sporting prowess and crime. The body's cor-poreal limits are also sites where accusations of weakness and deficiency in masculinity are directed. These criticisms take shape when a supposedly masculine desire to push through the "pain barrier" is rejected (Miller, 2001), when men are unable to manage their health and when "natural" heterosexual activity meets "unnatural" homosexual perversity (Connell, 2005, p. 45). Embodied *manly* experiences sit amongst legacies of myth making where men are the hunters and women are the consumers of men's productive activity. As Connell (2009) points out, these assumptions are relatively recent:

> In most hunter-gatherer societies, women collectively produce more food than men do. In peasant societies, women are a vital, regular part of the agricultural labour force, working together with men in the fields or raising their own specialized crops. In many African societies, women have been prominent as traders. (p. 27)

Women's—and men's—roles are not as strictly defined as heteronormativity would dictate. Differences between men and women are often seen emerging from over-simplified accounts of gender difference, and the complex rela-tionship between sport and masculinities has received considerable atten-tion (Connell, 1993; McKay, Messner & Sabo, 2000; Messner, 1992; Rowe & Gilmour, 2009). Messner (1992) has argued that the development of young boys into effective men owes much to sport, while Lawrence A. Wen-ner (1998, p. 310) argues that sport reinforces gendered myths that men are naturally superior to women. Wenner and Steven J. Jackson (2009) argue that the evolving roles for women in sport are linked to increasing commod-ification, viewing the "performance of gender roles" as problematic in the masculinized domain of male team sports. They prefer to see sport and its various forms of media representation as a "site of struggle" (Wenner and Jackson, 2009, p. 2). This struggle means that sports culture and its media representation promote and stabilize masculine identity, while simultane-ously acting as a site of resistance against hegemonic masculinities. This is a useful context from which to understand a group that emerged in response to particular coordinates of hegemonic masculinity in fantasy sports spaces. They are a group called Women Against Fantasy Sports (WAFS).

WOMEN, LANGUAGE AND FANTASY SPORTS

Our account of this long-running fantasy basketball league begins with the plight of women living amidst a space of privileged masculine excess. Kathleen Ervin (2012) describes WAFS as a "support group" for "fantasy sports widows" that was popular amongst "dispossessed wives and girlfriends":

> When Allison Lodish's husband first started playing fantasy football, she viewed it as an innocuous pursuit. "Had I known where it would lead, I may not have been so eager for him to take up this hobby," she says, having since reconsidered her initial stance. Over the course of the past five NFL seasons, her husband of 13 years has spent an inordinate amount of time reviewing player statistics, drafting teams, managing lineups, making trades, and trash-talking with fellow fantasy league participants—time that could have been better spent, in her opinion, with her and the couple's two children.

Being a dedicated fantasy competitor interrupts other hetero-manly pursuits such as keeping *the wife* happy and looking after *the kids*. Alison Lodish is a "fantasy widow", and one of the founding members of WAFS. But, while playing fantasy sports seems to be an almost exclusively male pastime (Levy's study puts the figure at about 97.9 percent; also see Davis & Duncan, 2006), being opposed to fantasy sports is not so gender exclusive. One of the three founding members of WAFS is a man and a "recovering" fantasy sports "addict". The WAFS website sold merchandise in the form of official WAFS shirts featuring the slogan, "I thought I was your fantasy," and women's underwear with an inscription, "Closed for the fantasy Season" across the crotch (Ervin, 2012). Gender matters to WAFS because gender matters in fantasy sports. Gender—with its contradictions and the realities it creates and sustains—was an important feature of the fantasy basketball league discussed in this chapter.

In shifting focus to the language of fantasy sports, Slavoj Žižek argues that a *tautology* can reveal deep significance and meanings in the contexts of everyday interactions (Žižek, 2010, p. 68). Tautologies represent linguistic redundancies and frustrations with the limits of language in describing complex emotions and life-worlds. Language has the mystical power to transform uncertainties *out-there* into speech acts and forms that act as realities *in-here* (Law, 2004), and also labels uncertain realities with particular words. In these moments we can never be sure that what is communicated by speech acts or written words will be received in the ways that we intend. When, for example, the phrase *boys will be boys* is used, the speaker is attempting to come to terms with something indefinable about boys and, in the process, confronts the limits of language. Yet, it is precisely the banal repetitiveness of the phrase that gives it its power—boys, *it seems*, behave in the ways that boys do. The team names chosen over twelve seasons reveal the masculine attitudes, ironies and jokes that have come to characterize the social networking spaces of the league under examination. They are cases of *boys being boys*. Table 16.1 displays the best examples of this pattern in relation to team names over a decade or more.

Table 16.1 Examples of fantasy league and team names.

Year	Team Name	League Name
2000	Chodreteam	Stonecutters
2000	Tong PO	
2001	Desert Knob	NBA Masters
2001	OBL Freedom Fighters	
2002	Pornstorestiffy	1 Ring to Rule Them All
2003	DirtyKuffarBitchslap	Return of the King
2003	Marblehead Johnson	
2003	Arizona Bay	
2003	THE SNIPER OF PUSs	
2004	The Cherry Poppers	Lucky Breaks & Heart Aches
2004	Espace	
2004	HST never forgotten	
2004	Titts McGee	
2005	Bloody Bitch Dead	How Kaine Got His Groove Back
2005	EataMuffADaySorority	
2005	Cobra Kai	
2006	The Love Generator	The League of Masculine Love
2008	My 5 Towns	Rising Up Against WAFS
2008	AQUAMAN	
2009	Madmen	Geelong Fantasy Ballers
2010	Gary Colemans Forarm (sic)	Geelong Fantasy Ballers
2010	Kenny Powers	
2010	Tastes Like Chicken	
2011	Thunderous Thrusting	Geelong Fantasy Ballers
2011	Badly Packed Kebab	

We want to draw attention to particular themes that emerge from these league and team names, and revolve around sex and sexuality, and television and popular culture. The team names that relate to themes of sex and sexuality see privileged men making manly, heteronormative jokes about female and male body parts and sexual intercourse—one might say typical "locker-room" banter. There are four references to male body parts ("Desert Knob", "Pornstorestiffy", "Marblehead Johnson" and "Gary Colemans Forarm"), all of which are penis references. There are three references to female body parts—one a reference to breasts ("Titts McGee") and two are vagina references ("Eatamuffadaysorority" and "Badly Packed Kebab"). There are three references to sexual acts among the team names that are squarely heterosexual ("THE SNIPER OF PUSs", "The Cherry Poppers" and "Tastes Like Chicken"), whilst a fourth is more orientation neutral ("Thunderous Thrusting").

The remaining team names are references to popular culture apart from two that have more political meanings ("DirtyKuffarBitchslap" and "OBL Freedom Fighters"—both refer to Muslim identity and the so-called "War on Terror"). The popular cultural references revolve around particular masculine themes and male-oriented pop-cultural experiences. The movies that are referenced in the team names are Matt Stone and Trey Parker's (of *South Park* fame) film *Orgasmo* (1997) ("Chodreteam"), *Kickboxer* (1989) ("Tong Po"), *American Psycho* (2000) ("Espace"), and *The Karate Kid* (1984) ("Cobra Kai"). The television programs are *Entourage* (2004–2011) ("My 5 Towns" and "AQUAMAN"), *Madmen* (2007–) ("Madmen") and *Eastbound and Down* (2009–) ("Kenny Powers"). There are two additional pop-cultural references—the *Tool* song "Ænima" (1996) ("Arizona Bay") and the literature of "gonzo" journalist Hunter S. Thompson and the films based on his writing ("HST never forgotten").

Fantasy sport supports masculine fantasies, but it is not limited to a desire to be involved in professional sport. The team and league names are highly suggestive in relation to hegemonic masculinities and the sexual team names are often misogynistic. The films and television programs referenced also tap into particular ways of being hegemonically male. In *American Psycho*, *Entourage*, *Madmen* and *Eastbound and Down*, women are directly and openly objectified—sometimes violently—in the name of "edgy" comedy. *Kickboxer* and *The Karate Kid* tell the familiar tale of boys (weak and feminine) becoming men (strong fighters), while *Tool* and Thompson represent intellectual forms of masculinity; the former calling for the total destruction of Los Angeles and the latter for the hedonistic, drug-fuelled pursuit of "truth". All are coordinates for particular masculine fantasies—everything from the desire for immediate sexual gratification, to easily "kicking somebody's ass", and even total and complete destruction (of a city and of oneself). An admiration for powerful male bodies is central to these mediated displays of masculine prowess.

Celebration of the masculine body is a central feature of discussion board dialogue during Fantasy NBA seasons. In recent years, the *Yahoo!* platform has expanded the available tools for discussion to include text altering (fonts, sizes and bolding, italicizing and underlining) and photograph uploading. Participants routinely supplement their discussions with photographs that display the masculine form of their favorite players:

Nov 13, 2:43 p.m.

Fast Neutrinos: A question for all managers. Which player on your team did you not really rate before the draft, but now after a mere couple of days of owning him, do you regard with a lot more optimism? For me, I am shocked and appalled that Tony Allen lasted to the last round. Dead-set gun! All trade offers will be refused (supplemented with a muscular image of Tony Allen).

Nov 13, 4:53 p.m.

Fast Neutrinos: I take it back, Jameer's value is trending upward now! (supplemented with an image of a shirtless Jameer Nelson posing in front of a mirror. A tattoo on his back reads "ALL EYES ON ME")

Nov 13, 5:08 p.m.

ReverseApacheMaster: Just like Wall St I'm ready to explode and make the top 50! (supplemented with an image of John Wall, smiling sweetly, biceps flexing).

Message board discussions like these are a way to "kill time", chat with people who are offline friends as well and brag about one's team and its collective physical abilities. Themes of sexual orientation are never far away from these images of muscular and often sexualized men's bodies, with issues of sexual orientation sometimes appearing as "jokes":

Dec 26, 12:04 p.m.

ClearEyesFullHearts: I love cock.

Dec 26, 12:59 p.m.

ReverseApacheMaster: Gay!!

Dec 25, 1:58 p.m.

Fast Neutrinos: That kind of honesty is refreshing Steve.

Dec 26, 7:25 p.m.

The blackPINO: What a gay dog. What a gay cunt.

Dec 26, 7:57 p.m.

ClearEyesFullHearts: I don't mind you guys knowing—just imagine posting it on facebook for the whole world to see!

Discussions sometimes take place after offline gatherings and involve in-jokes understood only by those in the "men's club" of this fantasy sports league. These related themes of admiration for the masculine male body and the open jokes about non-heterosexual orientation are combined with discussions of player performances. For example, the following discussion is about Phoenix Suns center, Marcin Gortat, in a thread titled "Marcin to his own beat":

Jan 12, 8:09 p.m.

Fast Neutrinos: (posts an image of a shirtless, muscular looking Marcin Gortat holding a sledgehammer and growling into the camera and a second image of Gortat landing an enormous slam dunk).

Jan 12, 8:56 p.m.

Badly Packed Kebab: what's with the sledgehammer?

Jan 12, 9:46 p.m.

Fast Neutrinos: He's breaking the hearts of all those GMs who passed on him on draft day (oh and they called him ugly too).
Fast Neutrinos: Just remembered Robbo, his nick-name is the Polish Hammer!
Badly Packed Kebab: Polish Hammer . . . has many different meanings I reckon!

According to Nikki Wedgwood (2003, pp. 185–86), sports operate within institutions where many young men "learn a physically assertive embodiment" that plays an important formative role in their "masculinity construction projects". The discussion on the league's message board suggests that these masculine projects take particular directions. There are few other contexts where it might be appropriate for heterosexual men to admire men's muscles, deploy penis metaphors and comment on how these muscular men have broken the hearts of other men. It is permissible here for straight men to declare—presumably for the laughs of other straight men—that they "love cock", and then not be criticized, persecuted or even taken seriously or believed. Wedgwood (2003, p. 186; also see Miller, 2001) has argued that men display their *sporting* masculinity by performing a spectacular physical feat, displaying "power and accuracy", and demonstrating "explosive speed and determination . . . [and] overpowering tackles and invasive, recklessly dangerous bumps". Hegemonic sporting masculinity in this fantasy sports league also incorporates "manly queerness", involving ironic public declarations that one is comfortable with being thought of as queer.

CONCLUSION: FANTASY SPORT AND THE GENDER ORDER

If "manly queerness" plays an important role in this heterosexual men's fantasy league, then what role, if any, is reserved for women? This question is not easily answered. Women have been viewed as central to men's sport for more than two decades, both as a category of analysis and as a bodily reality (McKay et al., 2000; Messner & Sabo, 1990). The evidence drawn from the fantasy sports league investigated in this chapter suggests that women might play little role, given that manly homoeroticism has a strong presence here, but so do misogynistic attitudes. Women are far less likely to be fantasy competitors and spend less money on their teams, although there is evidence to suggest that this pattern is changing (Hutchins & Rowe, 2012, pp. 173–75; Otto, Metz & Ensmenger, 2011). While Hutchins and Rowe (2012, p. 174) argue that fantasy sport remains a "male dominated environment", they also offer an avenue for women to occupy "subject position[s]" that would otherwise be rarely available; for instance, the opportunity to own and manage a professional men's sports team. Certain gender roles become, therefore, "imaginable" in fantasy sports leagues (Hutchins & Rowe 2012, p. 175).

This study is ongoing and involves interviews with the ten fantasy NBA players that form this league and their wives and girlfriends. The data collected will produce new accounts of fantasy sports as an everyday, mundane part of life, and of the ways that relationships with "significant others" are negotiated during time-consuming fantasy seasons and busy family and working lives. In this league there are no female players but there are prominent "others" in play. One of the long-term members of this league recently "retired", citing responsibility towards his wife and his two babies as the reason. Unlike the sporting seasons that are the focus of fantasy leagues, the fantasy season often lasts all year. It is the league's never-ending quality that made raising a young family incompatible with play for this participant.

The history of this league is, therefore, bound to the histories of the participants who have negotiated their development from male adolescence into adulthood. The changing circumstances that accompany different stages of life have travelled alongside an explosion of Internet-based technologies and witnessed the proliferation of sports spectatorship in spaces that exist far beyond broadcast television. Despite these many changes, the evidence suggests that fantasy sport fits within a cultural and media framework that acts as a "predominantly conservative force" in relationships between men and women (McKay et al., 2000: 2). Certainly, the fantasy sports league featured in this chapter is testimony to enduring masculinities, persistent hegemonies and an unremitting desire for frontiers where privileged masculinities can be practiced.

REFERENCES

Australian Coalition for Equality (2005–2006) Riewoldt in strife over gay slur. Online. Available from: http://www.coalitionforequality.org.au/index.php?option=com_content&task=view&id=693&Itemid=81 (Accessed 3 March 2012).

Bernhard BJ & Eade VH (2005) Gambling in a fantasy world: an exploratory study of rotisserie baseball games. *UNLV Gaming Research & Review Journal* 9(1): 29–42.

Big Footy Forum (2006) Nick Reiwoldt on MMM's the gospel. 7 July. Online. Available from: http://www.bigfooty.com/forum/archive/index.php/t-253345.html (Accessed 3 March 2012).

Campbell P & Kelly P (2009) "Explosions and examinations": growing up female in post-Saddam Iraq. *Journal of Youth Studies* 12(1): 21–38.

Connell RW (1993) *Which Way is Up? Essays on Class, Sex, and Culture*. Sydney: Allen & Unwin.

Connell RW (2005) *Masculinities*. 2nd ed. Crows Nest, NSW: Allen & Unwin.

Connell RW (2009) *Gender: In World Perspective*. 2nd ed. Cambridge: Polity.

Davis N & Duncan MC (2006) Sports knowledge is power: reinforcing masculine privilege through fantasy sports league participation. *Journal of Sport and Social Issues* 30(3): 244–64.

Drayer J, Shapiro S, Dwyer B, Morse A & White J (2010) The effects of fantasy football participation on NFL consumption: a qualitative analysis. *Sport Management Review* 13: 129–41.

Dwyer B & Drayer J (2010) Fantasy sports consumer segmentation: an investigation into the differing consumption modes of fantasy football participants. *Sports Marketing Quarterly* 19(4): 207–16.

Ervin K (2012) Women against fantasy sports. *Failure Magazine*. Online. Available from: http://failuremag.com/index.php/feature/article/women_against_fantasy_sports/ (Accessed 3 March 2012).

Esser L (1994) The birth of fantasy football. *Fantasy Index*. Online. Available from: http://www.fantasyindex.com/toolbox/birth (Accessed 27 June 2012).

Farquhar LK & Meeds R (2007) Types of fantasy sports users and their motivations. *Journal of Computer-Mediated Communication* 12(4): 1208–28.

Hu J (2003) Sites see big season for fantasy sports. *CNet*. 8 August. Online. Available from: http://news.cnet.com/2100-1026_3-5061351.html (Accessed 27 July 2012).

Hutchins B & Rowe D (2012) *Sport Beyond Television: The Internet, Digital Media and the Rise of Networked Media Sport*. Routledge: New York.

Ipsos Public Affairs (2011) For the first time, fantasy sports play tops 35 million North American players. *Ipsos*. 11 July. Online. Available from: http://www.ipsos-na.com/news-polls/pressrelease.aspx?id=5281 (Accessed 7 December 2011).

Law J (2004) *After Method: Mess in Social Science Research*. London: Routledge.

Levy D (2005a) Hegemonic complicity, friendship, and comradeship: validation and causal processes among white, middle-class, middle-aged men. *Journal of Men's Studies* 13(2): 199–213.

Levy D (2005b) *Sports Fanship Habitus: An Investigation of the Active Consumption of Sport, Its Effects and Social Implications Through the Lives of Fantasy Sports Enthusiasts*. PhD thesis, University of Connecticut, US.

Lomax RG (2006) Fantasy sports: history, game types, and research. In: Raney AA and Bryant J (eds.) *Handbook of Sports and Media*. Mahwah, NJ: Lawrence Erlbaum Associates, 383–92.

McKay J, Messner MA & Sabo D (2000) Studying sport, men, and masculinities from feminist standpoints. In: McKay J, Messner MA & Sabo D (eds.) *Masculinities, Gender Relations, and Sport*. Thousand Oaks, CA: Sage, 1–12.

Messner MA (1992) *Power at Play: Sports and the Problem of Masculinity*. Boston: Beacon.

Messner MA & Sabo DF (eds.) (1990) *Sport, Men and the Gender Order: Critical Feminist Perspectives*. Champaign, IL: Human Kinetics.

Miller T (2001) *Sportsex*. Philadelphia: Temple University Press.

Otto J, Metz S & Ensmenger N (2011) Sports fans and their information-gathering habits: how media technologies have brought fans closer to their teams over time. In: Aspray W & Hayes BM (eds.) *Everyday Information: The Evolution of Information Seeking in America*. Cambridge, MA: The MIT Press, 185–216.

Robinson M (2011) The naked truth about Nick Riewoldt and the naked photo affair. *Herald Sun*. 14 October. Online. Available from: http://www.heraldsun.com.au/sport/afl/the-naked-truth-about-nick-riewoldt-and-the-nude-photo-affair/story-e6frf9jf-1226166299181 (Accessed 4 February 2012).

Rowe D & Gilmour C (2009) Lubrication and domination: beer, sport, masculinity, and the Australian gender order. In: Wenner L & Jackson S (eds.) *Sport, Beer, and Gender: Promotional Culture and Contemporary Social Life*. New York: Peter Lang, 203–21.

Ruddock A, Hutchins B & Rowe D (2010) Contradictions in media sport culture: the reinscription of football supporter traditions through online media. *European Journal of Cultural Studies* 13(3): 323–39.

Shipman FM (2001) Blending the real and virtual: activity and spectatorship in fantasy sports. Online. Available from: www.csdl.tamu.edu/~shipman/papers/dac01.pdf (Accessed 25 June 2012).

Turkle S (1995) *Life on the Screen: Identity in the Age of the Internet*. New York: Simon and Schuster.

UFL.edu (no date) History of fantasy. Online. Available from: http://iml.jou.ufl.edu/projects/spring06/Antonio/historyoffantasy.html (Accessed 27 July 2012).

Wedgwood N (2003) Aussie rules! Schoolboy football and masculine embodiment. In: Tomsen S & Donaldson M (eds.) *Male Trouble: Looking at Australian Masculinities*. North Melbourne, Vic: Pluto Press, 180–99.

Wenner L (1998) In search of the sports bar: masculinity, alcohol, sports, and the mediation of public space. In: Rail G (ed.) *Sport and Postmodern Times: Culture, Gender, Sexuality, the Body and Sport*. Albany, NY: SUNY Press, 301–22.

Wenner L & Jackson S (2009) Sport, beer, and gender in promotional culture: on the dynamics of a holy trinity. In: Wenner L & Jackson S (eds.) *Sport, Beer, and Gender: Promotional Culture and Contemporary Social Life*. New York: Peter Lang, 1–32.

World Fantasy Games (2011) Fantasy sports demographics. Online. Available from: http://www.worldfantasygames.com/site_flash/index-3.asp (Accessed 1 December 2011).

Žižek S (2010) *Living in the End Times*. New York: Verso.

Contributors

Raymond Boyle is a Professor of Communications at the Centre for Cultural Policy Research at the University of Glasgow in Scotland. He has published widely on sport and the media, with books including *Power Play: Sport, the Media and Popular Culture* (EUP, 2nd ed., 2009) with Richard Haynes, and *Sports Journalism: Context and Issues* (Sage, 2006). His most recent book on the television industry is *The Television Entrepreneurs* (Ashgate, 2012, with Lisa Kelly).

Perri Campbell is located in the School of Education at Deakin University in Geelong, Australia. Her research interests are situated at the crossroads of gender studies, critical social theory, media studies and youth studies, with a particular focus on digital communication.

Steven Conway is Co-Convener of the Games & Interactivity course at Swinburne University of Technology in Melbourne, Australia. His research interests focus on the philosophy and aesthetics of modern digital game design. Conway's recent work examines the socio-cultural implications of consumer-oriented models of commercial videogame production.

Ann-Marie Cook is a Tutor and Researcher in the Creative Industries Faculty at Queensland University of Technology in Brisbane, Australia. Her current research activities include projects on transmedia, online audience engagement, fandom and the British teen series *Skins*.

Matthew David is a Senior Lecturer in Sociology at Durham University in the UK. He is the author of *Peer to Peer and the Music Industry* (Sage, 2010), *Social Research: An Introduction* (Sage 2011, 2nd ed., with Carole Sutton), and "Football's Coming Home" (in the *British Journal of Sociology* with Peter Millward).

Tom Evens is a Senior Researcher in the Media & ICT research group (iMinds-MICT) at Ghent University, Belgium, where he has also taught

"Media, Market and ICT" since 2011. His research focuses on the political economy of new media and ICT, business model innovation, and public policy. Together with Petros Iosifidis and Paul Smith, Tom is the author of *Playing to Win: The Political Economy of Television Sports Rights* (Palgrave Macmillan, 2013).

Mark Finn is Senior Lecturer in Media & Communications at Swinburne University of Technology in Melbourne, Australia. He has published widely on various aspects of new media, including the historical development of electronic commerce and the social implications of mobile computing technologies. For the past five years Finn has specialized in the social and cultural dimensions of video games, with his most recent work examining debates over game censorship.

Paul Gilchrist is a Senior Research Fellow in Sport and Leisure Cultures at the University of Brighton in the UK. His research interests explore the multiple dimensions of cultural politics, concentrating on people-environment relationships. He has published on a number of sport-related themes, including histories of climbing, sporting activisms, the sporting hero, countryside recreation and leisure theory. Gilchrist's current research is funded by the British Academy and investigates the institutionalization and transnational dimensions of parkour.

Gerard Goggin is Professor and Chair of the Department of Media and Communications at the University of Sydney in Australia. He has published widely on mobiles and digital media, with his books including *Mobile Technology and Place* (2012; with Rowan Wilken), *New Technologies and the Media* (2012), *Global Mobile Media* (2011), *Mobile Telecommunications: From Telecommunications to Media* (2009; with Larissa Hjorth), *Mobile Phone Cultures* (2008) and *Cell Phone Culture* (2006). Goggin has also published books on the Internet—*Internationalizing Internet Studies* (2009; with Mark McLelland) and *Virtual Nation: The Internet in Australia* (2004).

Ben Goldsmith is Senior Research Fellow in the Australian Research Council (ARC) Centre of Excellence for Creative Industries and Innovation at Queensland University of Technology in Brisbane, Australia. His research interests include sports television, media industries, the app economy, screen policy and Australian cinema.

Richard Haynes is Reader in Communications, Media and Culture, and a member of the Stirling Media Research Institute, in the School of Arts and Humanities at University of Stirling in Scotland. He is author of numerous articles, chapters and monographs on sport and the media, including *Power Play: Sport, the Media and Popular Culture* (EUP, 2009) with Raymond Boyle. Haynes is currently writing a history of BBC Television Sport.

Luke Howie is a Senior Lecturer in the School of Political and Social Inquiry at Monash University in Melbourne, Australia. His research interests include technoculture, social and cultural networking websites, security and terrorism studies, and critical social theory (particularly the work of Slavoj Zizek).

Brett Hutchins is Associate Professor in Communications and Media Studies and Co-Director of the Research Unit in Media Studies at Monash University in Melbourne, Australia. His books and edited collections include *Sport Beyond Television: The Internet, Digital Media and the Rise of Networked Media Sport* (Routledge, 2012, with David Rowe), *Environmental Conflict and the Media* (Peter Lang, 2013, with Libby Lester), and *Don Bradman: Challenging the Myth* (Cambridge University Press, 2005).

Deirdre Hynes is Principal Lecturer at Manchester Metropolitan University in the UK. She is a relative newcomer to football research having previously studied gender, technological domestication and everyday life. She has published several articles in media, technology and anthropology journals, and her current research focuses on female football fans and issues surrounding disenfranchisement, exclusion and empowerment.

Andrew Kirton is a Lecturer in Sociology at the University of Liverpool in the UK where he teaches Social Theory and Social Research Methods. His research interests focus on the relationship between media, culture and regulation in contemporary capitalist societies.

Katrien Lefever holds a PhD in sports law from the KU Leuven in Belgium and now works as a company lawyer at the commercial broadcast group, VMMa. She is also an affiliated researcher at the Interdisciplinary Centre of Law and ICT (iMinds-ICRI) at the KU Leuven. Lefever is the author of *New Media and Sport: International Legal Aspects* (Springer, 2012) and has published widely on media sports law.

David J. Leonard is Associate Professor and Chair in the Department of Critical Culture, Gender and Race Studies at Washington State University in the US. He is the author of *After Artest: Race and the Assault on Blackness* (SUNY Press, 2012), as well as several other works.

Peter Millward is Senior Lecturer in Sociology at Liverpool John Moores University in the UK. He has published widely on the sociological dimensions of contemporary football fandom (including supporters' collective actions and mobilizations), the political economy of sport and issues relating to sport and new/social media. Peter's second monograph, *The Global Football League: Transnational Networks, Social Movements and Sport in the New Media Age* (Palgrave, 2011), looks at the transnational networks connected to the English Premier League.

David Rowe is Professor of Cultural Research in the Institute for Culture and Society, University of Western Sydney, Australia. His books include *Globalization and Sport: Playing the World* (authored with Toby Miller, Geoffrey Lawrence and Jim Mckay, Sage, 2001), *Sport, Culture and the Media: The Unruly Trinity* (Open University Press, 2004), *Global Media Sport: Flows, Forms and Futures* (Bloomsbury Academic, 2011), and *Sport, Public Broadcasting, and Cultural Citizenship: Signal Lost?* (edited with Jay Scherer, Routledge, 2013).

Andy Ruddock is Senior Lecturer in Communications and Media Studies at Monash University in Melbourne, Australia. He is author of *Youth and Media* (2013), *Investigating Audiences* (2007), and *Understanding Audiences* (2001). Ruddock has published on topics such as media violence, political celebrity, media sport and its audiences, social media and marketing, pornography, the influence of media on attitudes to war and cultivation theory.

Jimmy Sanderson is an Assistant Professor in the Department of Communication Studies at Clemson University in South Carolina in the US. His research interests center on social media and sports media, sports organizations, and the interactions between athletes and fans. He is the author of *It's a Whole New Ballgame: How Social Media is Changing Sports* (Hampton Press, 2011).

Ethan Tussey is an Assistant Professor of Communication at Georgia State University in Atlanta in the US (PhD UCSB; MA UCLA; BA University of Arizona). His research interests include new media studies, media industry studies and audience studies, focusing on the relationship between the entertainment industry and the digitally empowered public. Tussey has worked for the Carsey-Wolf Center's Media Industries Project and has written articles on digital creative labor and workplace viewing practices.

Belinda Wheaton is a Principal Research Fellow in Sport and Leisure Cultures at the University of Brighton in the UK. She has research interests in, and has published on the sporting body, gender and race, leisure consumption and identity, leisure and the politics of the environment and sport, and sport and transnationalism. Wheaton's research on lifestyle sports, including windsurfing, surfing and parkour, has been published in a range of international journals, a research monograph, *The Cultural Politics of Lifestyle Sports* (Routledge, forthcoming, 2013), and two edited books, *Understanding Lifestyle Sport* (Routledge, 2004) and *The Consumption and Representation of Lifestyle Sports* (Routledge, 2012).

Haiqing Yu is Senior Lecturer of Chinese media and culture at the University of New South Wales in Sydney, Australia. She researches contemporary Chinese media, communication and popular culture, with a focus on the sociology of digital communication and emerging media and cultural forms and practices. She is the author of *Media and Cultural Transformation in China* (Routledge, 2009), *Sex in China Today* (Polity, forthcoming, with Elaine Jeffreys), and *Sports Media in China* (Sussex, forthcoming).

Index

Please note: italicized page numbers indicate figures and tables

CPSIA information can be obtained
at www.ICGtesting.com
Printed in the USA
FFHW020807030119
50051433-54842FF